# FALAFEL NATION

**STUDIES OF JEWS IN SOCIETY**

Harriet Hartman, *series editor*

# FALAFEL NATION

*Cuisine and the Making of
National Identity in Israel*

*Yael Raviv*

UNIVERSITY OF NEBRASKA PRESS
*Lincoln and London*

A section of the introduction was originally published as "Falafel: A National Icon" in *Gastronomica* 3, no. 3 (Summer 2003) © 2003 by the Regents of the University of California. Published by the University of California Press. A section of chapter 2 was originally published as "The Hebrew Banana: Local Food and the Performance of Israeli National Identity," in *Journal for the Study of Food and Society* 5, no. 1 (Summer 2001). It appears here with permission.

Library of Congress Cataloging-in-Publication Data
Raviv, Yael, author.
Falafel nation: cuisine and the making of
national identity in Israel / Yael Raviv.
pages    cm.—(Studies of Jews in society)
Revised version of the author's thesis
(doctoral)—New York University, 2002.
Includes bibliographical references and index.
ISBN 978-0-8032-9017-4 (hardback: alk. paper)
ISBN 978-0-8032-9021-1 (epub)
ISBN 978-0-8032-9022-8 (mobi)
ISBN 978-0-8032-9023-5 (pdf)
1. Cooking, Israeli—History. 2. Cooking—
Social aspects—Israel. 3. National
characteristics, Israeli. I. Title.
TX724.R385 2015
641.595694—dc23
2015021563

Set in Minion Pro by L. Auten.
Designed by Rachel Gould.

*To my parents,*

*Alona and Amiram Raviv*

# CONTENTS

List of Illustrations ix

Acknowledgments xi

Introduction 1

1. Putting Down Roots:
   Agricultural Labor and Icons 28

2. Patriotic Distribution:
   The "Hebrew" Watermelon 50

3. Kitchen Lessons: Educating Home Cooks 86

4. The Virtual Kitchen:
   Making Room for Pleasure 119

5. The Professional Kitchen:
   Articulating a National Cuisine 157

6. No Table Required:
   Consumption and the Public Sphere 182

Conclusion 209

Appendix: Historical Context 213

Notes 235

Bibliography 253

Index 269

# ILLUSTRATIONS

1. *Falafelman* cover, Dorit Maya-Gur, 2006     23

2. "A land of wheat and barley, of vines and fig trees and pomegranates, land of olive trees and honey" (Deuteronomy 8:8)     31

3. The Fourteenth Zionist Congress, Palestinian Exhibition     33

4. Ran Morin, *Oranger Suspendu*, Jaffa, 1993     38

5. Postcard from the Fifth Zionist Congress, by E. M. Lilien     40

6. "Buy Hebrew Watermelons," designed by Otte Wallish     56

7. A WIZO show advocating the use of dairy products, 1950s     72

8. Super-Sal advertisement in Tchiya Bat-Oren, *365 Shulhanot Arukhim* (365 set tables), 1961     77

9. Boys preparing luncheons in Talmus Torah Temini, Tel Aviv, 1930s     98

10. A young Moroccan girl learns to cook, 1950     105

11. Cooking class, late 1920s     108

12. The cover of Erna Meyer's *Aikh Levashel be-Erez-Israel?* (How to cook in the land of Israel?), 1935    122

13. Ad for Vita soup mix in Lillian Cornfeld, *Ha-Mitbah ha-Meshubah* (The superb kitchen), 1960    130

14. "White Meat Leg à la San Manold," in Amos Keinan, *Sefer ha-Ta'anugot* (The book of pleasures), 1970    133

15. Genuine mayonnaise, 1954    162

16. An army kitchen: meat and dairy pots    172

17. Cover of *Ba-Mahane*, 31 May 1995    174

18. Army kitchen pots    180

19. "I guess some servers are missing again," Gidi Keikh, *Efshar le-Hitpake'a! Karikaturot me-Hayey ha-Kibbutz* (You could burst! Caricatures of kibbutz life), 1966    186

20. "I am only 'rag'! I am only . . . 'soup'!" Hik, Kfar Giladi newsletter, 1956    187

21. "Today there is no bimkom!" Hik, Kfar Giladi newsletter, 1956    191

# ACKNOWLEDGMENTS

A project that was in the works for fifteen years accumulates a great many people to thank; I am indebted to all of them. However, I want to start by thanking my two Dalias, who were there from start to finish. Dalia Lamdani's curiosity, food knowledge, and friendship have been both instrumental and inspiring. She is one of the most knowledgeable food scholars I have encountered, a life-long student of all things culinary, and always sensitive to the greater context and implications of food work. Dalia Carmel is a dedicated cookbook collector and most generous spirit whose collection is all about the sharing of knowledge with others. I love them both.

I would like to thank my dissertation advisor at NYU, Barbara Kirshenblatt-Gimblett, for her guidance and insightful comments, as well as for not laughing me out of her office way back when. She inspires me to this day. I am also indebted to my dissertation committee members—Diana Taylor, Richard Schechner, Tamar Katriel, and Yael Zerubavel—for their comments and advice, as well as to the faculty at the Performance Studies Department, particularly Allen Weiss and Barbara Browning, for giving me great tools to work with. I would like to thank Darra Goldstein for her wonderful editorial comments and questions on my falafel piece (they informed much of what followed) and her encouragement over the years. I also want to thank Hasia Diner for her interest and support of this project. I am immensely thankful to Eve Jocknowitz for her friendship and help throughout the years and for bringing to my attention several important sources and documents.

I am grateful to Marion Nestle, Amy Bentley, Krishnandu Ray, and everyone else at the Department of Nutrition, Food Studies and Public Health at New York University for allowing me to think through many of the issues raised here and entrusting me with great students to think with. I appreciated the encouragement and the inspiration they offered in their own writings. I am particularly grateful to the members of the "Feast and Famine" colloquium hosted by the department and to my Comparative Cuisine, fall 2013, students for their insights and thoughtful questions.

I am indebted to Liora Gvion, Sheldon Rich, Avraham Weiner, Uri Guttman, Danny Angel, Tchiya Bat-Oren, Ya'akov Lishanski, Yehudit Hitron, Flora Shiryon, Amelia Uzeri, Gil Hovav, Eylon Goyten, Eugene Wolf, Ze'ev Ben-Gal (Zibon), and Moshe Gerti for their time and help in sharing their food stories and observations with me. I am particularly thankful to Hanna Heiman for allowing me to use the wonderful material she collected during her years as a food writer and nutritional instructor at WIZO and to Danny Plaot, Ilan Schwartz, and the entire Schwartz family for their help and support. A special thank you to Dorit Amir for her help in uncovering material in Kibbutz Kfar Giladi.

Thank you to Ran Morin and Dorit Maya-Gur for allowing me to use their work and to Gidon Barkani and Eri Wallish for graciously helping me reproduce their fathers' work.

I am also grateful to the following archives and collections for allowing me to use their resources: the Hadassah Archive in New York, particularly Susan Woodland; the Central Zionist Archives in Jerusalem; Sifriyat Beit Ariela, the IDF Archive, Ba-Mahane Archive, Sherut ha-Hadrakha ve-ha-Miktzo'a, Ha-Sade, La-Isha, and the Avi'ezer Yalin Archive: Arkhiyon le-Hinukh Yehudi ba-Aretz u-ba-Gola in Tel Aviv, particularly Nava Eizen. I am also thankful to the Memorial Foundation for Jewish Culture for its financial support.

A special thank you for the most recent contributors, who helped transform the manuscript from a private obsession into an actual book: Harriet Hartman, editor of the Studies of Jews in Society book series; and Kristen Elias Rowley, Marguerite Boyles, Joeth Zucco, and my diligent copyeditor, Mary M. Hill, at the University of Nebraska Press.

Finally, I would like to thank my family: my parents, Alona and Amiram; my sister, Vered Raviv-Schwartz; the entire Goldberg family; my husband, Noony; and my daughters, Maya and Leann. They all assisted me on occasions too numerous to list here, and without their help and patience this project would not have been completed.

# INTRODUCTION

*Food permits a person . . . to partake each day of the national past.*
—Roland Barthes, "Toward a Psychology of Contemporary
Food Consumption"

I was halfway through working on my doctoral dissertation at New York University in 2001 when violence erupted in my native Israel and gave me pause: Is it morally justified to be writing about food in faraway New York when Israel is in mortal danger? I could see why most critical writing about the Zionist project emerged only in the past few decades. It is difficult to take a critical approach to a venture that seems to be in constant, real peril, no matter if it is morally justified or not. I overcame my hesitations but have been faced with them again and again in the past several years. When I began this project I thought that approaching the study of Jewish nationalism through food rather than through political conflict might offer new insights. I later realized that political conflict is an unavoidable part of the discussion of any element of Zionist history, even food.

Most discussion of food in Israel in the popular media centers on particular foodstuffs and their implication in the political conflict: Who has the right to falafel? Whose hummus is bigger? I was concerned, instead, with the role food plays within the Jewish nation, the power struggles and moral dilemmas, the negotiation of religious and ideological affiliations of the different ethnic groups that make up the "Jewish state." How do we interpret the recent upsurge in the Israeli culinary scene, the transition from ideological asceticism to the current deluge of fine restaurants, gourmet stores, and related publications and media? I wish to explore the change in the relationship between Israelis and their food as mirroring the search for a definition of secular Jewish nationalism.

Two children and an American citizenship later, my thoughts on nationalism are less abstract. Whether I am making cheese-filled *bourekas* for a potluck dinner at my daughter's school or chopped liver for a Passover Seder with friends or even *not* making a turkey for Thanksgiving, I find my culinary decisions informed by thoughts of identity and identification. The traditional thinking of food as creating a sense of place and tradition has become more complicated in the modern world, where place becomes fluid and transient, and tradition is invented and reshaped with every generation. Recent scholarship, accordingly, takes care to complicate terms such as "authentic" and "nation," to focus on the minority and the marginal, the Diaspora over the land of origin. The case of Jewish nationalism carries within it the seeds of this conflict. Zionism revolves around the attempt to transform a new land into a homeland, to mobilize Jewish people from a conceptual Diaspora to a virtual homeland. Israel is a country of immigrants returning "home." In Hebrew the word for homeland is *moledet*, from the same root as *leyda*, "to give birth or be born." Homeland is literally birthplace. In elementary school, children in Israel study a topic called "moledet": local geography. This is a strange turn of phrase for a country of immigrants. It emphasizes the idea of Israel as the homeland of all Jewish people wherever they may have been born.

Food is central to our perception of "home" and identity. The items we buy, cook, and eat are everyday performances of affiliation with a greater community (or communities). The idea of nostalgia for mother's/father's/ grandmother's cooking or longing for a particular fruit or dish as denoting nostalgia for home or homeland is far from original. Taste and smell evoke memories. However, this work is not about remembering a homeland, it is about creating one. It is about the use of food not to re-create a longed-for past but to forge new connections, using food as a tool for building a nation, not only for imagining one. I use food as the key to understanding homeland and immigration, of negotiating old and new affiliations and identities. In the case of Jewish nationalism, food is not so much used to impact the land and the environment as it is used to remake the Jewish figure, to aid in the construction of an identity that is as different from the Diasporic Jewish image as it is from the local population of the land. It is used, among other tools, as a way to make the abstract idea of a Jewish nation into a concrete reality. This project looks at the role food played in the construction of a Jewish nation (distinct from the Jewish religion) and the Jewish national home in the land of Israel, focusing on the influence of immigration and its effect on the realities of nationalism in Israel.

The unique case of Jewish nationalism, physically transplanting people from a variety of other countries of origin and fusing them to each other and to the land, highlights the performative qualities of nationalism. Zionism is different from the ethos of other immigrant countries, such as the United States, for example, in that a significant part of the immigrant population, until very recently, has been motivated to move there for ideological reasons, in order to support the idea of Jewish nationalism. The case of Zionism shows Nation, as Homi Bhabha would have us see it, as ambivalent and temporal.[1] Every wave of immigrants shook the picture of national unity and influenced the social, cultural, and economic fabric of the country. The changes in the Jewish nation over time are not simply demographic changes. With each new wave of immigrants the idea of what and who is the nation shifts. S. Kalcik writes of ethnic identity as "processual and performative rather than fixed."[2] This study shows that not only do ethnic identities change and adapt, but so does the nation as a whole. The study of foodways is the perfect window into a study of nation as process rather than fixed construct, since they are processual and performative by nature as well.

This study looks at some historical materials, but it is not a historical study. It focuses on the manifestation, the performance of Zionist identity, the way Zionism shaped its voice, its self, both inward and for the world to see. As such, it affords the same value to archival documents, firsthand interviews, fictional writing, and caricatures. They are all evidence of the same phenomenon and are all parts of a greater picture.

The Zionist movement and, later, the Israeli state were engaged in shaping a (re)new(ed) Jewish nation from a multitude of ethnic groups in a very short period of time. In the service of this cause, the movement and the state employed any means available to them, including food and cooking.

In the early days of the Zionist movement, food played an important role in the construction of the new Jewish persona through agriculture. It is true that cooking and food consumption were marginalized, but this attitude to food can be just as telling as reverence or joy. The approach to food's production, distribution, preparation, and consumption transforms over time but always reflects the dynamic relationship between the nation and the multitude of ethnic, ideological, and political factions it contains.

The Zionist movement had another conflict to resolve: a wish to establish historical continuity dating back to biblical times, on the one hand, and creating a new and modern Jewish nation, on the other. Following food practices from production to consumption offers a window into this struggle. Food practices reflect both the Zionist attempt to forge a unified Jewish nation and the debates around the nature and character of this nation. Food practices were used as instruments of propaganda and acculturation, as well as a means to forge a literal bond with the land.

This book's main focus is the period between the Second Aliya (immigration wave) in 1905 and the Six-Day War in 1967, because this crucial period in the formation of Israeli nationality created a situation that was sufficiently cohesive ideologically and culturally to have produced distinctive food practices. The story I tell, however, begins with the First Aliya (1884–1903) and ends around the first decade of the new millennium, following the earlier culinary trends and tracing their effects on present-day Israeli society. With the Second Aliya food became ideologically charged, and the relative security and economic expansion that followed the Six-Day War transformed food again, as well as Israeli society and culture in general: by the early 1960s Israel had turned its attention outward and developed into a capitalist-consumerist culture. Food then became more of a leisure activity. Throughout most of the period between 1905 and 1967 the attitude toward food was utilitarian and functional, whereas during the following decades food increasingly became a vehicle of commercial culture, a source of pleasure, and a window into the outside world. This change in the approach to food coincides with a change in the perception of Zionism. In the past four decades, we see a growing wariness of Zionism and a corresponding awakening of new identifications rooted in concepts of globalization and transnationalism.

Approaching the subject of Jewish nationalism not only through the popular narrative and official ideology of heroic struggle and military history but also through concrete evidence in the field, factory, market, and kitchen and on the table allows incorporating the role of women, various ethnic groups, and different generations into the story of Zionism. It offers a "view from below" to a study of nationalism: the point of view of ordinary people as opposed to that of governments or activists. Eric J. Hobsbawm deemed this particular view extremely important to questions of nationalism, yet it is the most difficult to ascertain.[3]

## CULINARY NATIONALISM

Food offers a particularly good vehicle for an investigation of the tension between the public and the private spheres because of its role in both. As such, it is exceptionally effective for a study of nationalism, because this tension between the public and the private is one of the central concerns of work on this subject. Like other scholars who investigate the relationship between food and nation,[4] I, too, aim to use the concrete evidence of the development of a national cuisine to interrogate the abstraction of nationalism. But the case of the Jewish nation is unique in that Israel's small geographical space and its relatively homogeneous social structure (throughout most of the period discussed here) limit the influence of regional and class variations on food habits. What remains is the tension between the unifying and solidifying impulse of the nation and the multiple ethnic groups that work against this drive, pulling the cuisine and the nation in different ways, impacting both the nation and the groups that comprise it.

Because of their long histories in particular territories, nations such as France and China generated complex culinary histories that are difficult to disassemble for an investigation of modern nationalism. It is hard to trace the origins of culinary icons adopted and adapted by the modern nation-state. In the case of Jewish nationalism, the connection to land and history had to be created artificially because of the geographical transformation of Jewish people to the land of Israel; and because this process took place quite recently and under accelerated circumstances, it serves as a unique laboratory for examining the manipulation of food products as instruments in nation building.

Most scholarship on food and nation focuses on food-centered cultures such as France and Japan; however, the fact that food was marginalized throughout much of Israel's history does not make it any less influential or telling. Food can be influential even if ideologically it is presented as marginal. An ideology of frugality and asceticism shapes food habits just as much as one that savors individual comforts and pleasures and advocates consumerism. Trivializing food preparation and consumption while glorifying agricultural labor (i.e., production) characterized the attitude of the early Zionists and has left its mark on Israeli culinary culture to this day. This attitude facilitated the use of food as an instrument of propaganda by the national movement and later the state. When food is presented as "natural" and trivial, it becomes "innocent"; if it is unimportant, it is not interrogated and suspected, and so it can be used as a vehicle for influencing and shaping citizens. Unlike French culinary tradition, which exalted food the farther it departed from nature, Israeli culture deliberately glorified food's production and particularly its origins in nature. Food was an instrument for reconnecting with the land and with nature, as well as for the creation of a social revolution in which the workers in the field became the "elite."

Zionist ideology was concerned with creating a connection between the new Jewish immigrants and the land of Israel. Putting down roots through acquiring an intimate knowledge of the land was an ideal that was enforced in several ways. Creating a bond with a new homeland was a concern for every community of immigrants, and food was often used as an instrument for establishing concrete ties with an adopted country. There are several such examples of immigrant groups in the United States.[5] This is not only a story of a nation in the making but also the story of several groups of immigrants trying to negotiate former traditional ways with a new adopted home, and they too, like immigrants to America, negotiate traditional dishes with new products and influences. As Hasia Diner shows in her study of three groups of immigrants in the United States, food was used to define immigrants' attachment to their adopted new land, on the one hand, and to their community of origin, on the other. Food also mediated these two affiliations, but each group of immigrants used food in a unique way.[6] The immigrants who arrived in Palestine and Israel also came from many different countries of origin. Each group negotiated foodways in a distinctive way, making its own place and identity in the new country. The government and its agencies, the more established community, and various means of acculturation and propaganda often influenced food choices. However, these choices were also determined by the relationship to the immigrants' cultures of origin, as exemplified by the rejection of Diaspora culture by Eastern European immigrants, in contrast to immigrants from Middle Eastern or African countries who did not have the same relationship to their former culture (though their attitude toward the Arab cultures that they left behind would change in Israel with the influence of the dominant European population and the Arab-Israeli conflict, which positioned any Arabic culture as "the enemy's" culture).

In a discussion of food in a historical context, it is particularly important to note the complexities of studying ephemeral objects. Barbara Wheaton, in her study of the history of French cuisine, states, "Culinary history is the history of ephemeral social events."[7] Even though the historical period covered here is closer at hand, this study of food is still a study of traces and clues, since the object itself is obviously long gone, as are the situations of its making and consumption. The problem with such evidence is that it can create a distorted picture. When looking at the food habits of new immigrants to Israel following independence, for example, the more established population was responsible for the bulk of written accounts, and their perspective was tainted by their own viewpoint and agenda. Some surveys exist, but these too were often conducted by people with specific goals and tend to support preconceived notions. Cookbooks proved to be one of the richest sources for my research. They provide us with women's voices within the Zionist (hi)story that are missing from most official accounts. I follow Arjun Appadurai in viewing cookbooks as "revealing artifacts of culture in the making."[8] Following the changes in cookbooks in Israel reflects the shift in attitude toward new groups of immigrants within Israeli society in a way similar to that demonstrated by Jeffrey Pilcher in his study of the negotiation of class and region within Mexican national identity.[9] One of the significant differences in the case of Jewish nationalism is that the proportion of immigrants to established population was always such that the very face of the nation was altered with each new addition, and the nature of the nation had to be rethought. Cookbooks, as well as other food-related sites, reflect these changes.

When I started this project I wanted to show how looking at the construction of foodways reveals the process of forming the nation. I wanted to reveal the performative aspect of the nation: performative in the sense of showing, or displaying, an artificial "theatrical" act. Barbara Kirshenblatt-Gimblett eloquently theorizes the connections between food and performance. She describes their convergence in three junctions: *doing, behaving*, and *showing*.[10] As my project developed I realized that all three aspects applied to the performance of nation as well. *Doing*, or executing, applies to the production of food products and dishes in the field, factory, and, later, kitchen. It is linked to economic interests and to establishing literal ties between a physical land and the people occupying it. It is the creation of the fundamental physical structure for the nation. *Behaving* applies to all the customs, laws, and habits that define everyday food habits: following (or not) the laws of *kashrut*, buying local products, and participating in national holiday celebrations. All these contribute to the creation of the social and cultural fabric of the nation, reflecting political and ideological choices. Finally, *showing*, or displaying, applies to the creation of a nation's food symbols: food products and dishes that stand for the nation the way a flag or a national anthem might. Telling the story of the Jewish nation through the prism of foodways revealed a constantly changing and evolving process rather than a fixed entity, the result of constant negotiations and multiple influences and forces.

## METHODOLOGY

My original research for this project was in the context of my doctoral dissertation work at the Performance Studies Department at NYU, and it shaped my approach to this project and to the study of food in general. Since, as I mention above, I focused on process, on ephemeral objects and communal actions, on visual culture and multisensory events, performance studies' approach was remarkably well suited to my research. I relied on archival research for original documents, newspaper articles, advertisements, meeting minutes, photographs, and letters and treated them all with equal respect. I read fiction, poetry, cookbooks, and statistical surveys as valuable evidence, all illustrating with equal importance the shaping of the performance of nation in Israel. I also interviewed several people I thought would have a unique perspective and would offer me additional insights that would help me interpret what I read.

I believe that the inclusion of creative work and visual culture alongside historical evidence and theoretical investigations is one of performance studies' unique contributions. I agree with Dwight Conquergood's assertion that performance studies has the "capacity to bridge segregated and differently valued knowledges" and that it is "uniquely suited for the challenge of braiding together disparate and stratified ways of knowing."[11] I found cookbooks to be valuable texts bridging the gap between theory and practice, which seems to be an essential project for performance studies as a discipline. These practical texts, meant to teach concrete knowledge, offered layers of meanings and access to the workings of political processes and negotiations.

Additionally, performance studies is blatantly multidisciplinary in its approach. As I was reading academic sources from history, sociology, geography, economics, education, and more in order to understand the different aspects relating to food's production, distribution, preparation, and consumption and their negotiation within the political, economic, and social spheres I saw a clear parallel between the study of food and the study of performance in this respect. Both fields are inherently multidisciplinary because of the intricate webs they are implicated in, their roles in both public and private spheres, and their intimate relation to the body and to everyday life.

## A NATIONAL HISTORY

Zionism had to mobilize a dispersed community, few of whom lived in the geographical area of Zionism's projected homeland. Not all factions within the Zionist movement saw a concrete nation-state as their ultimate goal (just as Zionism was not the only national movement within Jewish communities in the Diaspora nor the only attempt to find a solution to "the

Jewish Question"). Advocates of cultural, as opposed to political, Zionism focused on developing the Hebrew language, literature, and other cultural manifestations independent of political autonomy. Cultural Zionism could be practiced under a foreign government and did not require national sovereignty.

Political Zionism combined a fight for political independence with the development of cultural products to reinforce its claim for a national existence in the particular territory of Palestine. Ya'akov Shavit argues that the Zionist movement consciously invented and shaped a national culture, seeing it as an essential component of identification as a nation (not an ethnic or religious community). Historical continuity or a common religion is not sufficient for recognition as a nation. Shavit highlights the role "planned culture" had in transforming a society of immigrants into a society with a national culture.[12] Food was one of the elements manipulated by the Zionists in this way. Attempting to forge unified cooking and eating habits artificially was another step toward fashioning a common national culture.

Food products were important in Zionist propaganda in that they were able to convey both a link to history and a new Jewish persona. Presenting certain food products or dishes as originally and continually belonging to the nation strengthens its claim for authenticity, communal origins in antiquity, and historical persistence.[13] Foodstuffs of biblical origin, like wheat, dates, and olives, were presented on Zionist commemorative postcards and on fund-raising posters.[14] Export products such as grapes and wine, olives and olive oil, figs, dates, and pomegranates "sold" Zionist ideology abroad. These foods, as well as agricultural tools that can be traced back to biblical times, evoke the sense of historical continuity and enforce the claim of an inherent bond between the Jewish people and their ancient land—a necessary condition for Jewish nationhood.[15] On the other hand, agricultural innovations and new, successful food products, like citrus fruit, advertised the new and modern Jewish existence in Palestine, which was divorced not so much from biblical times as from two thousand years of "spiritual" existence in exile. Zionist propaganda juxtaposed European Jews in attitudes of prayer or study with images of strong men plowing or sowing. Thus, food was used to convey both the authenticity of Jewish nationhood through historical ties to an ancient past and the Zionist vision of the future of the nation, a vital existence sustained by a direct bond with the land. The central place of agriculture in Zionist ideology and propaganda makes food an important part of Zionist iconography.

Yael Zerubavel, in her discussion of collective memory and national tradition in Israel, asserts, "The power of collective memory does not lie in its accurate . . . mapping of the past, but in establishing basic images that articulate and reinforce a particular ideological stance."[16] Accordingly, the Zionists' view of Jewish history presented antiquity—that is, the biblical period—as a positive period when there was a direct bond between the Jewish people and the land and when Jews had political sovereignty. The period of Exile, on the other hand, was a time that was dark and full of suffering.[17] Ben-Yehuda analyzed how the Zionists and later the state used the archaeological artifacts of Masada to establish both continuity with an ancient period of Jewish sovereignty and discontinuity with the period of Exile and spiritual existence in the Gola (Diaspora).[18]

Because of the role food and cooking play in the private sphere, because of the importance of agriculture in the early days of Zionist settlement in Palestine, and because of the importance of dietary laws and taboos in Jewish religion, examining foodways in Palestine and Israel offers a concrete angle to an exploration of the relationship between Jewish religion and Jewish nationalism. A study of the changes in food practices and in attitudes toward food and cooking allows an exploration of the changes in the perception and presentation of Jewish and later Israeli nationalism.

The place of Jewish religion in the new national culture was constantly negotiated and reexamined by different segments within the national movement. After independence and the establishment of the state of Israel as the "Jewish state," the question of the relationship between religion and nation was aggravated with the rise of questions regarding the government's involvement in the private sphere and separation between religion and state. Religion was largely shunned by the early *halutzim* (pioneers) who arrived in Palestine from Eastern Europe in their attempt to recast Jews as a modern nation and not a religious community. They were influenced by Marxist theories and the wish to replace the passive image of Jews in the Diaspora with that of the new Jew taking charge of his or her own destiny. Following independence, though, kashrut (the laws of ritual purity regarding Jewish dietary practice) was deemed an important factor in any national venture. To better understand the difference between Jewish and Israeli identifications, I examine the issue of kashrut throughout the history of the Zionist project and the Israeli state. The subject of kosher food (as a symptom of other issues relating to the [non]separation of religion and state) will return most prominently in the 1990s with the growing impact of the post-Soviet immigration to Israel.

The meaning of Jewish nationalism changed with the establishment of the state because the state offered a universal "seal of approval," legitimizing the Zionist cause. But independence also changed the relationship between Israel and the Diaspora. Before independence the Yishuv (the Jewish community in the land of Israel) needed to justify its existence, to prove to the world that it represented a modern nation and that the land of Israel was indeed its rightful place. It was in a fragile and tenuous position. The support (both moral and economic) of the Diaspora was necessary for its survival. Following independence, the power balance shifted, and Israel became that which provided security for the Diaspora. Jewish religion created a bond between all Jewish people and provided a network of support for its people; but whereas previously religion could be a hindrance to claims of nationhood (Jewish people as a religious sect or an ethnic minority, not a modern nation), by 1948 religion offered a ready-made common ground, a unified cultural product that would create a cohesive society out of a multitude of ethnic groups. Religion was also effective as a symbol of unity to present to the rest of the world. Creating a new and unified secular culture that carried the same weight was apparently a much more difficult and longer process. Looking to popular cultural products such as folk dances and songs or food provided the seeds for the creation of a secular Israeli culture. Because of the role food plays in Israel in both "high culture" (through religion) and popular culture, it provides a compelling window into the evolution of both.

Zionism, like other national movements of this period, is a nineteenth-century development that involves "imagining a political community" by establishing continuity with an ancient past.[19] The definition of nationalism as a "cultural artifact" involving elements of invention and social engineering, as suggested by Ernest Gellner, Hobsbawm, and Benedict Anderson, has been particularly useful for me, as it highlights the deliberate, the artificial, and the performative in nationalism itself.[20] The Zionist case is unique in that the transformation from the inception of the national movement to the establishment of a state happened between the First Zionist Congress in 1897 and the creation of the Israeli state in 1948. The "extroverted" nature of Zionism as a conscious ideological project makes the process of nation making explicit and has produced a wealth of documentation. Finally, the "ingathering" of Jewish people from a variety of countries to a new land created a clear historical break and a visible point of origin for a modern national project.

## A ROADMAP

This book focuses on food, yet political conflict, socioeconomic changes, and cultural shifts all influence food choices and habits. In an effort to streamline the narrative, I have opted to eliminate much of this background information from the chapters themselves; however, I offer some of it in an appendix. It includes a compilation of some significant annotated dates to help readers find their way and understand the discussion of food in a somewhat broader context.

The first chapter explores the role of agriculture in the Zionist narrative. Conveniently, the production and growing of food products, the high value placed on working the land, and an ascetic ideological approach to consumption are all characteristic of the initial period of Zionist immigration to Palestine, as well as offering a fitting place to begin a story about food. The chapter examines the concept of "Hebrew" labor, which I find particularly relevant now, as scholarship and popular media both devote growing attention to the role of labor in what we perceive to be "good" food. Questions around labor practices and divisions play a prominent part in current discussions of food security and food justice.

Chapter 2 follows the food chain with a discussion of distribution and the marketplace. The notion of selling Zionist ideology alongside locally grown—by "Hebrew" labor!—products is one of the central themes of this chapter, as well as a study of the evolution of the sale of nonkosher products, opening the way to a discussion of changing attitudes toward Jewish religious and cultural practices.

The following three chapters explore the kitchen. Chapter 3 focuses on culinary education in several forms: the "self-educated" early female pioneers, the women's organizations' role in educating both children and housewives of later immigration waves (and the complicated relationship between immigrants from different immigration waves and cultural backgrounds), and the "formal" state home economics education in the school system. All these sites share a similar evolution and an ongoing struggle to reconcile ethnic differences with national unity. The changing attitudes and rising status and professionalism of kitchen work are prominent topics, particularly as they are reflected in gender relations within Israeli society. In a way, chapter 4 explores culinary education as well, only this time through the prism of cookbooks and the media. The limited range in this field in the early years allows for a very thorough examination of influential texts, a task that grows much more difficult, as the cookbook-publishing field has exploded in more recent decades. I was not able to do justice to the on-line field in this book, but its influence is constantly growing, and it offers a view of the current culinary scene without the time lag and mediation that generally characterize printed cookbooks. It is a very direct expression of cooks' own voices. Websites, blogs, and social media outlets in Israel definitely merit closer additional attention. This chapter expands the discussion in chapter 3 on the struggle between national unification and the efforts to create a unified national cuisine, and the culinary variations practiced by each ethnic immigrant group. This chapter also reveals the tremendous change Israel has undergone in its attitude both toward pluralism and acceptance and toward food as a source of pleasure.

Chapter 5, the final kitchen chapter, explores professional cooking. I was not able to do justice to the many restaurants in Israel today and over the past few decades. I therefore opted to discuss hotel restaurants instead and to explore, through them, the professional kitchen's role in the representation of a national cuisine for the outside world. The first part of the chapter focuses on the role of a national cuisine as symbol, a performance of the nation, in the global arena. The second part of the chapter turns to army cooking as the site that is most influential within Israeli society. I decided to locate it in a chapter on professional cooking because of its central role in the public sphere and because the growing professionalism of army cooks is a telling phenomenon in itself.

Chapter 6 moves on to consumption. It completes the discussion of the communal dining rooms I began in chapter 1 and then centers on two types of events: the *kumzits* (outdoor dining) and the Mimouna celebrations (a Jewish-Moroccan holiday tradition). Both sites raise a range of themes that were explored in previous chapters, allowing the reader to revisit the entire evolution of the national movement's relationship with food and the land, in the case of the kumzits, and with a specific group of non-European immigrants, in the case of the Mimouna. The chapter highlights the nature of these events and sites as grounded in process, constantly evolving.

Taken as a whole, this book aims to paint a picture of the evolution of an Israeli cuisine as a reflection of the evolution of a secular Jewish nationalism in the state of Israel. It focuses on the ongoing negotiation between a clearly defined, unified national image and the multiple immigration waves, ethnic variations, and global forces and influences that tug at it.

## FALAFEL: A CASE STUDY

"So you're writing about falafel?" or "So what is there other than falafel?" or "I assume you are not writing about falafel" were perhaps the most typical responses I received upon announcing that I was writing about Israeli cuisine. As these responses indicate, falafel has become synonymous with Israeli food in recent years. My publisher's wish to include "falafel" in the title of this book is perhaps the latest example of its resonance with a wider public. It is but one of several food products that have become symbols of national identity. Usually, as in the case of Japanese rice and French wine, the products are so intimately joined to their cultures that it is difficult to excavate the historical origin of these associations. In the case of falafel, however, we have access to its historical origins. It has not assimilated into Israeli society by a long, slow, natural process; rather, its transformation into an icon-of-Israel status was rushed and deliberate, groomed by the national movement as a signifier of Israeli pride. The case of falafel also generated a unique controversy, since it became embroiled in the Arab-Israeli political conflict. How did a product that originated in Arab cooking achieve the status of an Israeli national icon?

Initially, I thought the story of falafel would make for a thought-provoking conclusion, but upon consideration (and on the advice of my wise readers), I have decided to present it here, in the introduction. This allows me to anticipate the entire story of this manuscript in a compact package, raising most of the central points presented later within a single example and, I hope, getting falafel out of the way so readers can see beyond it.

Falafel is generally made from fava beans (as in Egypt, where it is also known as *ta'amia*), from chickpeas (the version traditional to Palestine and encountered in Israel today), or from a combination of the two. The dried legumes are soaked in water, ground, mixed with spices, shaped into small balls, and deep-fried.[21] Falafel's origins have been traced to the Christian Copts of Egypt, who were not allowed to eat meat during certain holidays, especially Lent. Ta'amia served as a meat substitute. When the dish later spread to other regions in the Middle East, the fava beans were sometimes replaced with chickpeas.[22] The early Jewish pioneers in Palestine adopted the local Arab version made with chickpeas. By the 1920s falafel had become a popular snack with the younger generation, and by the 1950s it was common throughout Israeli society.

In her study of the bagel in the United States, Barbara Kirshenblatt-Gimblett has outlined a series of stages the bagel passed through on its way from an ethnic niche product to the popular American food it is today.[23] The same stages are useful to illuminate the transformation of falafel's status in Israeli society. By following falafel's progress through these stages, I would like to revisit the parallel transformations within Israeli society and culture discussed throughout the other chapters. In the first stage, which Kirshenblatt-Gimblett terms "self-evident," the product is taken for granted. The position of falafel in the everyday Arab diet was certainly "self-evident." The second stage, termed "self-conscious," is an accurate description of how the early Jewish immigrants adopted certain local Arab cultural practices in a deliberate attempt to relinquish Diaspora habits in favor of a new existence in Palestine. The halutzim of the Second and Third Aliyot chose to adopt certain Arab models that they perceived as related to the Jewish existence in the mythical biblical past. Here the ambivalent Zionist attitude toward the local Arab population comes to the fore. The Arabs were seen as models of behavior, on the one hand, and as primitive and in need of Jewish acculturation and modernization, on the other. As a street food, not a creation of a sophisticated court cuisine, falafel supported a view of Arab culture as unrefined and facilitated its acceptance by the Jewish community in Palestine at a time when home cooking was seen as part of the bourgeois existence the halutzim had left behind in Europe. Even as the initial marginalizing of the kitchen and the subjugating of the nuclear family by the community and the nation (manifested most clearly in the kibbutz system) gave way to the recruiting of food and of the traditional family structure to the national project, the ideals of productivity and efficiency remained powerful. As a quick, no-frills, affordable, and satisfying dish, falafel accorded with these ideals. It was seen as a functional food, not an indulgent one.

Most falafel was consumed at falafel stands. Even so, practically every cookbook published in Israel up to the 1970s included a recipe for it. As a high-protein vegetarian food, falafel fit the agenda that had been promoted by women's organizations since the late 1920s to reduce meat consumption and consume more local dairy and legumes (though the fact that falafel was deep-fried diminished its appeal somewhat). One of the earliest recipes appeared in 1940 in the daily newspaper *Ha-Aretz*. In response to a question by one of the readers ("How is falafel made?"), the anonymous writer offered the following recipe:

Cook the legumes (dried peas, *lubia* [fava beans], or another type), grind, mix with oil (preferably sesame) until thickened, add plenty of crushed red pepper and salt (you can also add fresh green pepper while grinding and add other minced vegetables at the end). Make small balls from the mixture and deep-fry in boiling oil until brown-yellow. You could also do an easier version with pea flour (if available) mixed with water until thick or cooked in water with a pinch of baking soda and finished as above.[24]

This recipe differs from all subsequent versions in its flexible attitude toward the main ingredient (not specifying chickpeas at all), the suggestion to include fresh minced vegetables, the use of oil in the mixture, and the absence of any of the traditional spices (like coriander and cumin).

Kirshenblatt-Gimblett's third stage in the cultural assimilation of food is "estrangement." For falafel, this process began with the campaign for the purchase of *totzeret ha-aretz* (local products) and its insistence on Jewish labor. The orange, which preceded falafel as an Israeli culinary icon, was seen as a symbol of the success of Jewish agriculture in Palestine (the cultivation of oranges had formerly been controlled by Arab labor). By "estranging" the orange from its Arab past, the Zionists were able to adopt it as their own while presenting Palestine as empty and desolate before their arrival. The insistence on Jewish labor as an essential part of the campaign helped the early halutzim to see themselves not as a colonizing force but as redeemers of the land. But the orange could symbolize the Zionist project only after it had been detached from its early ties with the Arab population. As the importance of agriculture diminished and the demographics of the Jewish population changed (following Israel's independence in 1948, a much larger percentage of non-European immigrants began to arrive), falafel underwent an evolution similar to that of the orange and, in many ways, took its place. Since falafel could now be linked to Jewish immigrants who had come from the Middle East and Africa, it could shed its Arab association in favor of an overarching Israeli identification. Furthermore, these newer immigrants did not share the Eastern European aversion to Diaspora culture and so could maintain certain elements of their own culture in Israel.

Following the 1948 War of Independence, Arabs began to be portrayed as the enemy, and Arab cultural products acquired negative associations. This process affected falafel, which was distanced from its roots in local Arab cuisine and attributed to Jewish immigrants from Yemen. Running falafel stands was popular with Yemenite immigrants in Palestine as early as the 1920s and 1930s. *Beyond Milk and Honey*, a collection of recipes distributed by the Israeli Embassy in Washington DC, attributes falafel's popularity in Israel to Yemenite immigrants and makes no mention of its Arab roots.[25] However, contrary to what many Israelis believe, falafel is not native to Yemen; the Yemenites had learned how to prepare it from the local Arabs.[26]

After independence, as the economic situation worsened and the percentage of immigrants from Middle Eastern and North African countries grew, falafel became even more popular. The Zena (rationing) regime, instituted by the Israeli government in 1949, restricted the consumption of meat and other products, thereby contributing to falafel's increasing favor in Israeli society as an affordable source of protein. Moreover, falafel was cheap, satisfying, and flavorful.

Falafel's growing fame was reflected in its appearance as the subject of popular songs, such as Y. Zukerman's 1949 "Falafel":

> *I had for quite a long while*
> *a dangerous ulcer,*
> *diet and remedies were no help at all.*
> *What need have I for medicine,*
> *I have a kind of cure*
> *better than penicillin.*
>
> *Chorus:*
> *Falafel, falafel,*
> *fresh, hot and aromatic.*
> *Honestly, you should taste it.*
> *Falafel, falafel,*
> *spicy and blood boiling,*
> *burning—fires of hell.*
> *What flavor!*
> *Everyone devours.*
> *And again!*
> *Salt and pepper.*
> *Falafel, falafel,*
> *An old man shouts and a young boy too,*
> *this is one spicy falafel.*
>
> *Shlomit has a baby,*
> *he has grown some teeth already,*
> *chatters constantly,*

*Shlomit tells him:*
*"Say Mommy to me!"*
*But the boy cries instead:*

*Falafel, falafel . . .*

*I have a girl,*
*this is what she told me:*
*"Know I have two loves."*
*And jealous then I asked her, "Who?"*
*"One is you—and the other's name is"*

*Falafel, falafel . . .*[27]

This song encouraged anyone unfamiliar with falafel to try it: "Honestly, you should taste it." By the late 1950s, however, such encouragement was unnecessary. A song by Dan Almagor called "Ve-Lanu Yesh Falafel" (And we have falafel) demonstrated that by 1958 the Israeli embrace of falafel was complete.

During the 1950s, greater exposure to a variety of ethnic influences through such institutions as the Israeli army and the school system further increased the popularity of some non-European foodstuffs. The 1948 cookbook compiled by the Women's International Zionist Organization (WIZO) does not include a recipe for falafel, but the 1956 edition does. It appears under the subheading "Oriental Dishes," "Oriental" serving as a common Israeli substitute for "Arab" at the time. The recipe calls for soaking chickpeas in water and a pinch of baking soda overnight; grinding them twice with water-soaked bread, garlic, and parsley; adding salt, red pepper (cayenne), coriander, and cumin (adding one egg is optional); and finally forming small balls from the mixture and deep-frying them.[28] In 1960 Lillian Cornfeld, one of the most popular and influential cookbook writers in Israel at the time, included a recipe for falafel in the section of her cookbook devoted to legumes, moving the dish closer to the mainstream of the Israeli diet. The recipe itself is similar to the WIZO recipe, but it eliminates the soaked bread in favor of a teaspoon each of flour and baking soda added to the mixture. Cornfeld also suggests serving falafel as the falafel stands do: in pita bread, with vegetable salad and tahini or accompanied by French fries.[29]

The detachment of falafel from its Arab origins allowed it to reach the next stage in its assimilation, "authentic." At this stage, the food is no longer taken for granted; the best variations are searched out and are upheld as prized products. By the late 1960s falafel had become "nationalized" into Israeli culture and cuisine to the point where it could be used with pride as a symbol of "Israeliness." As Israel devoted greater effort in the 1960s toward establishing images of a united nation, the "Jewish state" fell back on certain elements from Jewish tradition. In the realm of food, this meant that all "national" ventures, from the Israeli Defense Forces (IDF) to El Al Airline to state dinners, served kosher food. Falafel had an advantage in its status as a pareve food (neither meat nor dairy), which gave it flexibility in kosher menus. Thus, despite its original low status as a street food, falafel slowly gained entry into formal menus representing the state of Israel. When chef Uri Guttman prepared the annual dinner of the German Gastronomic Academy in 1998 with dishes native to his home country of Israel, he chose to begin the eight-course meal with an appetizer of hummus and tahini with a single falafel ball, pine nuts, and a drop of oil served on a spoon.[30]

Kirshenblatt-Gimblett's final stage, that of "naturalization," occurs when the product becomes common, part of everyday life. There is no question that falafel in Israel achieved this final stage. It can be found everywhere from ready-made supermarket mixes to modern fast-food chains, and it is consumed by all factions of Israeli society.

During the 1970s and 1980s, partly because of health risks (rumors regarding the use of engine oil for frying the falafel balls circulated for a while) and partly because of competition from other fast-food products such as pizza and hamburgers, falafel's popularity seemed to decline, but it has never disappeared from the Israeli diet.[31] In the past few years, its popularity has surged as new falafel chains offer a clean, modern environment. There are also new variations, such as the red pepper or sweet potato falafel offered at Tel Aviv's Malkot ha-Falafel (Falafel Queens), which opened in 1998.[32] One of the owners of Malkot ha-Falafel, Ella Shein, justified her falafel variations to the critics by saying that falafel is "not originally Israeli"; it was always influenced by a variety of sources and is a product of integration.[33]

As national icons, wine in France and rice in Japan seem to resonate with the people who consume them, but Israelis seem somewhat ambivalent toward falafel. Although it is a very popular snack, falafel appears to be most powerful as a symbol for outsiders (such as Jews living abroad or tourists) rather than for the people of Israel. Hanokh Levin, who was one of Israel's most prominent playwrights, wrote a short story describing a very unfortunate blind date. In an effort to salvage something from the evening, the woman tries to get the man to buy her dinner, but the man wants to spend as little money as possible. So they end up at a falafel stand. Levin describes their meal:

> Ishel and Romanechka are standing . . . , each one holding a pita stuffed with fiery falafel balls, stale salad, and runny tahini sauce, their bodies leaning slightly forward like animals at a trough so as not to stain their clothes with dripping tahini. . . . Both of them dislike falafel; they are swallowing it listlessly, Ishel forcing himself to pretend avid eating . . . and Romanechka pouring all her fury and resentment onto the falafel, and so to an observer it would seem as if two hedonists are drawing the utmost pleasure from the cheap Yemenite dish that has become—alas—our national emblem.[34]

Falafel is often presented as a proud national symbol on postcards, in tourist publications, and at meals served abroad. However, it appears to serve more as a representation of Israel to the outside world than as an evocative and inspiring image for Israelis.

More recently, Dorit Maya-Gur, an illustrator and comic book artist, published *Falafelman* (2006), a comic book detailing the adventures of a new Israeli superhero. Similarly to Levin's description, the hero here is an ambivalent figure: an overweight, procrastinating, underachieving slob who is transformed through a freak accident into a super strong and rotund (resembling a falafel ball) hero who fights for justice and punishes evildoers. The ironic use of falafel, as well as the particular choice for this first quintessentially Israeli superhero, serves as a perfect illustration of Israeli's ambivalent feelings toward falafel.

A photograph of falafel balls in pita bread adorned with a prominent Israeli flag, positioned as if to signify Israel's dominion over this particular

1. *Falafelman*, Dorit Maya-Gur (2006). Published with the artist's permission.

falafel landscape, is displayed on postcards, as well as on the cover of a small cookbook sold in tourist shops called *The Melting Pot: A Quick and Easy Blend of Israeli Cuisine*. The same company, Palphot Ltd., published both the postcard and the book. The cookbook is written in English, and its cover image seems to be the most nationalistic representation of falafel.[35] Oddly enough, Palphot also published a book titled *A Taste of Egypt: Quick and Easy Egyptian Recipes*, which features on its cover the very same image but with one small change: the Israeli flag has been replaced by an Egyptian one.[36] The Israeli publisher apparently had no problem "sharing" this national icon with Egypt, the country regarded as the originator of falafel, but actual Egyptian publications do not appear to regard falafel in the same manner. It might be a popular street food, but it is too lowly to be featured as a national emblem.

Outside of Israel, falafel retains its status as a marker for the Israeli nation and Jewish nationalism. Falafel and hummus have taken over as the popular offerings at Jewish social gatherings. Because falafel's origins are Arab, it is not directly associated with any one community in the Diaspora; since the entire Jewish population in Israel has adopted it, it is the perfect symbol for a proud, new, ethnically mixed, Jewish nation. By replacing bagels or pastrami with falafel, a Jewish community in New York, for example, can display its affiliation with Israel, its connection to the Jewish state, and its inclusion in the Jewish nation. So perhaps falafel has not lost its cachet as an emblem of Israeli identity.

Over the years, Palestinians have criticized Israelis for appropriating falafel and making it their own. Prof. Daniel Bar-Tal, a family friend, told me about a conference he participated in several years ago at which an Israeli woman was trying to break up an argument between the Palestinian and the Israeli participants. "Why are we arguing?" she asked. "We have so much in common! Even our food: falafel, for example," to which an outraged Palestinian woman objected, "You stole everything else from us, now you want to steal falafel too?!"[37] An article in the *New York Times* focused on the tension between Palestinians and Israelis surrounding falafel.[38] It presented a range of opinions on both sides regarding falafel's "ownership." From the article it appears that today most Israelis acknowledge the Arab origins of falafel, whereas some Palestinians concede that falafel is a regional food and therefore is not "owned" by any one nation.[39] Because food and eating habits are often products of cultural and commercial exchange, as well as mutual influences, tracing their origins can be problematic. Falafel became a particularly sensitive topic because of the tense political situation and because Israelis made falafel into a symbol for the Israeli nation.

In his cookbook *A Taste of Palestine*, Aziz Shihab reports that in Jerusalem "hummus and falafel shops are filled with customers. They are no longer Arab foods."[40] Shihab's observation is tinged with nostalgia, with a sense that the city of his childhood is no longer his. But the wider appeal of these foods in the global market is treated as a positive phenomenon in several modern cookbooks: "Falafel . . . is now part of the global menu," writes Anissa Helou.[41] In a brief survey of Middle Eastern cookbooks written mainly by Palestinian and Arab authors, I found that falafel is consistently described as popular throughout the Middle East: "The fast food of the Middle East, falafel has invaded restaurant menus of all categories in many parts of Europe and America," writes Christiane Dabdoub Nasser.[42] Sonia Uvezian is more specific: "One of Egypt's national dishes, falafel is also very popular in Syria, Lebanon, and Jordan, where it is avidly consumed at all times of the day."[43] Falafel's popularity in countries other than Egypt is not perceived as a problem. Jenny Ridgwell states simply that "falafel is popular throughout the Middle East, each country having a slightly different recipe."[44] A specific mention of Israel is conspicuously missing from all these examples. If Israel is part of the Middle East, then its citizens have as much right as those of any other country in the region to love falafel. Israelis' choice of falafel and hummus as markers of identity should perhaps be perceived as a reflection of their wish to become part of the Middle East. Would their motives not be more questionable had they insisted on gefilte fish or hamburger as the "national" snack?

Food is constantly implicated in economic and political processes, as well as in social and historical processes; it can serve either as a tool of propaganda or as an instrument of study and greater understanding. Because of the recent events in the Middle East, even something as innocent looking as a ground chickpea ball can be used as a weapon of sorts in a battle played out in the media and global public opinion. I admit that the history of falafel told here is a subjective one, as I have focused on falafel's role within the Israeli national project. I maintain that the iconic power of falafel for Israelis and for the Jewish people in the Diaspora derives from its ability to serve as a common, unifying marker for a variety of factions within Israeli society. That it was adopted from the outside and does not "belong" to any one particular ethnic group is, in fact, one of the reasons for its success. The history of falafel's vicissitudes within the Israeli nation also reflects the ambivalent attitude of Israelis toward the Palestinian population. Unlike other food products (e.g., sugar), falafel was never produced through the labor of a colonized population, nor was Palestinian land appropriated for the purpose of growing chickpeas for its preparation. Thus, falafel is not a tool of oppression. As considered here, the case of falafel can offer some insight into the complex nature of national icons and cultural preferences.

When I began exploring food in Israel I did not set out to create a list of popular foods, nor did I wish to describe what Israeli cuisine might be or to debate its existence. I was interested in exploring the idea of Jewish nationalism and the Israeli state through the prism of food because it was, in fact, difficult to list and to define. Food mutates. Food travels and shifts alliances. Sugar influenced the mobilization of entire populations, impacting the economy on three continents, setting in motion political and social processes that are still unfolding today; the tomato, a plant native to South America, became so integral to Italian cooking that the question of its authenticity is no longer relevant; rice, originating in China, became the national emblem of Japan, historically China's sworn enemy; falafel, an Arab street food, became an icon of the state of Israel. These are but a few samples from a vast array of mutations and unexpected transformations that, as our world shrinks with new technology and greater access, seems to unfold at a quickening pace. Food is intertwined in politics, the economy, religion, culture, technology, and art. It is multidisciplinary and multisensory. It is tangled, and changeable, and ephemeral: it is grounded in process. It is therefore a perfect vehicle for discussing "nation," a construct that was always presented as immutable, immovable, and unchangeable.

Through symbols and histories, nations are depicted as absolute, eternal, and uniform. The discourse of food exposes the vulnerability of the nation, its flexible and changeable nature, its many voices. Food products demonstrate that transplanted does not mean inauthentic, that "authentic" does not denote an absolute truth and may carry different meanings, and that a nation is not a complete, natural product but rather a complex, many-faceted, ongoing process.

Immigration waves have had a tremendous impact on the economy, ideology, and culture of Israel. Foodways reflect these changes and mirror socioeconomic processes. They embody the tension between ethnic affiliations and national identification. Going through the entire time period from the inception of Zionism to the present through the story of food rather than through a straightforward chronology, I wish to offer room for new voices and new questions in the study of Jewish nationalism. As I consider the role of immigration in shaping Israeli culture and society I wish to pay special attention to Israelis' effort to connect to the land and to forge meaningful symbols of secular, national affiliation and belonging.

# 1

# PUTTING DOWN ROOTS

## Agricultural Labor and Icons

*A land of wheat and barley, of vines and fig trees and*
*pomegranates, land of olive trees and honey.*
—Deuteronomy 8:8

Food has been used as a marketing tool for the land of Israel since ancient times. In biblical times the land of milk and honey was advertised with the aid of grapes, and ever since, food has continued to play a significant role in Zionist propaganda and Israeli tourism campaigns. These campaigns tend to use natural, whole foodstuffs such as grapes, olives, and oranges. These "fruits of the land" are perceived as direct links to the land itself, and creating and enforcing these links has been the primary concern of the Zionist movement. The most significant change in the treatment of these culinary symbols began with the First Aliya (immigration wave) toward the end of the nineteenth century. The members of the First Aliya had a new point of view: they not only were interested in consuming symbolic slivers of the promised land but also attempted to forge a more direct and powerful link with the land of Israel. They wished to put down roots by growing these products themselves; by working the land, they attempted to create an immediate and intimate bond between people and place.

This chapter focuses on agriculture in the Zionist project, particularly in its early years, as both practical tool and ideological trope and on the relationship between ideology and practice (sometimes supportive and often at odds). "Working the land" was a fundamental stage in the Zionist national project, a performance of Zionist ideology in the sense of "execution," "doing": connecting to the land of Israel in the most literal way and establishing an independent economic foundation. Growing food meant establishing strength and self-reliance in the present and the future, as well as forging a bond with the physical land both by working its soil and by consuming its fruit. In addition to the greater project of agriculture, specific agricultural products took on a similar role: growing and/or consuming them equaled the praxis of Zionism. Before the national movement could rely on official state symbols, it could use these products as physical markers of national identity.

One of the early challenges of the Jewish national movement was the first encounter of the young immigrants from Eastern Europe with the reality of life in the land of Israel. The Zionist movement could claim that the Jewish people are directly descended from the biblical Israelites, but in reality the new immigrants were raised in a different climate and were used to different foods. One of the most trivial-seeming yet essential steps to settling in a new land is being able to live on the available food products. The early Jewish immigrants felt this acutely because of the difficult economic situation and the limited products available to them.

The difficulty in adjusting to the unfamiliar foods of Palestine during this period is beautifully described in S. Y. Agnon's novel *Temol Shilshom* (Only yesterday). The "green" pioneer, Izchak, is offered a meal by a more experienced fellow pioneer after a frustrating day of unsuccessfully trying to find work in the *moshava* (village). The meal consists of tea, bread, tomatoes, and olives. Both tomatoes and olives are strange to Izchak and not quite to his liking even after he is persuaded to try them, but his friend admonishes him: "If you wish to be a son of the land of Israel, you have to learn to eat what you find."[1]

Agnon makes it clear that one cannot be "a son of the land" if one cannot live off what that land provides. We are later told that Izchak becomes accustomed to these new foods: "Even the foods that were foreign to Izchak at first became tasteful to him. The fried eggplants in oil and in tomato sauce and all manner of dishes that are common in the land, are his foods every day, and needless to say olives and tomatoes."[2] This is an essential step in the assimilation process of the immigrant Izchak. Agnon follows this with a lush description of the available seasonal fruits: apricots, grapes, prickly pears, watermelons, figs, dates, pomegranates, oranges, and mandarins. These fruits were more readily accepted by most immigrants, since they were already somewhat familiar with them. The immigrants had been exposed to them in Europe as very expensive, special, and prized products representing the land of Israel, the land of milk and honey. The sweet taste of dates, oranges, or pomegranates would symbolize the promise of the biblical land of Israel. These fruits are used in the novel to help present the land as bountiful, although one had to be open to trying the local products.

## CULINARY ICONS

As Agnon's story demonstrates, fruit as a symbol of the "promised land" was a familiar device. In the early days of Zionist settlement in Palestine, these symbols were extended and expanded to forge both emotional and literal links to the land. Several food products were employed both as concrete symbols of an intangible connection to a new land, a unifying device, and as an attempt at a practical solution, a crop choice for a new farming endeavor.

Four decades after Agnon wrote *Temol Shilshom*, Benyamin Tamuz wrote a fictional account of a young *halutz* visiting his family in a town in Eastern Europe during approximately the same historical period. He brings them olives as a special gift from the land of Israel. Tamuz highlights the gap between the idealized image and the sometimes literally bitter reality:

> As soon as he said it must be olives, immediately everyone almost fainted. Olives we have seen only in the Bible when we read "land of olive oil and honey," as it is written in the book of Devarim, as we have learned; and you must remember well that it is written there also "olives you will have in all your borders . . ." and in Prophets *olive* is written a thousand times. But who in his life has seen an olive? . . . "So a man walks into a store and buys olives?" asked grandfather in a whisper. "Sure," said Yehiel, "they are very cheap and the halutzim eat them a lot since they are very cheap."[3]

The family then invites most of the town (everyone who is anyone) to view and partake of the olives. They all gather promptly and wait for the

2. "A land of wheat and barley, of vines and fig trees and pomegranates, land of olive trees and honey" (Deuteronomy 8:8). From the collections of the Central Zionist Archives, Jerusalem.

rabbi, who, after a short deliberation, gravely announces that these are indeed olives from the land of Israel. The gathered crowd is beside themselves. They pass around a crystal dish with the olives for everyone to have a small taste.

> The taste was, may the *kodesh borech-hu* forgive me, as if you put a chicken's gallbladder in your mouth. Far be it from me to speak badly of the olive that is a holy fruit from the land of Israel, it must have spoiled in the meantime, since I cannot believe, and simple logic does not allow, that the olive would be so bitter. It must be sweet as honey, providing you eat it fresh off the tree like you would apples and pears. The entire world knows that you should not eat spoiled fruit, but because of the olive's sacredness you do not mind it.[4]

Both the writer of this letter and the other guests display their excitement over the olives through their connection with the biblical text by quoting relevant passages and sayings. The olive embodies the bond between Jewish religion and heritage, a mythical golden age, and modern Jewish nationalism. However, the encounter with the reality of the olive, the actual taste, is a clear marker of how alien it is to them, how removed they are from life in the land where the olive grows. The olive has a strong association with Arab foods. Its foreignness to the Eastern European Jewish palette stands in marked contrast to its role as a staple in the Middle Eastern Arab diet. The olive tree itself became a powerful symbol in Palestinian mythology, coming to signify the Palestinian connection to the land and the bearer of Palestinian memory and national identity.[5]

In the early days of Jewish settlement in the land of Israel, grapes and olives played a central role as culinary "ambassadors." They were both linked to biblical times through their place among the seven *minim* (species) the land of Canaan was said to be blessed with (the others were almonds, wheat, barley, pomegranates, and figs). As such, both grapes and olives support the Zionist historical narrative, which traces a direct line from the ancient Israelites to the modern-day Jewish nation. Concurrent with its attempt to shape a new, vital, and self-sufficient Jewish figure, the national movement wished to show the Jewish nation as natural, constant, and historically linked to the land of Israel. Grapes (and all their by-products, such as raisins and

3. The Fourteenth Zionist Congress, Palestinian Exhibition. From the collections of the Central Zionist Archives, Jerusalem.

wine) offered a perfect trigger to the collective Jewish imagination, encapsulating all these objectives in a small, sweet package.

The early Zionist settlers arriving in Palestine toward the end of the nineteenth century chose grapes as one of the main agricultural products for cultivation in their attempt to create a productive, self-sufficient Jewish society. Two unique ventures, Petach-Tikva, a moshava established in 1878, and Mikve Israel, an agricultural school established in 1870, were early attempts at agricultural work by Jewish people in the land of Israel prior to the First Aliya (1884–1903).[6] They represent the seeds of the attempt to bring Jewish people out from behind the city walls and into a new, more independent existence. It is important to note that despite the prevalence of the Zionist narrative of the First Aliya as the first to introduce agricultural work to the Jewish community in a significant way, Jewish agricultural work is in fact a much older practice. Historian Israel Bar-Tal attributes the encouragement of agricultural labor among Jewish people in the late 1800s to the Russian government's influence and to Eastern and Central European intellectuals' economic views. They regarded agricultural labor and craft as essential to a country's economic prosperity (unlike commerce and trade) and therefore encouraged mass migration of Jewish communities to rural areas and farming life throughout Eastern Europe in the nineteenth century.[7]

The members of the First Aliya founded twenty-five new agricultural settlements (*moshavot*, plural of moshava) between 1882 and 1903. These agricultural settlements should be distinguished from the *moshavim* (plural of *moshav*), the cooperative villages established in the early 1920s, because the early moshavot were not structured as communes or cooperatives but as more traditional villages with private plots and hired help. The emphasis on self-labor ("Hebrew" labor), particularly agricultural labor, was one of the main innovations of the First Aliya.[8]

The ideal of self-labor was difficult because of the harsh economic conditions in Palestine, lack of experience and agricultural knowledge of the immigrants, and shortage of capital. The moshavot established by the immigrants of the First Aliya survived largely due to the support of Baron Edmond James de Rothschild through a system of overseers and agricultural advisors and teachers. Later immigrants criticized the members of the

First Aliya for receiving this support from Rothschild. They saw it as akin to the money of the *haluka* (the organized distribution of financial support from communities abroad, viewed as a handout) that had been given to the old Yishuv. So despite the original intention of the First Aliya to create a new Jewish image, to change the Diasporic lifestyle into a productive and independent one, subsequent immigration waves believed the first wave betrayed these ideals.[9]

Rothschild's advisors helped the settlers develop crops such as grapevines and olives. New technologies gave a great push to citrus and orchard products. Creating a basis for an independent national economy was an important contribution by the First Aliya's members. It was the first attempt at a conscious national endeavor.[10] The settlers originally wanted to grow wheat. Producing bread, the staff of life, through their own labor was their ultimate goal, but they chose orchards when they realized the small size of their plots would not support wheat growing.

The decision to plant grapevines was due not only to Rothschild's influence but also to the financial reality: settlers generally invested all the money they had in purchasing land and therefore favored a crop that would give a fairly quick return. Vines give fruit after two years, while citrus produces fruit only four years after planting. Later, though, the settlers realized that in order to produce wine from the grapes, a much greater investment and longer period of time were necessary (including building production facilities and shipping the wine to Europe for sale), and citrus growing rose in popularity.

Oranges replaced olives and grapes in the late 1920s both as the main agricultural product and as a powerful symbol. Citrus growing was promoted as one of the main export branches of the Jewish community in Palestine. The climate in Israel appears particularly well suited for citrus growing, and it flourished. Over a period of about six years following the First World War, the area of Jewish citrus groves tripled. Ninety percent of these citrus groves were privately owned and influenced the growth of related industries. The orange is markedly associated with successful Jewish agricultural labor in Israel. It has no connection to the Bible, lacking the mystic and historical connections to land and forefathers that olives and grapes had, yet that lack of connection is also its advantage: like the new non-Diasporic Jew living off the land, productive and strong, the orange is a new agricultural product, a foundation for a national economy. Despite the later success of other products such as avocados and tomatoes, the continued importance of grapes and olives, and the addition of other citrus products, the orange remained for several decades the premier agricultural export of Israel.

The oranges were mostly of one particular type known as Shamuti—an almost seedless, elliptical, sweet fruit that was easy to peel. These were becoming known in Europe as Jaffa oranges. Initially, every company would ship oranges under a different brand name, but by the mid-1920s the brand name Jaffa had begun to appear on orange crates from the land of Israel. In the 1940s the Council for the Distribution of Citrus Fruit was established by the British Mandate. They realized that Jaffa was associated with a high-quality product and began distributing all citrus products from Israel under that brand name.

Despite the fact that citrus growing in the region began as a product of Arab labor (and, like the olive, the orange had also been adopted as a symbol of Palestinian nostalgia for a lost homeland), its increasing success as an export product was tied to Jewish labor and initiative. Oranges became identified with the Zionist project, and the Israeli state embraced the orange as "quintessentially" Israeli. The orange began to play the role of a national icon, invoking national pride much like a flag would. Carol Bardenstein offers as an example the uniforms of El Al Airline stewardesses in the 1960s. The idea of Israel as a Jaffa orange was translated into the stewardesses' bright-orange uniforms with orange-shaped helmets.[11]

This use of the orange in a tourist-oriented enterprise such as the national airline is particularly significant, since it projects a certain image of the Israeli state to the outside world. Stewardesses' uniforms could have been blue and white, for example, the colors of the national flag, but instead they were modeled after the orange. The orange indicated certain characteristics that the state wished to promote as part of its image, such as self-sufficiency and rootedness in the land. The orange not only stands for the nation but also presents a particular national portrait. Other examples show the use of oranges as emblems of Israeliness for the Israeli public as well: they grace the covers of folk-song collections and have been reconstructed and questioned by Israeli artists.[12]

The orange has lost much of its cachet as an Israeli national icon in recent years, with technology becoming a central Israeli export and the importance of agriculture declining both economically and ideologically. Today growers in other countries can purchase the right to use the Jaffa brand. They must pass an Israeli board that assesses the quality and characteristics of their oranges and then pay for the privilege of using the brand name. It is apparently a worthwhile investment, since consumers abroad associate the Jaffa brand with quality and are willing to pay a premium for it. Today it is just as likely that a Jaffa orange comes from Spain or South Africa as from Israel.

As often happens to national icons, the orange plays a new role within Israeli society today in the work of certain Israeli artists, who use the layers of meaning associated with the image of the orange to reflect on Zionism or the state of Israel today. One example is Ran Morin's *Oranger Suspendu* (1993), which incongruously hangs an (oversized) orange above the ground in Jaffa, disconnecting it from the physical land and highlighting its rootlessness. The orange remains a vital, powerful icon for both Israelis and Palestinians, even though its meaning has drastically changed over time.[13]

## HEBREW LABOR

Agricultural products are at one end of a process that begins with agricultural labor. Labor as an important factor within the food chain has been getting more attention in academia recently, in particular, immigrant labor's role in the production and preparation of Western foodstuffs in agriculture, factories, and restaurant kitchens.[14] Within the Zionist narrative, labor, specifically "Hebrew" labor, was a central and essential construct. Influenced by late nineteenth-century European thought and the valorization of workers and productive labor in agriculture and crafts, the Zionists promoted an ideology that prized agricultural labor above all other occupations.

"Hebrew" labor producing "Hebrew" products was a fundamental trope from the inception of the Zionist movement. It established a link between modern settlers and ancient Hebrews in biblical times; both were rooted in the land, knowing its nature and cultivating its soil.[15] At the same time,

4. Ran Morin, *Oranger Suspendu*, Jaffa, 1993. Published with the permission of the artist.

the trope promoted the image of a new people, proud and self-sufficient, severing ties with the Diaspora: the new Jewish settler relied on his or her own work, not money or products from abroad. Hebrew labor was essential in distinguishing the new immigrants from the old Yishuv, many of whom lived off donations from the Jewish Diaspora. Finally, the idea of Hebrew labor helped Jewish settlers to feel morally justified in their actions: they were not colonizers taking advantage of the local population but rather workers themselves, bringing the benefit of Western technology to a "primitive" country. Thus Jewish agricultural labor was central to early Zionist immigration, and those working the land were afforded the highest status. Agricultural labor lent a moral justification to the entire project of Jewish settlement in Palestine, distinguishing it from colonial projects elsewhere in the world, such as the Spanish in South America and the British in the Caribbean.

Throughout the early years of the Zionist movement, many of the visual images accompanying its campaign positioned young, active farmers as the new, vibrant alternative to passive, praying, old Diasporic Jews. This campaign promoted both a new Jewish persona and a literal, concrete connection to the new land. As the economic significance of agriculture in Israel was replaced with other industries (such as technology), the role of agriculture in Zionist propaganda changed as well. The focus in current Israeli government publications and the press is on scientific and technological innovation and on entrepreneurship as the core of Israeli economic successes. Despite the change in "venue" from rural to urban setting, the underlying ideology and value system are similar: self-sufficiency and a pioneering spirit still prevail. The ideal of "productivity" is central to both: for example, new technology companies in Israel create new products and innovations; they do not trade in products manufactured elsewhere.[16] The sense of agency, creativity, and vibrant, powerful youth has been transferred from the body to the mind, wielding a computer instead of a plow. The need to manufacture and enforce the link to the physical land is no longer paramount with new generations of native-born Israelis.

The employment of Palestinian workers in a variety of menial-labor jobs in agriculture and industry following the Six-Day War complicated the notion

5. Postcard from the Fifth Zionist Congress (Basel, 1901), by E. M. Lilien. From the collection of the American Jewish Historical Society.

of Hebrew labor and self-sufficiency, much as the control over new territories and people complicates Israel's position as a presence in the Middle East. More recently, a new element was introduced into Israeli society, raising further questions about the role of labor in the national project. Foreign workers on temporary visas, mostly from countries in the Far East, Africa, and Eastern Europe (such as Thailand, the Philippines, Nigeria, Eritrea, Bulgaria, and Rumania), are on the verge of becoming a significant factor in Israeli society. They began arriving in Israel in recent years as part of the Israeli government's solution to the diminishing numbers of Palestinian workers who were employed in all types of menial labor in Israel. These foreign workers are given temporary work visas and no citizenship rights, but some are slowly (and illegally) raising families and making Israel their home. Foreign and Palestinian workers make up about 10 percent of Israel's working force, according to recent estimates.[17] Their presence in Israel is becoming more significant, and the Israeli government must contend with their participation in Israeli society. One of the main difficulties is that they are not Jewish and have no interest in Judaism, which, of course, complicates their position in the "Jewish state." Baruch Kimmerling comments on the challenge these workers pose to the Zionist ethos of Hebrew (Jewish) labor.[18] Since the ideal of Hebrew labor was essential to the creation of a Jewish existence that was radically different from life in the Diaspora, an existence that was productive and rooted in the land, these changes in the makeup of the workforce impact the very definition of Jewish nationalism. The shift in Hebrew labor from the fields and factories to offices and laboratories may have retained some elements of the formative Zionist ideology, but it also forces Israeli society to reexamine some of this foundational ideology and to face the complexities inherent in its core values.

## ASCETICISM AT THE INTERSECTION OF IDEOLOGY AND NECESSITY

Another of the core values of the early Zionists was their ascetic ideology, which placed the future of the nation as paramount and superseded any individual concerns and comforts. Not only were the early Jewish immigrants unfamiliar with the local products, but the foods available to them were very limited in general, particularly in the more isolated new settlements. The situation in these settlements was aggravated by the inadequacy of the cooking facilities and by inexperienced cooks. These practical conditions were easier to bear, given an ideology of frugality and asceticism that characterized the Second Aliya (1904–14). These settlers' antibourgeois philosophy advocated setting aside individual luxuries and comforts. The pleasures of the individual, such as food and sex, were marginal compared to the greater good of society. The same applied to the nuclear family, which was perceived as an extension of the individual. Its interests, its very existence, had to be secondary to that of the community. Even joy in food could cause a distraction from pursuing the goals of a social revolution, so the immigrants of the Second Aliya prized the simple life: food beyond basic sustenance was deemed a frivolity and a waste. Resources would be better spent on creating or enhancing the means of production that would contribute to the future of the nation. Kibbutz Kfar Giladi, in the northern Galilee, published a brochure of memoirs from their old dining room in celebration of the inauguration of the new one.

One of the members, Manya Shohat, offered a story of an event in 1923 that provides an example of how this ideological stance translated into life in an isolated settlement: "We have been waiting for the truck carrying products from Haifa . . . for two weeks. In the meantime we have eaten everything in the house, and the storeroom is completely empty. No legumes, no rice, and not even a drop of oil. We've stopped even dreaming of tea and sugar. There is still a portion of bread for everyone and onions. Plenty of onions, which was a very successful crop this year." Shohat complained of the lack of food to a young man who walked into the dining room. He replied: "That's it? Now here's a tragedy! . . . What is the harm in not eating for a couple of days? You won't die from that, and it won't ruin your stomach either. Don't you know that we are only fertilizer for the next generation?" His words cheered her up, and she greeted the returning hungry kibbutz members by saying, "There is nothing to eat! . . . Only onions and bread. But don't worry: Luka says we are only fertilizer for the next generation." The members accepted the news in the spirit in which it was given, and the dining room quickly filled with songs and dancing. Shohat ends with: "This was the happiest meal I can remember in Kfar Giladi."[19] This type of story is common in early immigrant narratives and makes plain the reasons for the prizing of agricultural labor above food consumption and preparation. Cooking and eating were marginalized not only for ideological reasons, such as personal sacrifice for the sake of the future of the national home, but also in order to help withstand hunger and hardship.

## THE PRIVILEGE OF AGRICULTURAL LABOR

The women of the second and third immigration waves encountered a different reality when it came to agricultural labor in the new land. The ideal of coming to the land of Israel, working in the fields, connecting with the land, finding independence and self-reliance, and laying the foundation for the future of the Jewish nation was more difficult for women in the reality of life in the new settlements. The importance of agriculture to the future of the nation and productivity as a fundamental ideal were instilled in the young women pioneers, as well as in their male comrades. Achieving these goals, however, was more complicated. Deborah Dayan tells of her first attempt at baking bread for the *kvutza* (literally, "group," a small, communal working group):

> B., the skillful baker, has taught me everything. She told me exactly how long to knead the dough, she told me when to add the water, and was very emphatic about adding only a little at a time. She gives me her instructions and goes out. . . . [A] little time passes and my hands begin to tremble with exhaustion. . . . I put all my strength into it but the flour will not turn into dough. I know I oughtn't to do it, but I add more water and the flour turns into a sticky, sloppy mess. I can't pull my hands out. . . . My back aches, I am tortured by thirst. . . . "Bread for fifty people!" I repeat to myself and attack the mess of flour and water again.[20]

When Dayan finally manages to make the flour and water into dough her torture and doubts are replaced by joy: "My comrades are in the field, mowing the harvest that we have sown. Close by I hear the mill grinding grain. And the flour from the mill comes straight to me and I bake the bread for all of us. Bread is surely needed."[21]

Dayan's account is an example of the high value placed on productivity and contribution to the collective. Bread baking, unlike other kitchen tasks, gave Dayan a sense that she is indeed contributing to the kvutza as a productive member. Since bread has the image of being a basic necessity and not a luxury item, baking bread can qualify as a productive activity. Her satisfaction does not derive from her success in mastering the dough or standing up to the intense physical hardship but from her sense of direct connection to the work in the field and from the "productivity" of her labor.

The total lack of culinary publications such as cookbooks, recipe booklets, and cooking advice in the newspapers during the first twenty years of the century is glaring. It exemplifies the halutzim's view of cooking as a "natural" female task and not as a profession or a serious, print-worthy subject. There were quite a few references to food in the daily papers, but practically all dealt with the element of production or agriculture and not with consumption. The focus on production in the press also serves to mirror and enforce Zionist ideology. It is part of the process of shaping the new nation as productive, working the land, facing forward to the future rather than looking back.

Members of a collective were valued according to their contribution to the group: creating material products that could be used in building and strengthening the collective and the nation was the criterion by which value was assessed, along with the efficiency and productivity of each individual member. The collective and its future (and the future of the greater collective, which is the nation) preceded any one individual. According to the halutzim's value system, those involved in food production (i.e., agriculture) were highly valued members: they were developing an economic base for the future of the nation. Women's work in the services was considered nonproductive and therefore afforded low prestige, since it involved food preparation for consumption by individual members. As Yosef Baraz complained in the daily newspaper *Davar*: "To discuss eating, food, and rest openly or, heaven forbid, in public, is not nice! . . . The first thing they take care of is the livestock: it is unthinkable for the animals not to receive their full portion [of food], but who takes care of the people?"[22] Remembering her efforts to improve the situation in public kitchens, Rivka Givalder wrote some years later: "The life and health of the individual were treated with disrespect."[23]

Wages were one indication of this value system, offering women lower pay for their work. Even when they were able to get agricultural work, they received lower wages because they were deemed less productive compared to men in the same position. Ida Friber's story is one of many similar examples: "My friend Haya pretended she knew how to cook, and did this task with little success. I announced immediately that I am completely ignorant in cooking and took on the task of cleaning, laundry, and mending. . . . Pay was not allotted me because it was 'obvious' that if I did not work in the citrus grove, I would do the housework, since 'the girls must clean, wash, and mend, and anyway is this work?' so they said. Food alone was my payment."[24]

This value system may seem at odds with the principle of equality characterizing the socialist ideology, but it was "justified" by the centrality of the collective and the nation to the halutzim's worldview. Tzipora Shtozin's account shows that the women adopted the same value system as the men, regarding kitchen and other service work as less worthy: "We cleared the field of stones. That was my first work in agriculture. It was a pretty boring task, but I was happy because this was the first time I worked with the comrades, rather than just in services. I was equal to all the comrades, an agricultural worker like them."[25]

One of the first attempts at formal training of women for their life in Palestine was at the Women's Farm at Kinneret. This farm, established in 1911, was geared toward educating young Jewish women for productive farm life. The idea was to train women for certain types of agricultural labor and to develop new branches of agriculture that would be more suited for women and would aid the local economy in areas such as growing vegetables, raising chickens, and performing certain dairy work. The farm's director, Hanna Meisel, included training in cooking and efficient housekeeping as part of the duties of a farmer's wife, to the protests of the young women: "The girls object [to home economics]," Margalit Shilo cites Shoshana Bluwstein. "What sort of subject is that! All their lives women have worked in the kitchen. . . . [T]he kitchen is a bitter necessity, but to make a goal of it?"[26]

The Women's Farm is the central site in Shulamit Lapid's 2006 novel *Havat ha-Alamot* (The damsels' farm). This work of historical fiction highlights the women's conflict between the wish to show their value, play a productive role, and demonstrate an ability to work in the fields, on the one hand, and the fact that in reality they would be expected to do kitchen and laundry work wherever they go, regardless of their abilities, as "natural" feminine duties, on the other.

> Everyone knew that here was a group of fine [female] workers who are able to work in the field and would not be satisfied with kitchen work alone—the work they were repeatedly offered. . . . The Farm's workers still received only half the wages of their male counterparts but forbore it, knowing they were making not only their own way but also the way for those female workers who will follow in their footsteps. . . . They decided that wherever they go they must join as a group of six. That way, if they are assigned running the kitchen and cooking, which is what will most likely happen, they would be able

to take turns in that task, so that each one could continue her work in the vegetable patch, the dairy, the chicken coop, and perhaps even the yet to be breached fields.[27]

Women were willing to work in the kitchen and dining room, but not exclusively. As Lea writes in the *Sefer ha-Kvutza* (The kvutza book) in the 1920s: "We have not tired of housework as part of everything, as one corner of our lives, but we are tired of it as an 'everything' for such an extended period of time."[28] Lapid's fictional treatment of this subject in 2006 is indicative of the more recent shift in Israeli culture: a more critical approach to topics and historical periods that at one time were "untouchable." As Israel matures it can afford to reexamine and question some of the central myths established by the Second Aliya and its close followers, among them the myth of equality.

New branches of agriculture such as vegetable cultivation (a branch that was dominated by Arab labor up to this point) developed quite rapidly (especially with the need to rely more on local products during the First World War) as an attempt to answer women's complaints. Both cultivating vegetables and raising chickens (for both eggs and poultry) can be linked more directly to the kitchen and consumption (they are traditionally raised in proximity to the kitchen, in small plots, requiring no further processing), which probably helped in their acceptance as female pursuits by the halutzim. They became a "women's domain," providing women with greater access to agricultural labor but confining them to particular jobs. The rapid development of these two branches, as well as that of dairy production, can be attributed in part to nutritional education and propaganda in the 1930s and 1940s. The new immigrants from Central Europe, some of whom had been trained in new home economic practices, inspired the publication of new cookbooks and recipe booklets, cooking courses, and newspaper columns and articles. These were used as devices to encourage the use of locally grown vegetables, eggs, and other dairy products as mainstays of the Jewish diet in Palestine, further enhancing the status of these branches of agriculture.

Despite recent economic shifts, the relegation of agriculture to a lesser role in the Israeli economy, and the employment of Palestinian and foreign workers in many physically demanding roles, in the twenty-first century agriculture remains linked in the national imagination with images of "greening the desert" and self-sufficiency. This high status and positive image are largely a result of the constant reiteration in the last several decades of the importance of "Hebrew" agriculture in a variety of cultural products. The circulated imagery and positive language became part of the "canon" of Israeli culture.

## SINGING THE PRAISES OF AGRICULTURE

One example of using food as a device for propaganda can be seen in Israeli popular songs. These songs were an informal means of educating children and instilling in them the nationalist value system. They were taught in the schools and in the youth movements and published in magazines. Food products and agriculture were extremely common topics in the early decades of Israeli folk songs, which generally "endorsed" a particular product, encouraged participation in the growing of vegetable gardens, or promoted agricultural labor. One brochure published in the 1960s and intended for preschoolers and first and second graders included seven different songs describing vegetable gardens.[29] One example is a song by Haim Nahman Byalik (known as Israel's "national poet"), "In the Garden":

> *In the garden plot,*
> *right around the barrel,*
> *cabbage and cauliflower*
> *joined in a dance.*
>
> *When the beet saw this,*
> *he hurried to join in,*
> *together with a tomato—*
> *oh, what merriment!*[30]

Another song, "My Garden," by Refael Sporta, a popular children's poet, includes these lines:

> *My tiny little garden!*
> *Row after row:*
> *peas, onion, chubby radish,*
> *carrot, sweet lettuce.*

*Morning comes, my eyes open,*
*to the garden with joy I run.*
*With watering can I'll water*
*every seedling and begin to plant.*[31]

Vegetable growing was, until recently, part of the elementary school curriculum in what was known as agriculture classes. It was seen as a first step to getting young children closer to the land and instilling in them respect for and love of agricultural labor. It is important to note that this was a common practice in urban schools, as well as in rural ones.

Some songs "promote" a variety of produce, while others focus on a single product, as in A. L. Yaron's "Onion":

*Son of onion green am I,*
*no one like me in the garden.*
*Sweet and spicy all at once,*
*everybody loves me.*[32]

They all share great enthusiasm for the vegetable in question:

*Tomato, tomato!*
*We have only just arrived by boat,*
*and already you peek out of the borscht.*
*You're in a salad, in meatball mix—*
*Oh joy, delight, and bliss!*[33]

This particular song was written in the 1930s but acquired special significance after independence: like the tomato, new immigrants who had only just arrived in Israel were already assimilated in their new homeland. Thus, the song not only promoted the tomato but also used it to paint an optimistic picture of integration in a new country.

As the children grow a little older the songs change slightly. A songbook intended for eighth graders no longer includes gardening songs but instead includes six songs on agricultural labor. The songs combine descriptions of the hard work involved in working the land, presenting it as a heroic task rewarded by the joys of its accomplishments:

*Row, row, plow,*
*my land is hard,*
*but my horse is brave, strong,*
*and my hand firm.*
*Horse son of horse,*
*pull with might!*
*Plow, sing a song:*
*the song of bread, song of wheat,*
*song of field and garden.*[34]

Like the previous example, this song attempts to present a difficult situation as a temporary one and current hardships as a necessary price for future success. It depicts the agricultural laborer as a hero and role model taking on a difficult challenge that can offer great rewards.

Another approach to highlighting the importance of food products within the national project was in detailing the entire process of production, from plowing to harvest, to grinding of flour, to baking of bread, ending with a mother serving bread to her children: "Warm slice they chew / heroes they become."[35] This is a common tactic because of the ideological importance of productivity. Situating food products as part of a greater process highlights their economic and nationalistic contribution. From the work in the field, to the production of bread, to its consumption, the child/consumer becomes part of the nationalistic endeavor.

The 1950s marked a change in Israeli poetry and literature in general. The "committed" or nationalistic poetry and fiction that idealized the values of Zionism and the figure of the Tzabar (a native-born Jewish Israeli) began to give way, slowly, to a more personal approach and a more critical tone. New poets and writers gave voice to the individual and his or her concerns rather than to the nation, the community, or the party. This marked a change in Israeli society and culture that would blossom more fully in the following decades.[36]

# 2

# PATRIOTIC DISTRIBUTION

## The "Hebrew" Watermelon

*When the smell of baked bread began diffusing the air, everyone*
*was filled with excitement and smiled at each other. . . . In less than*
*two minutes a commotion began outside. The village people came*
*running. . . . [T]he smell from the bakery wafted like a cloud over their*
*plain shacks, washed over their dusty street, exploded through wooden*
*walls and shabby blankets and hit their nostrils. They brought cheese,*
*tomatoes, and olives, they even got hold of hard liquor somewhere and*
*kippers. . . . Their joy filled the air. "Now we have a bakery," they said.*

—**Meir Shalev,** *Esau*

This scene from Meir Shalev's novel *Esau* is set in 1927 in an unnamed village in Palestine. It illustrates the beginning of a shift in the Yishuv's approach to food: embracing consumption and not regarding it only as a by-product of agricultural labor. The sense of joy in the smell of freshly baked bread might be only fictional, but it does reflect a real shift in the Yishuv in the second half of the 1920s.

Whereas in the period of the Second and Third Aliyot (1904–22) a preoccupation with food was associated with bourgeois values and the traditional family and therefore seen as an obstacle to social revolution, by the late 1920s the Yishuv embraced food as a useful tool for Zionist propaganda. This transformation was due largely to the immigration wave known as the Fourth Aliya (1924–26), which was comprised chiefly of immigrants from Central Europe. These immigrants, many of them family men and women, merchants and craftsmen, gravitated toward the urban centers and away from agricultural labor. They helped bring about a shift in the role of food products within the Zionist campaign for a national home. These immigrants advocated that merchants and craftsmen be awarded the same prestige as agricultural laborers, and so commerce and the distribution of food products became as important as their production.[1] Buying and selling food became a matter of national significance.

This shift in values blossomed some decades later following the Six-Day War in 1967, when Israel enjoyed a period of greater security and stability accompanied by a rise in the standard of living and increased buying power. Israel's transformation into a capitalist-consumerist society can be said to have started in earnest at this point, spurred by greater openness to the outside world and a corresponding ideological shift. By the late 1980s and through the 1990s, Israeli consumption patterns changed again, influenced by new immigration waves from Ethiopia and the Former Soviet Union (FSU). Both groups maintained close ties to their countries of origin and, for different reasons, maintained a clear, separate identity within Israeli society.

Occupying a dual position within the nation is not unique to these immigrants to Israel, but it is in line with global changes that have affected immigrants throughout the world. These changes are not so much in the essence of the immigrant condition, positioned, as it were, between two affiliations, but are more visible or accentuated due to technological development and the circulation of products as well as people. David Bell and Gil Valentine, as well as Bob Ashley, Joanne Hollows, Steve Jones, and Ben Taylor, have written on the need to complicate our view of globalization in the context of food studies.[2] The perspective on globalization as creating a world that is more homogeneous is too narrow and, in fact, inaccurate. As Ashley and colleagues have shown, technological changes have helped people establish and maintain connections across great distances. Lisa Antebi-Yemini has shown how these connections (both social and economic) help form communities that can maintain distinct identities, finding more individual interpretations for national identity.[3] The link between consumer culture, market forces, and globalization is well established. One of the results of these processes is the greater diversity of products available to consumers, which in turn allows them greater choice and a way to display affiliations with faraway communities in everyday life.[4]

The most obvious effect of the FSU immigration wave on the Israeli marketplace is the change in the visibility and availability of nonkosher products. Dietary restrictions and rituals play an important role in Jewish religion, which, in turn, is inextricably linked to Jewish nationalism, so any public breach of these restrictions within the Jewish state has significant implications regarding the representation of the national identity. The change in the availability of nonkosher products and dishes goes hand in hand with the greater percentage of non-Jews within this immigration wave, as well as the secular orientation of those who are of Jewish descent. In both cases, the change in the marketplace reflects a change in perception and a need to rethink the definition of Israeli national identity, complicating the original distinctions put forth by the Zionist movement in its early days. This chapter examines the relationship between these changing definitions and their reflection in the Israeli marketplace in the context of an evolving perception of national identity and affiliation.

## THE CAMPAIGN FOR *TOTZERET HA-ARETZ*

By the 1920s, the Zionist movement had begun employing food directly as a tool in its campaign to establish a unified and homogeneous Jewish nation in Palestine. By "nationalizing" food products, the Zionists set themselves apart from the Arab population while establishing themselves as productive and self-sufficient. They wanted to assert themselves not as a foreign colonial force capitalizing on the work and resources of local inhabitants but as a legitimate and separate national entity. In her article "Zionism in the Kitchen," Sulamith Schwartz described her struggle to remain devoted to purchasing only *totzeret ha-aretz* ingredients ("products of the land," or food grown or produced locally by Jewish labor). She explains that the theory is simple: "The more we use the products of Jewish fields and factories, the more we encourage the development of Palestinian Jewish industry and agriculture, thus creating room and work for tens of thousands of new immigrants, strengthening the Palestinian Jewish economy, making it sounder and more self-reliant." Practice, however, can be another matter, and Schwartz concludes by saying: "The practice in our own kitchens in Palestine makes housekeeping nothing more nor less than a complicated kind of religion."[5] Schwartz is not referring here to the issue of consuming kosher food according to Jewish religious laws but to the idea of purchasing food products as a conscious act for the sake of the nation's future. In the case of the Yishuv, this often means not using what is most readily available, freshest, or most economical, as local products usually are, but rather making a special effort to support new crops, new settlements, and more expensive workers. Buying and eating certain food products becomes tantamount to a patriotic act.

The campaign for totzeret ha-aretz resulted in the transformation of everyday food products into markers of national affiliation through a concerted effort on the part of the national movement and related agencies such as women's organizations. In addition to the influence of local conditions and circumstances, Zionist ideology determined the content of national cultural products through consistent encouragement to change former eating habits and consume locally available products. Consumption of local "Hebrew" products becomes a way of "performing" the new, or renewed, Hebrew nation.

The campaign for the purchase of totzeret ha-aretz began in the 1920s through the work of the Department of Commerce and Industry of the Zionist Administration, an important tool in promoting the Zionist political agenda before independence. In 1925 the daily newspaper *Davar* published an ad by the Zionist Administration informing the Jewish population that the store Totzeret ha-Aretz in Jerusalem was no longer in any relationship with the Zionist Administration and was considered closed. This was due to the owner's many breaches of the contract with the agency, selling foreign goods instead of local products made by Jewish people. The Zionist Administration announced the establishment of a new authorized store and urged the public to patronize it instead.[6] In 1936 the Union for Totzeret ha-Aretz started operating as an initiative of the Jewish Agency, the National Committee, the United Industry Owners, and the Hebrew Workers Union. All these agencies had economic interests in promoting the purchase of locally made products. Since Palestine was under the rule of the British

Mandate at this time, it had to operate within the confines of the British government's own economic agenda. The various political agencies formed by the Yishuv were prevented from using instruments like tax incentives to regulate imported products that an independent government might employ. The Hebrew Workers Union, therefore, acted mainly through propaganda and trade agreements with importers and traders to stimulate the purchase of local Jewish products. The union called on housewives to purchase only totzeret ha-aretz, claiming that in doing so they held the power to influence the nation's future in their everyday grocery shopping. Some of this work involved introducing housewives to various local products through exhibitions and tours of local factories. The union also appealed to store, café, and restaurant owners, as well as to wholesale traders, to use and trade what was produced by local Hebrew labor. Flyers distributed to owners of eating establishments in December 1936 read: "Subject: a complete cancellation of the use of canned milk, milk powder, etc. of *totzeret hutz* [foreign sources]. . . . As of today, December 1, there will begin strict control of all coffeehouses, restaurants, and eating establishments regarding the use of milk. . . . [T]he experiments and tests done by Tnuva supplied satisfactory results, and all coffeehouses, restaurants, and eating establishments must begin using Hebrew milk immediately."[7] A later flyer appealed to all produce stores, grocery stores, and shopkeepers: "We hereby announce that the Hebrew *meshek* [local economy / farms] supplies the following kinds of vegetables in plentiful quantities: cabbage, carrots, beets, cucumbers, eggplants, radishes, beans, zucchini, kohlrabi, spinach, peppers, lettuce, and spring onions. You are required, therefore, to buy and sell these kinds of produce coming only from the Hebrew agricultural meshek. Our inspectors will visit stores and markets to insure that the instructions of this flyer are followed in full."[8] Other such flyers introduce various products, from cauliflower to strawberries, in a similar way.

The Agricultural Department of the Union for Totzeret ha-Aretz published a survey of its actions for the summer of 1938, stating satisfaction with the results of the practice of labeling produce with a tag marking it clearly as "Hebrew." For example, every watermelon grown by Hebrew labor was marked with the union stamp "Hebrew Watermelon." According to the report, watermelons not graced with this stamp could not be sold, and the prices for the "Hebrew" watermelons were far lower. The report continues to discuss the advantages of clear labeling and distinguishing packaging for recruiting the public's help in controlling the sale of totzeret ha-aretz.[9] This "nationalizing" of foodstuffs was not limited to watermelons: there were ads for the "Hebrew Banana" and the "Hebrew Egg" as well. "Hebrew" became a preferred brand name for marketing purposes. This form of labeling transformed these foodstuffs from everyday objects into national symbols. Through this campaign, food products were presented as part of the national project in a very literal way. Consuming a "Hebrew Banana" could be a conscious political statement, a deliberate performance, whereas eating a nonnationalized piece of fruit was an everyday, unmarked act.

Tnuva was the marketer and distributor of the produce and dairy products of the kibbutzim and *moshavim*. In her article, Schwartz mentioned the importance of seeing Tnuva's logo or mark on produce bought as totzeret ha-aretz. By 1937, according to an article in *Ha-Aretz* newspaper, it had established itself as the largest wholesaler of agricultural products. The reporter, Max Yakobson, asserted that, being synonymous with totzeret ha-aretz, Tnuva had certain responsibilities. He claimed that as of that year, Hebrew vegetable growing would not be able to survive unless the entire Yishuv bought Hebrew products. He urged Tnuva to amend its marketing strategy. Yakobson explains that when Hebrew products made up only one-tenth of the Yishuv's consumption, five or six years earlier their sale had depended on the national consciousness of a tenth of the population, but now nationalistic propaganda would no longer be sufficient, since there was no possible way to awaken the national consciousness of the entire Yishuv. Therefore, professional marketing strategies were needed. Due to the competition with Arab traders and imported goods, Tnuva needed to attract customers and not simply wait for them to appear.[10] Such a "capitalist" attitude presented in 1937 would have been unthinkable twenty years earlier.

Other marketing strategies began appearing at this time, including the distribution of Hebrew honey door to door before the Jewish New Year by the Union for Totzeret Ha-Aretz and advertisements boasting the health benefits and high vitamin content of a product. In fact, scientific information

6. "Buy Hebrew Watermelons" (1930s), design by Otte Wallish. From the private collection of Eri Wallish, published with permission.

was very common in both food columns and advertisements during the late 1930s and 1940s. These strategies served to bolster sales but were used in conjunction with nationalist propaganda.

Unlike steak-frites serving as a "sign of Frenchness" or rice as a metaphor for Japanese identity, totzeret ha-aretz products did not develop their symbolic power slowly over time but were adopted and adapted as symbols by the national movement.[11] As in the case of other elements of national culture (see Ya'akov Shavit's 1996 essay, "Bein Uma Yotzeret Tarbut le-Tarbut Yotzeret Uma" [The Yishuv between national regeneration of culture and cultural generation of the nation]), the Zionists wished to consciously shape eating habits, fashioning them as essentially different from eating habits in Eastern Europe and from those of the local Arab population. Totzeret ha-aretz implied not only local products but also ones created by Jewish hands, which gave the Zionists a pragmatic prism for presenting their views of past and future life in the land of Israel: it drove the lesson home at every meal. Buying and using totzeret ha-aretz strengthened the bond of the Jewish people with their land and promoted the image of a new people, proud and self-sufficient. This campaign advocated "Hebrew" products not only over imported goods but also over Arab products, helping play down the Arab presence in Palestine in the process. If foods were to be transformed into carriers of national significance for immigrants who were often completely unfamiliar with them, they indeed required a special mark and an accompanying campaign in ads, newspaper columns, and cookbooks.

The great burden of carrying out this national struggle was placed on the shoulders of housewives in Palestine, who became responsible for the fate of the nation with every purchase they made in the store or market. In a report compiled in preparation for an exhibit on food, agriculture, and groceries in 1939, the writers claimed that according to estimates, about two-thirds of the Yishuv's food consumption was imported from abroad or bought from "our neighbors." Among the imported goods were many that the local industry could supply but did not because of either consumers' established habits or their lack of knowledge. The exhibit could remedy the situation by introducing women to the available local products.[12]

In some cases, though, weak adherence to the principle of totzeret ha-aretz was attributed to more than lack of knowledge. Old-fashioned guilt was used to encourage compliance. A letter by Miryam Baraz, addressing the "women comrades in the city," appeared in *Devar ha-Poelet*:

> Is it true what we are being told, that you mothers, you housewives, you are causing Hebrew agricultural products not to take their rightful place on your tables? . . . We are all aspiring for a wide-ranging settlement [of the country]. How will this settlement survive if there is no market for its products? . . . [I]n your hands is the management of the home, in your hands the fate of Hebrew products; and remember, you set an example for your children. . . . [C]arry the burden of Hebrew agricultural products, they are the foundation for a Hebrew meshek [local economy], for a Hebrew worker and for the building of our land![13]

On the cover of an issue of *Devar ha-Poelet* a map of Palestine appeared with a question printed across it: "The *olim* and *olot* [new immigrants] for whom the land is their hope ask you, *havera* [female comrade], who buys for her home foreign products: why do you deny us work in the homeland?"[14] The issue of buying totzeret ha-aretz for home consumption was presented not as a personal choice and a private decision but as a civic duty that had radical implications for the entire nation's economy and future survival.

Not all factions of the Yishuv embraced the campaign for totzeret ha-aretz without reservations. Ytschak Ziv-Av, a citrus grower, wrote a bitter article in 1935 describing his frustration with the system. He refers to the recent decisions of the members of the Traders Union in Tel Aviv–Jaffa to use only fruit coming from citrus growers employing Hebrew labor, appoint a supervisor to monitor those growers, and come to an agreement with the Pri Hadar (citrus fruit) partnership regarding the use of the symbol "Hebrew Labor."[15] Ziv-Av offered a more capitalist and pragmatic perspective, stating that for the citrus grower Hebrew workers are much more costly than Arab workers, who accept lower wages, and that additionally he ends up receiving lower compensation for his efforts than do his Arab competitors. Ziv-Av stated that when the citrus grower tries to compete in the marketplace by employing cheaper Arab workers, he is "punished" and his products are boycotted, whereas if he would have gotten financial support beforehand, it would have enabled him to pay Jewish workers and still compete with the Arab suppliers. At any rate, he writes, the boycott would be useless, since the Hebrew juice was being sold next to imported cigarettes and candy, and "that is not what will save the homeland."[16]

A major percentage of citrus growers in Palestine were living in the *moshava*, a type of capitalist settlement, where each farmer owned his own land and employed workers (not to be confused with the *moshav*, a later, socialist type of settlement). They saw this version of Hebrew labor as a financial problem and not as a political ideal. Since the citrus growers in the *moshavot* owned their own land and were personally responsible for the means of production and distribution, they had to be more conscious of costs in order to remain profitable and support their families. They did not subscribe to the socialist ideology of the members of the second and third immigration waves and did not concede that self-labor was an ideal in itself. Their priorities were thus guided by the necessity to compete and survive in the free market. They believed that establishing a successful export industry was essential to the survival of a Jewish national home. Their view was that the national home could only be established "naturally," over time.

The campaign for totzeret ha-aretz, on the other hand, is an example of the Zionist movement's attempt to expedite the process and encourage it by artificial means. The movement transformed the act of cooking and eating from an everyday activity to a conscious performance of national ideology. Food became a tool for making concrete such intangible ideals as "nationality." Through the act of purchasing Hebrew products, the people of the Yishuv could actively participate in the national effort; by changing their shopping and eating habits, they could grow closer as a community and demonstrate their unity and national affiliation. As Sulamith Schwartz stated, when she went without bananas or walked farther or paid more to get fowl or lamb officially marked "totzeret ha-aretz," when she shopped for and cooked dinner, she believed she was contributing to the future of the nation.[17]

### RATIONING

The Zionist movement, prior to Israel's independence, did not have some of the tools available to other independent governments to influence consumer choices and so had to rely on propaganda and advertising, but twice over the course of Zionist history the sale and purchase of food products were regulated and directed by the government in a much more direct manner. The first instance, in the early 1940s, was initiated by the British government, and the second, in 1949, shortly following Israel's independence, was initiated by the Israeli government. The difference between these two programs offers a window into the distinction between colonial rule and an independent government in its dealings with its citizens.

## "A FAIR PORTION FOR EVERY HUMAN BEING"

The rationing program initiated in Palestine by the British government in the early 1940s was based on a "point system." Each family was allotted a certain number of points per month, and particular food items were assigned a point value instead of a price. Coupons were used for the purchase of the rationed products (or they could be bought illegally on the black market). Lists detailing the "prices" of various products in points and the changes in these "prices" appeared in the daily newspapers. They were presented under the slogan "A fair portion for every human being." The size of portions for products such as meat and fish was also specified. The newspaper *Ha-Tzofe* published such a list in April 1945 with a message from the food controller. It specified the size of a beef portion at 110 grams (about 4 ounces) per person per week and that of mutton at 200 grams (7 ounces) per person per week. The ad gave the prices in points for flour, standard biscuits, rolls, noodles, spaghetti, macaroni, beef and mutton with or without bones, oil, margarine, tea, and coffee.[18] On a different day the paper ran another ad by the food controller, this time calling for the public not to pay higher prices for products than those set by the government. Here, too, appeared a list of products and their prices. This time they were not rationed products, and they had monetary prices and not points. These products included rice, dry cake, bulgur (crushed wheat), local honey, standard chocolate, dried potatoes, dried eggs, powdered milk, canned fish of various kinds, salami, sausages, fresh and pasteurized milk, butter, and various kinds of cheese and other dairy products.[19]

The public was not "wooed" into cooperation with the program but rather required to follow the policy. Other countries, for example, the United

States, created complicated campaigns to justify rationing programs with arguments for the democratic and equal division of food and descriptions of the importance of women's patriotic contributions to the war through the kitchen, but the British government did not see the need for this type of propaganda in Palestine.[20] The British Mandate did need housewives in Palestine to cooperate with the rationing system and avoid hoarding and the black market, but it was not concerned with getting their votes or moral support. Women's organizations, newspaper columnists, radio show hosts, and cookbook writers all joined the effort of assisting the housewife in Palestine to cope with wartime shortages and the rationing system, but not in convincing her of their benefits. Publications by the Women's International Zionist Organization (WIZO) during the war years include a number of brochures dealing with this topic or with foodstuffs that are particularly cheap and accessible: *Dishes for a State of Emergency, Dishes According to the Products Available in the Land Today,* and *Small Fish Dishes and Seasonal Vegetables* in 1940; *Cheap Recipes for the Family* and *What Shall We Eat at This Time, 1–4* in 1941; and *What Shall We Eat at This Time, 5–7, Lakerda* [bonito] *Recipes, Recipes for Cabbage, Cauliflower, and Spinach, Lakerda and Sweet Potato Dishes, Cheese and Vegetable Dishes, How Shall I Use the Points,* and *Menus and Recipes According to the Point System* in 1942.[21]

WIZO's brochure *Menus and Recipes According to the Point System* explains how to divide the points per day per person. It offers lists of weekly and daily grocery shopping for a family of four and encourages the housewife to supplement the foods limited by the point system with legumes, vegetables, citrus fruit, dried fruit, and milk.[22] A number of menus follow with specific quantities for each product, as well as the number of points required for its purchase and recipes for the preparation of some of the suggested dishes. One menu suggests the following daily plan:

Morning: Cheese, margarine, radishes, carob honey or jam, coffee, and fruit.

Lunch: Half a grapefruit, lentil salad, lakerda and vegetable stew, unpeeled cooked sweet potatoes, and dried fruit salad.

| Supper: | Noodles with cheese in tomato sauce, radish and pepper salad, margarine, figs, peanuts and tahini spread, and tea. |
|---|---|

To the daily menu was added a quantity of bread, oil, and sugar.

Lakerda, peanuts, and sweet potatoes are featured in many of the accompanying recipes, such as the one for "Herring-Flavored Peanut and Lakerda Salad": "Cook sliced eggplants in salted water and chop up. Add lakerda that has been soaked and bread soaked in vinegar. Mix together with chopped onion, ground roasted peanuts, a bit of sugar, and mustard." Lakerda and peanuts were cheap and available protein sources that could replace scarce and expensive beef, but they were unfamiliar to the housewife and required the aid of professional advice.

The brochure *Menus and Recipes According to the Point System* was published in conjunction with an exhibit by the same name. Displays and demonstrations were popular tools used in nutritional education by both women's organizations and the government. They were helpful in reaching women in an immigrant society, some of whom had difficulties reading Hebrew. An accompanying brochure was handed out with the recipes of the exhibited dishes, but the idea was that the displayed dishes and expert advice, as well as the interaction with other housewives, would influence housewives' shopping and cooking habits.

Another example of a WIZO publication dealing with the same problems is *Our Nutrition at a Time of Emergency in the Summer Months*, published in 1940. WIZO's Practical Committee for Questions of Nutrition and Housekeeping put this brochure together. It offered a list of menus within a strict budget of 25 and 35 mils per day per person "without harming the nutritional foundation."[23] One such menu option was:

| Breakfast: | Vegetable salad, hard-boiled eggs, margarine, tea with milk, and bread. |
|---|---|
| Lunch: | Beet borscht with potatoes, zucchini stuffed with meat in tomato juice, rice porridge, and fruit. |
| Supper: | Cheese spread, vegetable salad, and rice pudding with fruit. |

Again, the use of peanuts and dairy as replacement protein sources is apparent in this brochure. Also interesting is the tendency to combine traditional Eastern European dishes with Middle Eastern ones (like borscht and stuffed zucchini), trying to provide the comfort of the familiar alongside available local products.

Amy Bentley's study of food rationing in the United States during World War II raises the question of protein substitutes. The U.S. government made a significant effort to induce women to serve meatless meals, to deviate from the traditional structure of serving "A + 2B" (protein plus two vegetables or side dishes). Despite the efforts of nutritionists and government agencies to "infuse 'non A + 2B' meals with the same kinds of symbolic connotations of security, love, and abundance that the 'A + 2B' meal contained," they were ineffective.[24] The government was in fact sending a double message: alongside its promotion of soy products and other meat substitutions, it sent many "reassuring images" that featured a traditional, meat-dominated meal. As soon as Americans were able to consume meat, particularly the more prestigious cuts, they did so with as great a relish as before the war, if not more so.[25]

A comparison to the situation in Palestine is quite telling. The main difference between the campaign Bentley describes and the situation in Palestine was that the British government had no interest in circulating "reassuring images" in Palestine. As a result, the message transmitted to the public was more consistent. Certain wartime substitutions did not leave a lasting mark on the local diet, but others have remained. Peanuts, soy products, and most offal were largely neglected, but dairy consumption remained high, and chicken and eggs offered a popular substitute for meat, which remains of secondary importance in the Israeli diet to this day. The success of dairy, poultry, and eggs can be attributed largely to the extensive campaign to support local products, presented as beneficial for health reasons, as well as patriotic ones.

A poem entitled "Agira" (Hoarding), published in *Olam ha-Isha* in 1948 just prior to Israel's official independence, sums up certain attitudes toward the British control over food distribution at the time.[26] The author ridicules a housewife who, in her panic in this "abnormal" time in the face of changing governments, hurries and buys anything and everything to prevent her family from going hungry without comparing prices or preferring local over foreign products. The poem ends on an optimistic note, blaming all the woes of tasteless food on the "foreign cook" and prophesying that as soon as this cook leaves the kitchen,

> *we will cook ourselves,*
> *add eggs to taste,*
> *we will cook and succeed,*
> *our dish shall exceed.*[27]

### POSTINDEPENDENCE RATIONING

After Israel's independence, rationing was employed again as necessary in a time of crisis and as a way to marshal a young country's resources and facilitate the absorption of the multitude of new immigrants arriving on its shores. This time, rationing was imposed by a government of the people and not by colonial rule and therefore took on an entirely different character. The tactics used to persuade the public, particularly housewives, to cooperate with the rationing program were much closer to the ones used in England and the United States—they were the tactics of a government concerned with the views of its potential voters.

Prime Minister David Ben-Gurion announced the implementation of the Zena program of rationing on April 26, 1949. The following day the daily paper *Ha-Aretz* published the government's declaration of a rationing program. It gave the government's primary objective, stated by Ben-Gurion, as the absorption of new immigrants. According to the paper, Ben-Gurion rejected any notion of limiting immigration in any way. The other goals of the Zena program listed in the paper were lowering the cost of living, encouraging the consumption of local products, saving foreign currency, and expanding production.[28] The plan, proposed by the minister of rationing and supply, Dov Yosef, included restrictions on the production of luxury items, controls on the black market, and significant expansion of the "portion" system for food products and cloth. The purpose of the plan was to guarantee every citizen nutritious food in equal portions and a daily menu of 2,700 calories. "We will guarantee the country a supply of food and other necessary products, we will determine a rational and modest menu, which will be the only one available to the public," stated Yossef.[29]

The British government's experience with rationing during World War II was used as a model by the Israeli government for a division of rations according to a point system. Despite initial sympathy for the program, it provoked complaints and resentment after a short time. This was partly due to the tedious bureaucracy tied to the distribution of the ration (points) books and the long lines that ensued, as well as the government's choice of what would constitute "basic ingredients," which disregarded the different tastes and customs of the variety of ethnic groups making up Israel's population. Bentley cites a similar problem in her discussion of the rationing program in the United States during the war. The unfamiliarity of the deciding bodies with the diet and ingredients of certain ethnic groups resulted in inadequately allotted rations.[30]

By the end of April 1950 the basic "food basket" of every Israeli citizen included the following monthly rations: potatoes, 4 kilograms; beets, 150 grams; eggs, five for a child and two for an adult; coffee, 100 grams; tea, 50 grams; chicken, 250 grams. By 1952 the rationing regime had begun to diminish slowly, and by 1958 the rationed products included only sugar, jam, oil, margarine, coffee, chocolate, cocoa powder, imported cheese, and red meat. In 1959 the rationing era was officially over.

A number of mechanisms were developed to encourage and facilitate cooperation with the rationing program. Different instruments targeted different groups within Israeli society. Cookbooks, newspaper articles and columns, food shows, government publications and advertisements, and cooking courses were all employed in an effort to encourage cooperation with the rationing system and the establishment of a common, unified cooking and eating culture. In this initial phase of independence and mass immigration of new ethnic groups, the Israeli government was as concerned with unifying its population as it was with feeding it. The strong focus on eating local products supported both the economic cause and Zionist ideology.

*Print Propaganda*

The several cookbooks and recipes discussed below are largely inspired by the need to contend with the limited availability of products and, therefore, with limited choices. "What can I buy/get?" is the question that drives most of these recipes. Their point of origin, as well as their reason for being, is rooted in the marketplace.

The significant influence of housewives on the local economy and their contribution to the "future of the nation" were sentiments echoed by newspapers, magazine columns, and cookbooks alike. In her 1949 cookbook, *What Will I Cook from the Zena Rations?*, Lillian Cornfeld states: "Her strength and her talent are recruited to heal our economy. She has been assigned the crucial role of knowing how to produce the utmost benefit from her rations, and with her success we all shall succeed in decreasing the cost of life."[31] Cornfeld emphasizes that cooking with rations may be more difficult, but it is essential for the sake of the country's future. It may require careful planning and frugality, but tasty and healthful meals can be prepared with rationed foods.[32] This approach was much like campaigns that accompanied wartime rationing in other countries such as the United States and England. Positioning the housewife as "healer of the economy" was a phenomenon that did not accompany preindependence rationing. The elected Israeli government was more concerned with having the nation's moral support and its compliance than the British Mandate had been. This strategy was much like the one used in the campaign for totzeret ha-aretz: recruiting the housewife to support a political cause.

The issue of substitutions appears in numerous articles and columns during this period. In fact, it seems to have been the main concern of nutritionists, food writers, and housewives. Ziona Katinski-Rabao wrote of what she called "instead-of" nutrition, discussing the situation created by the Zena regime of a constant state of substitutions (this *instead of* that). Katinski-Rabao's major complaint of the Zena regime, echoed by various other writers, is the lack of consideration for public opinion in the choice of many of the available substitutions, mainly canned meat, fish, and vegetables. She suggests conducting a survey among housewives to determine which canned products the majority of the population would prefer.[33]

In a column titled "Nutritional Policy and the Woman Consumer," Cornfeld wrote that housewives should be included in managing nutritional policy: "The main flaw in the government's propaganda for the Zena regime is too much esteem for the intelligence level of the Israeli homemaker. Most women cannot read the Hebrew newspaper.... [M]any cannot write down the recipes read over the radio. The entire propaganda method is too complicated for the average woman ... with long articles and complicated lectures on the political—economic situation."[34] The problem, she explained, is quite common to an immigrant society where Hebrew is not the native tongue of most women. Since "we are dealing with ingrained habits from many generations," it is not enough that the government tells the public that milk is better than meat. The government must be aware of these customs in order for the propaganda to be effective. Cornfeld concludes by calling for more women to be included in the related organizations within the Ministry of Supply and Rationing, since they understand women's needs and know the best way to approach them.[35]

The campaign directed at more established housewives often cloaked propaganda in a cover of "helpful suggestions." A typical column from Ha-Aretz's For the Woman and Home section in 1950 was titled, disarmingly, "Nutritious and Refreshing Meals." It included a recipe for mock "chopped liver" made from beans: it was prepared by grinding cooked beans with fried onions and adding breadcrumbs and a boiled egg. Other meal suggestions included boiled potatoes, chopped cucumbers with lebeniya (a mild version of yogurt), and, for dessert, apricots and "bread fingers" (bread that had been cut into strips, dipped in milk and flour or egg, fried, and served with sugar or jam); or fish soup with vegetables and milk, potato pancakes with applesauce, and orange pudding with whipped cream.[36] This column is interesting because it makes no mention of the Zena or of the dilemmas housewives were faced with but offers suggestions for meals that utilized the limited products available at the time, treating the need to save by limiting meat consumption as obvious. The recipes have a distinctly Eastern

European flavor while promoting local products such as dairy, cucumbers, and oranges.

An anonymous writer in the newspaper *Ha-Boker* complained:

> It seems our women never experienced such a difficult holiday. . . .
> [D]espite having our own food controller, not a *goy* but a Jewish person
> in an independent government, there appears a lack of any concern
> for supplies for the holiday. . . . The housewife is now experiencing . . .
> a week of worries and troubles accompanied by bitterness and disap-
> pointment with the entire food control system. . . . It is hard to advise
> the housewife on how to manage her kitchen during Passover, since
> there is no knowing what each one has succeeded in acquiring.[37]

A similar complaint appeared in the same column a month later. This time
the author, Daniella, lamented the neglect of a different holiday: "Independence Day was a great holiday, but not in the housewife's kingdom. . . .
Only one thing was neglected: a special ration in the food distribution so
we could feel not only in the head and heart but in the stomach as well that
it is a holiday for Israel."[38] According to Daniella, there was no addition of
eggs or margarine to allow baking a cake or coffee to serve guests.

These complaints are related to the issue of a psychological sense of
deprivation. They argue that the two holidays, Passover and Independence
Day, have an important connection to national sovereignty—they symbolize
a release from a foreign oppressor and the beginning of an independent
existence—and as such, their celebration is particularly important. The
lack of appropriate supplies is a glaring omission. The Israeli public began
demanding greater influence in the decision-making process. Because this
rationing program was implemented by a democratic, elected government,
its actions were scrutinized and critiqued, even in the patriotic environment
following the Declaration of Independence. Even though the government
had more control and influence over food consumption, its citizens had a
stronger voice as well (a strength that comes with democracy), and they
began asserting their right to be heard and to affect food choices.

Cornfeld's cookbook *What Will I Cook from the Zena Rations?* was based
on her cooking advice columns, which appeared in *Olam ha-Isha* magazine.

Many of these columns responded to readers' pleas for help with food shortages and the need to use substitutions. This book is reminiscent of the author's 1942 publication, *How to Cook in a Time of War?*; both deal with rationing imposed by the government, only this time the government is not the colonial British rule but an independent Israeli one. Dov Yosef wrote an introduction to the book. His words are reminiscent of the campaign for Hebrew products, encouraging the public to support the program for the future of the nation and for the good of the greater community: "The need to strengthen the foundations of the economic life of our young state forces us to plan the people's diet. We are bound to use local products as much as possible and to minimize the import of food products from abroad. . . . [W]e must act this way out of the necessity to expand our agricultural production and through that expand the possibilities of absorbing the multitudes of olim [new immigrants]."[39]

The differences between Cornfeld's two books are indicative of some of the changes between pre- and postindependence Israel. The first book's cover shows a neatly dressed, European-looking woman holding a tray bearing a covered tureen. The postindependence book, *What Will I Cook from the Zena Rations?*, shows a row of figures marching across its cover bearing different foodstuffs. Significantly, only one of the figures appears to be non-European, a Yemenite woman in traditional dress.[40]

The second cover tells the story of a more diverse, multicultural society (though the bias toward Western culture is still apparent). The book appeals to both urban and rural communities as its potential audience, as well as to different generations. Finally, this cover speaks of the existence of professional chefs and restaurants, reflecting both the greater buying power and the ideological makeup of Israeli society. Not to judge these works solely by their covers, the same changes are reflected in the books' contents. Despite featuring several recipes for "special cuts," which include liver, tongue, and lungs, the meat section in the later book is not limited to "inexpensive meat dishes," as it was in the earlier book. The meat chapter also includes a new paragraph on how to make meat kosher and on how to keep a kosher kitchen. This reflects a change toward religion in the country at large: from intentional, ideological disregard by the early halutzim, to observance by many of the newer immigrants. Also, with independence the official attitude toward the Jewish religion changed, and it became an important element in formal representations of the "Jewish state." The later book no longer has a separate chapter for "Oriental dishes"; rather, "Oriental" recipes (i.e., Middle Eastern dishes) can be found dispersed among several chapters along with recipes from Hungary, Argentina, and Romania. This, like the cover, demonstrates the growing acceptance of a variety of ethnic influences within Israeli society and an acknowledgment of their contribution to the local diet (though not yet to other cultural spheres).

Finally, Cornfeld points out that several basic components mentioned in the book carry a particular "Zena" meaning: "butter" should be taken to mean margarine or any other available fat. When the words "sour cream" appear, *lebeniya,* or milk curd, should be substituted. When eggs and milk are mentioned, they must be substituted by egg powder and milk powder as long as the fresh products cannot be obtained (according to a chart that is provided separately). When fresh produce is not available for soups, it may be replaced with dried vegetables. This use of "normal" terminology to indicate "Zena" products has an important psychological effect. By writing "butter," "sour cream," and "eggs," the sense of deprivation is not as visible; the need to make substitutions is acknowledged but not continuously reiterated with every recipe. It also implies that rationing is a temporary situation and that the difficulty the housewife now encounters is necessary for the sake of a better, soon-to-arrive future. Cornfeld ends by saying that the book is based essentially on foodstuffs produced in Israel, which adds to the sense of a positive spin on a difficult time.

Cornfeld was one of the champions of studying and adopting local Arab food practices as one of the models for a new Israeli cuisine. In her chapter on nutrition, Cornfeld inserts a note on "local foods": "We must learn a great deal from the *local population* [Cornfeld's emphasis], who use plenty of vegetables, yogurt, and spices, who prepare fish in all ways and limit their use of meat."[41] The "local population" is not mentioned by name (i.e., Arab inhabitants), which seems more "politically correct" for the time of publication, just following the War of Independence against an Arab enemy. Cornfeld makes a point in all her books to turn to Arab cooking in an attempt to create an Israeli cuisine that is suited to the local conditions and climate. Some recipes, which are integrated into different chapters of Cornfeld's book, include *megadarra* (rice or bulgur with lentils), shish kebab, baba ghanoush, hummus, and falafel. In an interview, Ya'akov Lishanski, cookbook author and culinary figure, commented on Cornfeld's work, saying how much he respected her openness and willingness to learn from the local, Arab population.[42]

A recipe for "Zena Cookies" in the book is attributed to Mrs. Zehava Yosef of Rehavia (a neighborhood in Jerusalem). It is but one of several recipes marked as contributions by women from different parts of the country. Some of them are "Meat and Rice Stew," "Potato Salad," "Eggplant Pie Sally," "Zucchini Geula," "Light-as-a-Feather Lemon Pie," and *burekas* (savory pastries with a variety of fillings). This element of a community cookbook combines with the author's own recipes of various ethnic origins to represent different ethnic groups within the new state and introduce them to each other. By bringing these recipes together, Cornfeld not only legitimized them but also offered a picture of Israeli cuisine as a collage of ethnic foods with local influences and adaptations. Recipes for gefilte fish, fish in spicy tomato sauce, roast beef, Hungarian goulash, pigeon *bisteeya* (a traditional Moroccan festive meat pie), and potatoes au gratin appear side by side. This is an example of the wish to create a common, unified cuisine, but one that is based on inclusion.

*Food Shows*

This recipe for fish pie is said to have "won a prize in the food show held in Jaffa": "Half a kilogram of mixed frozen fish [defrosted] combined with chopped onion and parsley. Add salt, pepper, lemon juice, two tablespoons of oil, paprika, an egg, a half-cup of breadcrumbs, and flour. Place the fish mixture between two layers of spaghetti previously cooked in salted boiling water and bake until browned."[43]

Food shows, which were fairs open to the public, were a popular device in addressing the variety of new immigrants in the young state. They were mainly geared toward more established housewives and not the very recent immigrants arriving after independence. Aliza Holdheim described the food

7. A WIZO show advocating the use of dairy products, 1950s. From the private collection of Hannah Heiman, photographed by Julian Furst, Haifa.

shows in an article for the newspaper *Ha-Aretz*. According to her, the shows were held in large cities on a weekly basis. She wrote that she herself went to the shows out of frustration: "For days [she] could not think of a single thing [she] would be able to cook."[44] Holdheim stated that the shows offered some ways to vary the available basic products and to enrich the obtainable resources, and she described the shows as "well presented" and offering housewives typed copies of recipes. One of her main points of contention, though, was that often there was no consideration for the housewife's time limitations: for example, the shows suggested that housewives spend hours grating pounds of vegetables (these were pre–food processor times). According to Holdheim's experience, the shows were not very popular, perhaps due to the complexity of the recipes (a criticism raised by Cornfeld as well) or because they were difficult to access by public transportation.[45] Despite their limitations, the shows were a common device for the education and persuasion of housewives during this period.

WIZO held weekly shows aimed at Tel Aviv housewives, attempting to teach them how to use the available products and "what to prefer from a nutritional point of view." In the report on its activities for 1948–49, WIZO declared it had held 221 food shows under the title *What Shall I Cook This Week?* in conjunction with the food controller's office.[46] Tikva, writer of The Woman's Column in the newspaper *Ha-Boker*, described a particular show that dealt with the current shortage of oil (each show was structured around a central topic). The lunch menu included vegetable soup, filet of fish wrapped in noodles, red cabbage salad, and frozen semolina dessert. Another option included rice in mushroom broth soup, spinach and cheese cutlet (*shnitzel*), and orange slices. The writer made a point of saying that "all these foods are available in the market, they were presented in an appetizing fashion, with maximum camouflaging of ingredients we have grown tired of eating."[47] Tikva also specified that, unlike previous shows, these recipes were simple and "unadorned," so that "even a housewife who hasn't graduated from a WIZO school could make them."[48] This column discussed the demographics of the shows' audiences, describing them as mostly older women with families and children. The women interviewed by the writer claimed that they went because the show "saves them from thinking." As one of them said: "'It used to be simple. . . . [Y]ou cooked meat . . . ; now you have to be an artist in order to prepare a meal.'" The author was impressed, though, that the women did not complain about the Zena regime: "I suppose they got used to it [the education on the radio and in the press made an impact], and they are trying to cope with the disaster whose name is the Ministry of Supply and Rationing with the aid of the [food] shows."[49]

A final interesting note in this column deals with language. The writer was impressed with the level of Hebrew spoken at the show, which was apparently surprising even for people fluent in Hebrew: "How many men know what a *mirvah* (gap) is, what a *krukhit* (blintz) is, and what is the difference between *miktzefet* (something whipped) and *mirheshet* (a cooking implement)?"[50] These words were all new to the language—they are terms invented to supplement biblical Hebrew and aid in its transformation into a modern everyday spoken language. It is not surprising that names of cooking and food products needed special attention, as the Bible never dealt with many specific recipes to begin with, and technical innovations and imports introduced many new cooking methods, tools, and products. Creating, using, and teaching Hebrew names and cooking terms was an important part of the project of homogenization and nationalization.

A final note on rationing should acknowledge its opposition. Not all consumers and traders adhered to the rationing plan without complaint and with full patriotic commitment. The existence of a black market was a constant problem for the government during the Zena years. The issue of product adulteration was particularly sensitive in this context, since producers would choose to increase their profits by sending out materials to the black market and substituting them with cheaper alternatives. Both consumers and suppliers had to be deterred from participating in black market activity. This "resistance" was sometimes the result of a wish to make an extra profit, of course, but it also allowed consumers to personalize their diets and "correct" governmental bias in creating food rations with no regard to ethnic preferences. The black market also allowed restaurants to stay in business. Some restaurants would surreptitiously provide certain diners with extra point vouchers to allow them to order meat, for example. Just imagine how hard it would be to draw customers to dinners of minced fish filet and spaghetti pie.

## HAIL TO THE SUPERMARKET

The black market serves as a reminder of the role of the consumer and individual choice in shaping the marketplace. Even though Israel's government practiced some control over products and prices (e.g., in the form of subsidies for basic products), other forces have shaped the marketplace in Israel in different periods of time. Several scholars have recently demonstrated the idea of consumption patterns as an important factor in the formation of identity. Marilyn Halter showed how consumption of specific ethnic products can supplant other community affiliations, particularly in a "postmodern life" where people might revive ethnic traditions as a response to a sense of displacement and transition. Halter shows how American consumers use the marketplace as a site for reviving ethnic values, demonstrating how commercialism can in fact enhance ethnic identifications.[51] Ashley and colleagues show how supermarkets, criticized as the epitome of homogenization, can also offer individuals a way to negotiate a variety of products and create a more heterogeneous shopping basket.[52] (Though we should keep in mind Bell and Valentine's cautionary remark on the controlled environment of the supermarket, which manages and directs shoppers' "choices," while they reiterate its importance in the urban fabric.)[53]

Over the past five decades there has been a major shift in consumption patterns in Israel due to the growing role of supermarkets. Previously, shopping for food took place at small, conveniently located grocery stores and at the markets (these too are made up of small stall owners and are not centralized). Supermarkets, in contrast, offer one-stop food shopping and self-service, implying more uniformity. The latest supermarket mutation in Israel in the late 1990s was sprawling, supermarket-like, gourmet, nonkosher delicatessens. These serve as an example of how consumerism can be employed to enhance a particular ethnic affiliation and how in turn this commercial choice influences Israeli society in general, as demonstrated below.

> *Make it a rule: grab a basket*
> *and go shopping at the Super-Sal.*
> *Air-conditioning, incredible selection,*
> *and the lowest price in town.*
> *Instead of suffering, running, asking—*
> *with no effort, take it all.*
> *You can see row upon row,*
> *eggs, milk, meat, fruit,*
> *boxes, drinks . . .*
> *all clean, all excellent,*
> *fresh every day, tomorrow too.*
>
> . . . . . . . . . . . . . . . . . . . . . . .
>
> *It's good, convenient, cheap, and easy*
> *to buy it all at the Super-Sal!*[54]

According to the Super-Sal website, the first supermarket opened in Israel in 1958 in Tel Aviv.[55] The store's main competitor, Co-op or Ribua Kahol (Blue Square), claims to have been in operation since 1937. The co-op stores that opened in the late 1930s were owned by a public company and not by an individual, and they offered some degree of self-service. They grew to be large national chains in the 1980s. The main competition for these large, self-service stores were small, privately owned grocery stores (*makolet* or *tzarhaniya*). One of the main differences between the two was their location: there were many grocery stores located within easy walking distance, whereas supermarkets were fewer and farther between, often requiring the use of public transportation or a car.[56]

Supermarket advertisements stress convenience, one-stop shopping, lower prices, and greater selection, in contrast to specialized stores, which might offer personal service or better quality. Supermarket ads tend to stress modernity, shopping as a leisure activity, plenty of items to choose from, and economic security (customers in fine, Western-style clothes pushing shopping carts heaped with products). The supermarket shoppers in these advertisements have a clear Western, particularly American, look that was synonymous with modernity. Western culture, as opposed to the Orient, has been an ongoing trope in Zionist ideology since its inception, and, much like Americans in the 1950s, Israelis during the 1960s and 1970s were attracted to the idea of the modern world and all its scientific and technological advances. The supermarket offered not just a modern shopping experience but also a variety of "modern" products like canned goods and prepackaged and prepared foods, allowing shoppers to bring the modern world into their home kitchens. Thiya Bat-Oren's 1961 cookbook, *365 Set Tables*, featured an advertisement for Super-Sal that highlights the difference between the earlier shopping experience (running from one store to the other, dragging heavy bags) and the "modern" convenience of shopping in a supermarket.[57]

Only in the 1980s, however, did supermarket shopping in Israel become the dominant alternative, tied to a large degree to growing ownership of private cars. In 1978 the first large supermarket opened outside urban centers: shopping by car became the preferred method, and large stores outside city centers offered ample parking space, as well as more shelf space within the store itself. Several scholars have remarked upon the significance of supermarkets' locations just outside the urban centers, requiring a car

8. Super-Sal advertisement in Tchiya Bat-Oren, *365 Shulhanot Arukhim* (365 set tables) (Jerusalem: Hagal, 1961).

for food shopping. Peter Luntz and Sonia Livingston observed that the car trip "encodes distance from the local," reaffirming the supermarket's position as representing the global and homogeneous (unlike the textured, heterogeneous space of the local).[58]

In the 1980s supermarkets began offering more prepared foods, breads freshly baked on the premises, and extended hours (some remaining open twenty-four hours a day). A newspaper article from 1998 claimed that the supermarkets served 44 percent of the Israeli public and that the forecast was that this would grow to 60 percent over the following few years.[59] This statistic is somewhat problematic, since it does not distinguish between different sectors of the population in Israel. The very religious, for example, prefer to rely on local shops that maintain higher standards of *kashrut* and are sanctioned by the religious authorities. The large supermarket chains have tried to court this population in recent years by opening separate minichains of low-cost, certified kosher food prepared according to the strictest standards (e.g., Shefa Shook, part of the Blue Square chain of supermarkets). The other way these chains expand is through offering home shopping via their Internet sites, as well as one-stop shopping by carrying an ever-growing array of nonfood products (pharmacy, home décor, toys). The growing competition for the Israeli consumer appears to have resulted in a greater specialization of shopping experiences. All stores offer convenience, a wide selection of products, and low prices in a self-service, modern environment, but while some offer strictly kosher products, others developed to fill the growing demand for gourmet and specialty products and offer nonkosher and specialty items in a supermarket setting.

## TO SELL OR NOT TO SELL NONKOSHER PRODUCTS

Israel was established as the Jewish state. As such, it maintains a public face that is in line with certain Jewish traditions; one of them is the consumption of kosher food. All government and public ventures (the army, the national airline, government offices, and consulates abroad) offer only kosher food. Hotel restaurants, catering largely to tourists, also offer kosher food. Most restaurants in Israel, however, as well as a significant percentage of the population, do not keep kosher kitchens.[60] Most supermarket chains, not wishing to alienate the large kosher-keeping portion of potential shoppers, carry only kosher products (no pork or seafood products). In Israel's early days, nonkosher products could be purchased in small delicatessens or kibbutz stores, in particular stalls within some markets, or from seafood purveyors in Arab population centers. With the role of these smaller, more specialized retailers shrinking, what has been the impact on the purchase of nonkosher products?

*Early Nonkosher Product Sources*

Ma'adaney Mizra is a manufacturer of a variety of sausages, salamis, and meat products made from turkey, chicken, beef, and pork. The plant was established by kibbutz Mizra in the late 1950s. Initially, the pork came from locally raised pigs, but due to a ban on raising pigs on Keren Kayemet lands (land "redeemed" by the Keren Kayemet, the Jewish National Fund, established in order to buy and develop lands for Jewish settlement and then leased to kibbutzim or kept as public land), the company moved the livestock initially to Nazaret and, more recently, to two Arab villages. The pigs are slaughtered there, and kibbutz Mizra then purchases and processes the meat. In 1959 the plant was renewed with the assistance of a professional consultant from Haifa. The company started selling its products to several kibbutzim in the area and slowly expanded its business. Ma'adaney Mizra supplied kibbutzim and some high-end delicatessens, whose development it encouraged. This changed in the second half of the 1990s. Mizra had to compete with the large supermarket chains and could no longer rely even on kibbutzim as a market, since the demand for kosher products there actually grew after many kibbutzim opened their communal dining rooms to tourists. The company therefore contracted with Tiv Ta'am, an upscale chain of nonkosher supermarkets, to sell its products through them.

According to Moshe Gerti, who ran the plant from 1968 to 1978 and is still working there as a retiree, immigration from the former Soviet states affected the company's sales and production profoundly: "They [these immigrants] are used to eating nonkosher food."[61] The plant always had a large percentage of hired labor from outside the kibbutz. Earlier these were mostly Arab workers, but by 2007 80 percent of the ninety employees were post-Soviet immigrants. Ma'adaney Mizra has always engaged in the development of new products, but with the opening of this new market it began developing products targeting the "Russian" market. Gerti thinks that the greater availability and visibility of these products influenced their sale in Israeli society as a whole, since all the products are displayed side by side on the supermarket shelves (implying also the effect of the change in food-shopping practices and the influence of the supermarket as the main shopping site). As a result of the greater demand, Ma'adaney Mizra has developed other nonkosher products for the local market, such as a line of chicken "schnitzel" with various fillings (including chicken Kiev, with garlic butter, and chicken cordon-bleu, with ham and cheese) and a type of cheeseburger (the cheese is stuffed into the patty).[62]

A somewhat unique source for nonkosher meat in Israel has been hunting. Though not widely practiced, it is still telling. In an interview with Ze'ev Ben-Gal (Zibon) in Kibbutz Rosh ha-Nikra (located in the northernmost corner of the western Galilee), he spoke about hunting wild boars.[63] Zibon is a "self-taught" hunter. He recalls that when he first moved to Rosh ha-Nikra in 1949, there were no boars in the area, but when he returned to the kibbutz after a long absence in the 1970s, there were many. Much of the area's Arab population escaped during the war for Israel's independence, and the wild boars from beyond the northern border were quick to find a relatively quiet area with no natural enemies, where they multiplied. They are considered a pest and so can be hunted legally year-round.

After a hunt Zibon does not bring the meat to the kibbutz dining room, since "they keep kosher a little there," but the members would organize a *hafla* (the Arabic word for "feast") on the lawn outside. In some kibbutzim there is a reluctance to consume pork "officially" or to break with kashrut in an obvious manner, though cooking and eating boars outside the dining room is completely acceptable. The feast is accompanied by alcohol (which is not part of everyday eating habits in the kibbutz either) and takes place in a space that is outside the formal dining area. According to Zibon, the kibbutz members were not very accomplished boar cooks, and the meat was therefore often tough and chewy, but the hunting stories and the accompanying homemade alcohol were the important part of the experience (much like the coffee and singing of the early *kumzits*). Sometimes they would have the Christian-Arab neighbors butcher and smoke the meat. The Arab villagers used to eat the boars in the form of *kube-naye* (ground rare meat mixed with spices), but that method does not kill any of the bacteria in the raw meat. Recently, these boars have developed a particular strain of bacteria that not only prevents any raw preparation but also put a stop to their consumption in general. Zebon mentioned that even the Thai foreign workers who live nearby and were happy to have the boars before refuse to eat them now. His comment reminds us that new, non-Jewish groups have been added to the Israeli society mix in recent years and that their cooking and eating habits vary from the familiar Israeli ones and influence them in return, beyond the consumption of nonkosher products.

### Recent Nonkosher Product Sources

Tiv Ta'am, as well as the latest addition, Maniya, are supermarket chains that cater largely to the former-Soviet immigrants but have developed to fill the nonkosher product niche for secular Israelis as well. According to the Tiv Ta'am website, it is "a privately held company founded in 1990 by Mr. Kobi Tribtich engaged in importing, manufacturing, and marketing nonkosher food."[64] Today (2015) the company owns thirty-four retail stores throughout Israel and distributes to many other small delicatessens and restaurants throughout the country. The stores are open seven days a week. In fact, the only day they are closed is Yom Kippur. The chain openly targets the former-Soviet population with many specialty items, from particular cuts of meat and special sausages to dairy products, sweets, and alcohol; but, highlighting the stores' status as purveyors of gourmet food, they also offer such convenience, as well as a wide range of products and a "modern and sophisticated" shopping experience, that their appeal is much broader. Initially, the company had a small stall in the Carmel market in Tel Aviv; later, a large supermarket near Netanya (where there is a large concentration of former-Soviet immigrants); and later still, more large supermarkets opened, offering restaurants on the premises, as well as retail shopping. The latest addition has been smaller stores conveniently located within urban centers such as Tel Aviv. This development is one indication of the chain's growing popularity among secular Israelis in general. It also indicates the greater acceptance of nonkosher products at the corner store, alongside milk, eggs, and bread, and not simply in specialized stores.

The list of pork products offered by Tiv Ta'am (including both fresh and frozen, smoked meat, and sausages) numbers over 140 different items. The items include offal, ears, head, and tail (as do the beef products). The website offers information about cooking methods and recipes, presenting an interesting mix that reflects the site's audience; the site includes a recipe for *tshulnt*, labeled "the family Sabbath meal" (referring to the Ashkenazi specialty of a slow-cooked one-pot stew of meat, beans, and potatoes), rolled chicken with figs wrapped in bacon, dim sum, red curry and jasmine rice, chili con carne, "classic" goulash, and many more. The main difference between this website and earlier examples of recipes for pork is in the illustrations accompanying some of the recipes—they are clear and obvious, no longer "shy" about their main ingredient.[65]

### The Future of Nonkosher Products in Israel

The greater availability and visibility of nonkosher products has enabled greater choice in the private realm but has made no impact on public representations of the Jewish state: any and all formal events and ventures are strictly kosher. The army, the national airline, and state dinners all offer strictly kosher food. They aim not to exclude kosher-keeping citizens and to maintain the representation of Israel as the Jewish state. However, there is a clear distinction between formal, state-sanctioned events and public culture. The greater visibility of nonkosher products and businesses open on Saturday (the Sabbath) has changed the Israeli street, creating a growing rupture between Israel's public face and the reality of public culture.

The shift in public culture has had several effects. One is the focus of traditional Jewish life returning to the home. The home and family can reclaim many of the elements of Jewish tradition that were relegated to the public sphere with Israel's independence (such as holidays, the Sabbath, the Hebrew language). These traditional elements are different, however. Today, a greater diversity of Jewish ethnic experiences are seen as "legitimate" and vital. There is greater ethnic pride and more room for maintaining ethnic traditions than there was in the 1940s and 1950s. No longer do we see a blatant attempt to unite and unify, to shape a Jewish state with one clear "right" Jewish character. Instead, the traditions practiced in the home are more closely linked to those in each family's country (or countries) of origin.

In the past, formal representations often followed the street (the growing role of Middle Eastern food and the iconic status of falafel are good examples). Can nonkosher products follow the same pattern? The greater visibility of these products in Israel, their very existence in plain sight, reminds us that the Jewish nation is an ever-changing construct. By displaying greater openness in the culinary arena, do we signal greater openness in the definition of Jewish nationalism?

Another side of the trend represented by Tiv Ta'am and similar stores is the increased availability of imported products. These products form one of the links to other countries and cultures. The abundance of imported products not only enhances transnational affiliations, it also speaks to the decline in both the power of Zionist doctrine and the call for consuming local ("blue and white") products as a way to strengthen the local economy and the future of the nation. Creating physical links to the land of Israel was always an important trope in the Zionist canon. The decline of agriculture as an important economic factor went hand in hand with its ideological significance in a transnational environment. On the other hand, as a result of the growing market for gourmet products in general, there has been a growing local economy of "boutique" farms. Small local wine, cheese, and olive oil producers are becoming more visible in the Israeli market. This kind of local product is more in line with French notions of *terroire*, indicating a new kind of connection between the land of Israel and its citizens: not an ideological construct, a device in the hands of the national movement, but a more "natural" tie between people and the land they were born and raised on.

### IMMIGRATION IN AN AGE OF TRANSNATIONALISM

Larissa Remennick describes the way Russian Israelis are able to maintain dual affiliations by creating cultural and social networks that allow them to participate in life in more than one country.[66] Her description of the cultural products and attitudes of Russian Israelis can be applied to Israelis living abroad. Many Israelis maintain close ties to Israel even though they have emigrated elsewhere for business or other reasons. Many maintain business ties with Israel, some keep two residences, many continue to watch Israeli broadcasts and follow Israeli news online or through Israeli newspapers and to consume Israeli cultural products such as literature, music, and food.

Bell and Valentine have shown that "changes in identity . . . are articulated on individuals' plates."[67] They refer to changes in what people purchase, where they shop, who prepares the food, and where and when it is consumed. Bell and Valentine are referring mostly to life changes (age, occupation, marital status, etc.), but their conclusions are very well suited to a study of immigration. The degree of acculturation can be seen on the plate as well. The products embraced and incorporated into the daily diet in relation to the products and dishes retained from the country of origin speak to the way immigrants are negotiating two identities.

Julia Bernstein and Yoram Carmeli studied the Zastolie (literally, "gathering around a table") gatherings of FSU immigrants to Israel as a site for negotiating identity. These gatherings involve elaborate meals that in Israel include many traditional Soviet dishes but also some local additions and variations. Some of these changes are the inclusion of local popular foods such as hummus and tahini, stuffed filo-dough pastries, broccoli, and carbonated drinks (Sprite and Coke). Another change is the inclusion of dishes that were unaffordable in the country of origin, such as caviar, smoked salmon, and squid. A significant change is the inclusion of traditional dishes from other parts of the Soviet Union (not the participants' original area).[68] The last change is indicative of a change in identity, not only to include an Israeli component but also to refigure the Soviet element to include a greater Russian-speaking community that before immigration to Israel was seen as different. Bernstein and Carmeli focus on a particular food event, but looking at immigrants' eating habits in daily life would show similar processes. The inclusion of imported products from the country of origin and traditional dishes supplements local products and new ingredients and dishes.

Immigrants' plates often display complex, dual, or even triple identities and affiliations. This is not a novel phenomenon, of course. Immigrants have always brought their traditional dishes with them and combined them with local foods. However, the FSU immigrants to Israel are different in two respects: first, the greater availability of and access to imported products (ingredients and ready-made dishes) allow them greater accuracy in re-creating dishes from their country of origin and making fewer adaptations using local products. Availability and access also allow a display of affiliation with and support of their country of origin. Second, the change in attitude is marked: rather than wishing to assimilate quickly into the new society, these immigrants wish to maintain their dual affiliation, and their "plates" display a conscious effort to maintain a separate existence within the national community. This transnational identity is not an indication of the end of the power or viability of nationalism; rather, the growing mobility and multiple influences and alliances may result in more nuanced identifications. Instead of one Jewish national identity, we see more room for individual interpretations, variations, and choices, both culinary and otherwise.

# 3

# KITCHEN LESSONS

## *Educating Home Cooks*

*I am Iraqi-Pajama, my wife is Rumanian, and our daughter is the*
*thief of Baghdad.*
*My mother continues to boil the Prath and the Hidekel.*
*My sister learned to make pierogi from the Russian mother of*
*her husband.*
*Our friend, Morocco knife, sticks a fork of British steel in a fish*
*born on Norway's shores.*
*We are all discharged workers brought down from the scaffolding*
*of the tower we wished to build in Babylon.*

—**Excerpt from Ronny Someck, "Shir Patrioti" (Patriotic song)**

The story of the domestic kitchen in Israel is a story of culinary education: learning to use new ingredients and techniques, learning about other traditions and ethnic variations, learning about balancing ideals and reality, multiple ethnic traditions and a single national character. The early female pioneers were reluctant students, struggling to learn basic cooking skills in a harsh and unfamiliar environment while simultaneously attempting to escape the kitchen altogether in favor of agricultural work. The kitchen became a site for questioning women's roles within the national project. New immigrants arriving in subsequent immigration waves had to adapt to cooking in a new country with new ingredients, as well as to learn the already established common repertoire put forth by the more established population. The kitchen offered a place for immigrant "education" and acculturation, or it served instead as a battleground between the national movement's attempt at unification and the pull of different immigrant groups to maintain their individual culinary traditions. This "battle" became more subdued in later years with growing tolerance and flexibility on the part of the national movement as national ideals bent and adapted under the pressure of reality. These two stories—women's roles and status and new immigrants' acculturation—are often intertwined, as some women find more influential roles within the national project by working with new immigrants and teaching them the "national" culinary repertoire. Similarly, greater openness to ethnic culinary traditions went hand in hand with greater appreciation of the value of individual pleasures, among them the pleasure of cooking and eating, thus raising the status of those who cook.

This chapter follows the transformation of the Israeli kitchen from its shaky start in the days of the early halutzim and pioneer women's attempt to teach themselves the necessary, basic culinary skills, through Zionist women's organizations' educational work with the communal settlements, with children, and with new immigrants. After independence, children's education was taken up by the state and evolved over time to allow for socioeconomic and ideological changes within Israeli society. By the late 1970s, rather than trying to eradicate all difference in favor of a single, national identity, we see a growing openness to outside influences, as well as greater acceptance of variations from within. School curriculums, communal settlements' kitchens, and nonformal educational devices such as the Queen of the Kitchen competition all reflect the attempt to articulate ethnic difference within the national culture.

## ESCAPING THE KITCHEN?

The predominant socialist ideology of the early days of Zionism assumed equality among all members of the future society, naturally implying equality for women as well. Young women who joined the movement and immigrated to Palestine aspired to the same ideals as the men and tried to gain access to "masculine" roles, particularly agricultural labor (the most prestigious position, according to Zionist rhetoric of the time). Upon arriving in Palestine, however, the women encountered a harsh reality that challenged their lofty ideals and optimistic visions of the future. All immigrants had to face an inhospitable climate, a mostly antagonistic local population, rigorous physical labor, a difficult economic situation, and, often, hunger; moreover, women also had to cope with a shattering of their expectations of equality and of working the land. Women, who were only a small percentage of the Second Aliya (1904–1914), reaching a few hundred by 1911, were even fewer in number in the *kvutzot* (plural of *kvutza*, a small, communal working group): 11 women out of 165 workers in 1909, and 30 women out of 522 Jewish workers in 1912.[1] The few women who joined a kvutza expected life in a collective to afford greater opportunities for agricultural work. It was a way to break traditional family structures and, with them, traditional female roles. However, these women found themselves assigned to kitchen and laundry work for the entire group. Their fellow halutzim saw this as the women's "natural" position. The Zionist movement trained and sent young single women to Palestine to take part in the national revival. Upon arrival in Palestine, however, these women had to live and work with men who had difficulty embracing these ideals of equality, particularly in light of their own tenuous situation. The gap between the national ideology and its realization in Palestine placed the kitchen as a dreaded site and a potential trap for these women.

According to Dafna Izraeli, who wrote extensively on this subject, "The conscious rebellion against the traditional occupational structure of Jewish society did not extend to women's work."[2] Most women found themselves in service work instead of in the fields. Aliza Shidlovelski recounts her experiences in Palestine during the early years of the twentieth century:

> . . . These were torture hours for me, for I suffered one failure after another. Once, the porridge became a kind of inedible dough; another time, I wasn't able to light the fire in the stove. . . . One day . . . I was assigned to watch over the lentil porridge so it wouldn't burn. I stood and stirred with a wooden spoon. The lentils began boiling and bubbling . . . until they splattered all over the stove, the wall, and my hands, and I was burned—but it never occurred to me to lower the flame. . . . [A]fter that incident they decided to try me at work in the

fields, where I might be more successful. . . . [I]t was the first time in Dganiya that a woman went to the fields. I was ecstatic: this is how I imagined my work in the land [Palestine] before my immigration.[3]

The gap between expectations formed in Europe and the reality of life in Palestine was often a difficult one to bridge. Kitchen work became a hated task for these women, not only for the hardships it involved but also because it was a symbol of their frustration and exclusion from the prestigious agricultural labor. In Shidlovelski's case, her inaptitude in the kitchen actually facilitated her move to the coveted agricultural work, but often the results of such inexperience were humiliation and even expulsion from the group.

The difficult situation was compounded by the fact that these pioneers were in fact young, inexperienced girls: their average age was seventeen, and they came from fairly affluent families that generally had domestic help. They found themselves in a new land with very limited, unfamiliar facilities and supplies, they worked extremely long hours, and they were subject to criticism and ridicule.[4] Kitchen work was anything but "natural" to them. Not only did they lack experience and training in cooking (particularly for a large crowd of thirty or more), these women labored under particularly difficult conditions even for an experienced cook. One or two women had to bake bread and cook for the entire group using primitive, often makeshift stoves, which they had to stoke with firewood they gathered themselves. These cooking facilities were often outdoors, exposed to rain, smoke, and heat. Finally, the women worked incredibly long hours, as M. Baraz, Y. Zenter, and R. Machnimit described in their memoirs: "from 3:00 a.m. to 8:00 or 9:00 p.m."; "there was no set time for work, we worked from dawn to late in the evening, from 5:00 to 8:00"; "my work hours are from 4:30 a.m. to 9:00 p.m."[5]

Much of the criticism directed at these cooks by their fellow group members concerned the restricted variety of dishes. This was partly due to the limited available ingredients and partly to the inexperience of the cooks both in cooking in general and in using the local products in particular. Looking back on the early years of her kvutza, Rivka Givalder describes a typical lunch: different barley porridges and soups, usually burned, and eggplant three times a day, always prepared in the same manner.[6] The difficult work and harsh treatment of the women cooks by the other group members resulted in the rapid turnover of kitchen workers, which, of course, did not help the problem of inexperienced cooks. R. Bonik raised this issue in his examination of the "workers' kitchens" in an article for the daily newspaper *Davar* (1925): "If not for the rotation method, we would have had by now professional cooks with experience."[7] He questioned the training that would slowly become the central means of changing not only the situation in the dining room but also the image of kitchen workers: "The common opinion is that every female worker knows how to cook and that there is no need for expertise. This opinion is completely incorrect. Every kitchen requires a professional [female] cook."[8] This account demonstrates the beginning of a new perception of the task of cooking. By calling for the training of cooks, Bonik implies that he does not consider cooking women's "natural" task but rather a profession that requires special training and knowledge.

The necessity of training in these areas becomes obvious fairly quickly. B.B. tried to become a kvutza member for a long time until someone who needed a person to work in the kitchen finally took her on: "Kitchen? . . . I don't know how to cook. What am I going to do there?" She wrote of the damage she did in the kitchen, forcing the kvutza to find her a new role and trying her in laundry work, where she rubbed her hands raw before finishing the first batch of clothes. One of the older women in the kvutza complained: "She is not much help . . . we've made an unlucky choice. She wants to work, but she doesn't know how."[9]

Introducing men to kitchen tasks was never an option for men and women alike. The word "cook" in articles and accounts always takes the female form (*mevashelt* or *tabachit*). N. Gerdi describes the establishment of a kosher workers' kitchen for the single religious workers in Petach-Tikva: "Here arose the question of the cook [*tabachit*, female cook]. We did have among us a member who knew how to cook, and he ran the kitchen for a short time, but he did not want to continue this. We found one female comrade, the only woman to join the Poel Mizrachi then. . . . [T]he above-mentioned comrade did not particularly excel in the task of cookery, but that fact did not affect our high spirits."[10]

Establishing a kosher kitchen was one of the first actions of the Poel ha-Mizrachi movement (a separate movement for Zionist religious workers). The absence of kosher eating establishments in Palestine was one of the problems facing religious halutzim at the time. As part of the break with Jewish existence in the Diaspora and embracing a nationalist-socialist ideology, the majority of Eastern European halutzim forsook religious practices. The majority of political Zionists viewed religion as a bourgeois construct, and their main goal was the (re-)creation of the Jewish people as a political nation. As such, eating nonkosher food was almost a matter of principle.

In future decades the approach to kosher food, particularly in the public sphere, would alter dramatically, but during this early stage, the problem facing religious Zionists in finding kosher food was aggravated by the fact that they had to rely on communal kitchens. Whether they were single men following available work around the country or part of a kvutza, they did not have access to a private kitchen and were therefore forced to establish separate communal kitchens. As Gerdi's story demonstrates, the percentage of women among the religious halutzim was even smaller than their numbers in the rest of the early immigration waves due in part to the break the halutzim made with the traditional family structure, living arrangements, and even traditional dress. The women in the kvutzot fought to work side by side with the men, a radical concept for traditional, religious Jewish society.

What the women of the Second Aliya achieved was quite different from the image most Israelis have of this period in their history. The image of men and women working side by side in the fields to redeem the land is part of the iconography Israeli children are raised on. It is part of an idealized era in Jewish and Israeli history. Because of that image's significance to the national project and its influence on future generations, both fiction writing and school curricula glorified the immigrants of this period, presenting the halutzim as selfless heroes who could do no wrong. The "idea" of equality for women, as part of the equality of all workers, was indeed part of the agenda of the Eastern European Zionists, but achieving this equality in reality was far more difficult. As Yael Feldman wrote, "Wasn't the Pioneering movement—indeed the Zionist ethos in general—supposed to have promoted the equality of women? . . . [T]he answer is yes . . . but only as long as we remember to add the qualifier—in theory."[11] Feldman's study of women's fiction in Israel is one of the latest of several recent studies that dispute this popular myth.[12] These studies highlight the essentially conservative attitude of the halutzim in the second and third immigration waves toward their women comrades.

Women's struggle to bring the reality of Palestine closer to the ideal model conceived in Europe takes on another dimension with the births of the first children. In communal settlements, this struggle resulted in solutions such as shared childcare. Shared childcare and communal dining are the two obvious examples of the attempt to restructure traditional family roles by the early halutzim, replacing the nuclear family with the collective.

## The Communal Kitchen

During the time of the Third Aliya (1919–22), several of the institutions created by the Second Aliya were enhanced and organized. One example is the kibbutz, a further development of the small kvutza. Henry Near, who wrote extensively on the history of the kibbutz movement, suggests a definition of the kibbutz to include communal childcare as one of the central characteristics that distinguish it from the earlier kvutza and from other settlement types. Near defines the kibbutz as a community in production and consumption, as well as permanence in population and in location on nationally owned land.[13] The kvutza was initially a transitory and temporary settlement, but, as Near suggests, establishing communal childcare was the stage that sealed the structure of the kibbutz as a permanent settlement.[14] The halutzim saw communal childcare as well suited to their antibourgeois ideology and therefore antitraditional family ideology, as well as to the idea of equality of the sexes. It was also a practical solution for new settlements with very limited facilities and resources: initially it was easier to build one kitchen and one solid shelter for children while adults lived in tents. The kibbutz offers a distinct example for the community taking over traditional family roles and restructuring them. Zionism preached the same ideological shift on a grander scale, replacing the role of the nuclear family with that of the even larger community, that is, the nation.

Communal childcare might be the most glaring break with the traditional division of labor within the family, but one of the main contributions of kib-butz life to equality between the sexes was in establishing communal cooking and dining. Since economic survival is such a central part of the family unit in society, providing, preparing, and sharing food are closely linked to the traditional family structure and the division of labor between men and women. It is true that the overwhelming majority of workers in all the services in the kibbutz, including childcare and cooking, were women, but the new structure of communal cooking in the permanent settlements contributed to the representation of kitchen work as professional work, work requiring special training. As such, it could be fitting for both men and women. The kibbutz dining room is not like a cafeteria in a factory or a restaurant in the city but replaces the home kitchen and dining room. By literally taking the kitchen outside the home into the public sphere, the kibbutz eventually contributed to a change in perception of this element of housework.

Ziona Katinski, a WIZO (Women's International Zionist Organization) instructor who worked with the kibbutzim in the 1920s, described the state of the kitchens she found on her visits: "In the entrance to the kitchen piles of empty cans, inside the kitchen a 'primus' standing on two legs and his third leg a rock, on it a blackened pot and in it the famous bean soup. . . . A rickety table, smoky ceiling, dripping faucet, a dozen spoons for fifty mem-bers, partially baked bread, fried onion in oil for breakfast and tea. Many of the members have stomach problems, the women in the kitchen rotate every day."[15] One of the problems of kibbutz dining, according to Katinski, was the monotony. Despite the availability of a very limited number of products, the WIZO guides tried to introduce variety through new recipes such as liver-flavored eggplant, fish-flavored eggplant, mushroom-flavored eggplant, and apple-flavored zucchini.[16] But whatever improvements Katinski may have made, everything seemed to return to its previous state shortly after she left, since the women she worked with left the kitchen themselves for other jobs. In Katinski's opinion, this rotation of kitchen workers was the central problem of the kibbutz kitchen. She claimed it was essential that kibbutz women see kitchen work as professional labor that required dedication, training, and responsibility while offering them satisfaction and a sense of pride in return.

Other sources echo Katinski's observations: an anonymous report on the state of the workers in the *moshavot* (the capitalist settlements) from 1926 notes that "the cooking is done by young women who do not know how to cook, and even those rotate every two weeks or every month." Not surprisingly, "the food is very bad."[17] A typical menu included tea and bread (sometimes with jam or halva) for breakfast, soup and porridge for lunch, and soup and porridge or a bit of meat, or pickled herring, vegetables, and bread for supper.[18] Rivka Givalder writes of her memories from an assembly in 1931: "'From now on the *haluzkot* [young woman pioneers] will work'—states the 'veteran' cook who has been working an entire month in the kitchen. In the kibbutz assembly it was decided to put the three new immigrants in the kitchen."[19]

The problem of unskilled labor moving on to a new job within the kibbutz economy just as they had achieved a degree of knowledge and experience remained an issue for kibbutz kitchens for a long period of time. The famous kibbutz rotation of necessary tasks has certain advantages in creating equality among all members of the community (even though men began participating in kitchen rotation only at a much later time), but it also has one central flaw. It took several decades and much public relations work for the kibbutzim to have trained personnel occupy the central positions in the kitchen while rotating only the unskilled tasks such as dishwashing and vegetable peeling.

A publishing house affiliated with the kibbutz movement published a reader for second and third graders in 1952 titled *We Are Cooking*. The book offers a unique perspective on communal cooking; since this is an educational text aiming to "mold young minds," the ideological position behind everyday practices becomes transparent. The introduction states: "In the kitchen and bakery they are laboring to prepare our meals, the store room keeper struggles to get the products, . . . and we sit before the set table and do not think for a moment of the labor that was invested in the preparation of this meal. . . . Why don't we try to make for ourselves such a meal with our own hands?"[20] The section addressing the teacher at the end of the book offers advice on the right time for a discussion on "the value of the common [i.e., communal] kitchen, which offers advantages such as saving on workdays and ingredients and equality in nutrition for the entire population."[21] Some of the songs and jokes in the book are reminders of the bad reputation of kibbutz cooking, as well as of the fact that the quality of cooking is secondary to other values: camaraderie, equality, and a good sense of humor are supposed to make up for a lack of cooking expertise, as the anonymous song "We Are All Cooks Here" demonstrates:

*We are all cooks here,*
*we will work far and near.*
*In frying and cooking*
*we are experts!*

*A fish we'll set in the pan,*
*immediately burnt it will be!*
*A roast of beef or a hen*
*into black coal will transform.*[22]

Among other topics, the book includes stories about the origins of several foodstuffs, such as milk and butter, eggs, vegetables, coffee, and spices. The focus on the origins of foodstuffs and not on their consumption corresponds with the value placed on productivity by kibbutz ideology. It also details common ingredients and dishes and their cost, painting a picture of what the common diet on the kibbutz in the early 1950s might have looked like. That diet included chopped liver, vegetable salad, eggplant salad, borscht, cabbage borscht, fish filet, stuffed fish, spleen stew, and raw carrot salad, among other things. It is obvious that, despite the book's audience of second and third graders, the diet they are assumed to be familiar with is the same as that of the adults. It is also clear that the diet is highly influenced by Eastern European eating habits and that a child from a different background might feel somewhat at a disadvantage in this class.

## FROM RELUCTANT STUDENTS TO
## DEDICATED TEACHERS

The involvement of WIZO in the communal kitchen is but one example of the greater role women's organizations began playing at this time. WIZO volunteers brought with them from Europe a newfound scientific approach to nutrition and home economics. The growing numbers of immigrants from Central Europe in the late 1920s encouraged this approach and its application to the acculturation of new immigrants to life in Palestine, as seen in this article in the daily newspaper *Davar* from 1925, "The Science of Nutrition."

> Nutrition has been grounded in a scientific base only in recent years. . . . [F]or us [in Palestine] this science is particularly important, since we are moving here to new conditions of life and a new climate. We must look to the local inhabitants and their foods, which are the result of instinctive selection over generations. . . . [T]hey are completely different from our foods, which we have been accustomed to in the Northern lands. . . . The Arab instinct shall be replaced rationally in the ordering of our nutrition by knowledge and science.[23]

This quotation illustrates the ambivalent attitude toward the Arab population, presenting it as both "authentic" and archaic. The scientific attitude was instrumental in the attempts to create a local Jewish cuisine that would be distinct from local Arab eating habits and from Jewish eating practices in the Diaspora. By positioning food in the realm of science, nutritionists were able to present it as "productive" and "useful" and not as a bourgeois luxury. By working toward the creation of a rational and homogeneous system of nutrition, they tried to present food as a possible unifying force, an instrument in nation building, instead of a distraction and hindrance.

WIZO was founded in London in 1920. Its main goal was to train Jewish women in Palestine in agricultural labor. One report described its goal as "the education of Jewish women in productive work for the upbuilding of Palestine by [among other things] . . . the instruction of women in Palestine in all branches of agriculture, domestic science, housekeeping and dietetics, and infant welfare."[24] By 1927 WIZO was operating a school for domestic science and agriculture in Tel Aviv (established in 1922), an agricultural school for young women in Nahallal, and three "stations" for the guidance of young mothers in caring for their babies. At this point WIZO also began nationwide instruction of women in home economics and agriculture (mostly developing vegetable gardens) through roving instructors and cooking courses for housewives. In 1928 WIZO began working with women in the kibbutzim. They were taught, in addition to cooking and nutrition, laundry, sewing, and other household tasks.[25] The schools operated by WIZO often had public kitchens attached to them that were run by students and teachers and served food to many new immigrants.

This formal training served to replace the instruction a woman might have received from her mother or from another more experienced woman in the immigrants' communities of origin. The unique situation of a population that was transplanted into a new environment, leaving the older generations behind, made formal training in such traditional female roles as mothering and cooking seem necessary. This training also suggested a single "proper" way of accomplishing these tasks, in accordance with the idea that these women could contribute to the "good of the nation." This contribution was generally perceived both as economical (such as promoting certain products over others and using them efficiently) and as a unifying force: if all women adhered to the same system, unified eating habits would ensue.

Hadassah—established in the United States in 1912 as Daughters of Zion—was a women's organization that began activities in Palestine in 1913 in the areas of health and infant welfare. In 1923 Hadassah began a school lunch program in Palestine. Hadassah's focus remained health care (establishing hospitals, welfare stations, nurse training courses, and the like), but it was also involved to a great extent in children's welfare. Establishing the school lunch program in the 1920s to ensure that all children received proper nutrition and a hot meal fit in with the ideological shift described above. The school lunch program was also intended as an educational tool to teach children about nutrition. By working with the children, Hadassah volunteers hoped to influence their mothers as well. Giving growing attention to the feeding and nutritional education of children as one of the first steps in elevating the status of food within Zionist ideology in general was in line with the ideological climate inherited from the second and third immigration waves. The ideology of the new halutzim had a futuristic bent, that is, a willingness to make sacrifices in the present for the sake of a better future. Thus, when it came to children, "the future of the nation,"

9. "Boys in sixth through eighth grades preparing luncheons in Talmus Torah Temini, Tel Aviv," 1930s. 18 HMO / Programs Medical Education–Nurses–School lunch–Supplies, 1913–1960, box 7, folder 1, Hadassah Archive.

the rigid approach to individual comforts and needs could be bent and stretched. One of Hadassah's publications reads: "Children come first in Palestine, for the future of the Jewish National Home is bound up with the future of its children." It continues: "Proper food is the best medicine for children."[26] The reference to food as medicine is significant because it is similar to the scientific approach mentioned above in positioning food in the realm of science, not pleasure. With these objectives Hadassah began not only serving food to children but also organizing classes in nutrition and cooking.

Tracing the activities of these women's organizations shows two main shifts in the attitude toward kitchen work: treating it as a profession requiring study and training; and viewing the kitchen as another possible arena for Zionist education for women and children, helping those who were not agricultural workers per se forge a literal bond with the land through the products they prepared and consumed. These changes enabled some women to achieve a degree of political influence and empowerment through their work in the Zionist women's organizations by embracing the kitchen as their specialized turf instead of fleeing it.

During the second half of the 1920s, publications geared toward women and dealing, at least in part, with matters of home economics began to appear in Palestine for the first time. This material provides another example of the changing view of cooking and home economics in Palestine at the time. Hadassah began publication of the journal *Ha-Isha* (The woman) in 1926. In 1927 the journal published several pieces dealing with the issue of training in home economics. A. Chahanski wrote one of these pieces, titled "Our Attitude toward Housework."[27] In it she described the importance of housekeeping knowledge in small settlements that offer no alternatives to home cooking. Mothers cannot always teach this topic to their daughters, according to Chahanski. This is a significant argument in a country of young immigrants who left their parents and grandparents behind. This point also highlights the close connection between transmitting cooking knowledge and traditional family structure, as well as the rising importance of cookbooks and related instruments of instruction in modern times when the traditional frameworks are no longer available. Chahanski's main point is the importance of raising awareness of the value of kitchen work. She argues that it should not be considered an addition to a woman's other roles in the field of agriculture but as work in its own right. Chahanski states that the change in attitude is necessary not only for men but also for women, who do not see housekeeping as "work" and therefore always take on an additional job, which in turn only allows them to care for their home and family during their spare time. Chahanski concludes that it is necessary to open a school for the teaching of home economics. It should be a mandatory subject in schools for girls and considered a necessity, not an indulgence. Furthermore, Chahanski calls for publishing a cookbook suitable for the climate in Palestine written "by experts" and devoting more space to questions of home and kitchen in *Ha-Isha*.[28] By 1929 *Ha-Isha* was no longer publishing debates on the merits of home economics but instead had a regular home economics column that included articles such as "How to Cook Vegetables."[29]

WIZO began publishing recipe booklets at around the same time. The first booklet appeared in 1927, published by WIZO's Instruction Department. *Vegetable Dishes* and *Potato Dishes* were both published in 1927, as well as a booklet titled *Home Economics*. In 1928 *Broad Beans, Peas and Carrots*, and *Cabbage and Cauliflower* were published; in 1929 *A Booklet on Baking* and *Citrus Recipes* appeared. From 1930 on, the number of publications increased gradually, ranging from eight to eighteen different topics a year.[30] These booklets differ from formal cookbooks in that they typically do not include any introductory words, illustrations, or additional information apart from the actual recipes (thirty or forty of them). The information on the cover offers only the topic of the booklet and the publisher, for example, "WIZO, The Department of Home Economics Instruction." There is no mention of an individual author or authors and often no date of publication. These booklets demonstrate, on the one hand, a growing awareness of the need for cooking instruction and information and, on the other, the slower rise in the prestige of kitchen work, since there is no mention of the specific recipes' authors.

In a different piece in *Ha-Isha* from 1927, Esther Rozov-Uzieli wrote that "[now] there is growing and expanding immigration: other than the immigration of halutzim and halutzot, thousands of families are beginning to arrive [in Palestine]. The woman is a total stranger to the climate in our country, and adjusting is very difficult." Rozov-Uzieli therefore suggests introducing more roving instructors and publishing popular literature on housekeeping to aid in this transition.[31] Rozov-Uzieli's comment is significant because she specifically mentions the change in demographics of the new immigrants, from young, single halutzim to families. Creating alternative models to the nuclear family is more complicated when you have actual families to contend with, a fact that forced a change in Zionist priorities and rhetoric.

## "EDUCATING" NEWLY ARRIVED HOUSEWIVES

*Here is the bread that with cheap cosmetics*
*becomes dark*
*and the olives on a little plate*
*on the tablecloth.*

*. . . I was a child in the home that was called a shack*
*in the neighborhood they said was a ma'abara.*

　　—**Ronny Someck,** "Kav ha-Oni" (The poverty line)

The wave of mass immigration from North Africa and the Middle East following Israel's independence in 1948 (continuing through the 1960s) created
tremendous challenges for the young country. A rationing program (Zena)
was established by the Israeli government as part of the attempt to find an
economic solution to the absorption of so many new arrivals. However,
these newly arrived immigrants needed "encouragement" to cooperate
with the Zena program. Both the government and related agencies treated
new immigrant housewives as a separate entity from the more established
population and created different campaigns to win their cooperation with
the rationing program. This was part of a larger campaign of acculturation
of these new immigrants into the European-centered, hegemonic Israeli
culture at the time. A WIZO report from 1954 included the statement: "Let
us not forget that in addition to the customary roles in the area of home
economics teaching in the rest of the world, we are also constantly aware
of our important educational role to guide *olot* [new female immigrants]
from backward countries. These olot need, first and foremost, guidance
regarding new ways of life in their old-new homeland. This task requires a
staff of well-trained workers who are ready for *pioneering* [emphasis mine]
efforts."[32] This statement reveals the general position adopted by the WIZO
workers toward the new immigrants: full of dedication and Zionist zeal, but
also paternalistic and patronizing. The very terminology used to describe
each group is indicative of their different status in Israeli society: the early
halutzim (pioneers) comprising the more influential and politically powerful segment of Israeli society vs. the new *olim* (immigrants). The word *olim*
means "ascending," positioning Israel as a coveted higher plain and those
already living there as superior to those living in the Diaspora.

The massive immigration following independence triggered certain fears
and anxieties in the more established population. The new immigrants
threatened the Zionist claim for a common Jewish nationality based not only
on religion but on a shared culture and history. Since the new immigrants

appeared to have more in common with the Arab world than with Ashkenazi Jews, they destabilized the Zionist representation of a homogeneous Jewish nation.[33] The Jewish population of European origin that comprised a significant part of the Yishuv held negative stereotypical perceptions of the new immigrants and feared that the sociocultural character of the Yishuv would be compromised. The fact that the new immigrants were not screened in any way, did not have any Zionist education or inclination, and had no training in agriculture or modern Hebrew all added to the common prejudices within the established population that the new immigrants were primitive, ignorant, and unproductive, with low moral standards and no ideological commitment. They felt that the Socialist/European nature of the Yishuv was in danger of levantinization and Orientalism.[34] There was a consensus regarding the need to guide and direct the new immigrants, to acculturate them into the existing Westernized culture in Israel. The Yishuv thus adopted the "melting pot" ideology in the sociopolitical field and in the cultural sphere. The latter area, however, encountered some resistance. According to Moshe Lissak, the overarching philosophy of the melting pot dictated the eradication of all individual ethnic traditions and the creation of a single cultural frame that incorporated a variety of cultural elements but was governed by one dominant element: Western European culture.[35] This philosophy was later amended, and a slightly more pluralistic approach was adopted, but particularly during the 1950s this policy implied major involvement of the government in all areas of new immigrants' everyday life, from education and employment to personal hygiene and eating habits. One example is the choice of government subsidies for basic foodstuffs: the Israeli government subsidized the price of European-style bread but not pita bread, preferred by Oriental Jews and Palestinians.[36]

Food was one of the vehicles used to acculturate new immigrants and to integrate them into what previous immigration waves had established as the national standard. A similar attitude toward new immigrants can be seen in Harvey Levenstein's discussion of the absorption of Eastern European and Italian immigrants into American society: "New York City social workers . . . considered dietary change an essential element of 'Americanization.' Many believed the newcomers would never accept the social and political values of the United States until they abandoned the lifestyles and eating habits of the old country. One social worker described an Italian family as 'still eating spaghetti, not yet assimilated.'"[37] This description could easily be applied to the work of WIZO volunteers in Israel with new immigrants from the Middle East and North Africa. One of the differences between the two situations, however, is that the immigrants who arrived in Israel after independence hailed from countries that were in closer geographical proximity to Israel than the immigrants who arrived in earlier periods. The eating habits of immigrants from North Africa and the Middle East should have been better suited to Israel's climate than those of immigrants from Eastern Europe, yet they were put through a process of "education" in order to assimilate them into the new Israeli society. It was essential to the Zionist project to demonstrate that these Jewish people had more in common with their fellow Jews from Europe than with the Arab population they lived amongst prior to immigration. With the War of Independence, any cultural product that was associated with Arab countries was deemed "the enemy's" and therefore shunned.

WIZO took action to further the cause of homogenization and acculturation in the area of nutrition and food habits. The 1948–49 report described the organization's work with the immigrants in conjunction with the Ministry of Welfare: forty-five women would be specially trained to work with the new immigrants, and bilingual recipe booklets would be published and handed out to the immigrants at no charge. These booklets were published in a Hebrew/Yiddish version and a Hebrew/French version, which indicates that they were mainly geared toward European and North African immigrants. A 1950–51 report showed the same type of activities only in increasing numbers: the course for instructors for new immigrants in Tel Aviv and Haifa numbered sixty-eight participants in 1949 and ninety-six in 1950. The number of instructors who worked with immigrants in the *ma'abarot* (temporary camps) doubled from 79 in 1949 to 160 in 1950. The report includes more information on the nature of the instruction provided to the immigrants. Special cooking demonstrations were held in the ma'abarot and in new housing developments. Instructors explained how to use the products available at the market during this time of economic rationing, products like "fish filet," fresh "soft" cheese, powdered milk and eggs, and a variety of local vegetables. The instructors also demonstrated how to put together a nutritionally "correct" menu and gave explanations in laymen's terms on the importance of each product and technique. The WIZO members worked with a guide from among the immigrants who tried to help the instructors persuade the new immigrants to cook the new dishes in their homes.[38] The need to enlist an immigrant guide points to the main problems WIZO faced in working with this community: winning immigrants' trust and getting them to practice what was preached to them. Cooking and eating habits seemed more resistant to change than some other practices, perhaps because they did not seem essential to future economic success (unlike learning the Hebrew language or dressing in a Western manner) or because it is harder to change what has to be ingested, actually put into the body.

Most of the help offered to new immigrants by the various agencies and women's organizations was given during the first year of their arrival in the country. Mina Meyir, in a conference lecture in 1950 on working with olim, called for extending this assistance. She said that only after the first year are the olim more or less settled in terms of housing and employment; then they can devote more attention to issues of housekeeping and cooking.[39] Meyir pointed out the difficulty in assisting the post-1948 immigrants compared with previous immigration waves: these more recent immigrants were housed in isolated housing projects, cut off from the rest of the population; therefore, they could not learn from the more established residents and so continued the same practices they were used to in their countries of origin. This, according to Meyir, slowed their acculturation significantly compared with previous immigration waves. Meyir and other WIZO workers raised the question of gaining the new immigrants' trust: "There were times we were able to come straight into the home of a new immigrant and guide her, but today we must first win her trust by helping her in the difficult state she is often in, and only indirectly can we awake in her the desire to change her lifestyle."[40]

Meyir and the other WIZO guides did not refer at any point to the demand on the new immigrants to forsake all ties to their cultural heritage

10. "A young Moroccan girl learns to cook for her own household and maybe economically for . . . an institution too. The class is one of many held for new immigrants at WIZO's Center," May 1950. Hanna Heiman, private collection.

and tradition. Unlike the European immigrants, the immigrants from Arab countries had no desire to adopt a new lifestyle, and the ferocious campaign to assimilate them into a Westernized Israel did not leave them many links to their previous community and cultural identity. Awakening "the desire to change her lifestyle" effectively meant awakening a woman's desire to forsake her traditions and cultural heritage in favor of a homogeneous Jewish nation. Simha, another instructor working with immigrants, wrote: "They had many complaints. . . . 'Why do you come and explain all sorts of strange things to us while we have no dresses? . . . [O]ur husbands have no work. . . . Give us houses instead of tents, give us work. Then we shan't need all your explanations and lectures!'"[41] WIZO volunteers continued undaunted despite this reception. They proceeded to teach immigrants, mostly from the Middle East and North Africa, how to plan menus for their families, make sandwiches, understand the "right meaning" of Jewish festivals, and set a festive table.[42] They were guided by a belief that these invaluable skills would help their charges settle in the new country and adjust to a "modern" way of life.

The work done by the various women's organizations demonstrates a shift in the Zionist movement's approach to food and to the family beginning in the late 1920s and developing further after Israel's independence in the late 1940s and 1950s. In effect, Zionism learned to "recruit" the family and consumerist values to further the nationalistic agenda. Sociologist Oz Almog demonstrates Zionist propaganda's influence on all areas of life, including those of popular culture, such as advertising, toys, clothing, and food: "The Zionist spirit has succeeded in invading every corner of our being."[43] The national movement was able to unite the different social factions within the Yishuv through nationalist propaganda aimed at different groups in different ways.

### NUTRITIONAL EDUCATION IN THE SCHOOL SYSTEM

After independence the Israeli state had access to new instruments of socialization and acculturation of its citizens. One obvious agent was the education system. The direct influence of the school system on children's eating habits and the system's indirect influence on parents through their children is obviously not unique to Israel. In this case, both home economics classes and school lunches were "recruited" to teach students "correct," as well as unified, eating habits designed to promote not only children's health but also state ideology.

### The School Lunch

Hadassah had begun a program of hot school lunches as far back as the mid-1920s. Henrietta Szold, aiming to both feed hungry children and educate the Yishuv on the importance of proper nutrition, established the program in 1925. The ideas behind the school lunch program were to assure children of a daily hot meal, to teach them how to cook and serve food, and to develop in them "proper eating habits and elementary knowledge of the science of nutrition."[44] In addition, Hadassah hoped to influence indirectly the eating habits of the children's parents and families and thus raise "the standard of health and well-being" in the population in general.[45] A teacher described the effects of the program on the students and their parents in the late 1920s: she wrote that at her school in Jerusalem, there were many children from the "Oriental" community that were very poor. They came from families of fugitives from the Middle East and North Africa, "people of low cultural level . . . [who] cling to the old customs and habits, which have become second nature to them [even when their economic situation improves]."[46] She stated that most Sephardic children, when asked, said that for breakfast they had bread and coffee or leftover lentils from last night's dinner. Only seldom did they have milk or eggs. Some children actually stole food from the school's trashcans. The program, according to the writer, helped the children understand the limitations of their situation at home. Many children brought their mothers to school to learn how to make the dishes the teacher had made. With time, the children adapted and adopted the changes: "cleanliness, order, table manners, proper nutritional habits."[47] Reading her reflections, it is clear that this kind of approach aggravated tensions between different generations of immigrants, complicating a younger generation's feelings toward the traditions of their parents' generation and portraying non-European habits as backward and primitive.

Reports on school kitchen exams for eighth graders reveal some of the

11. Cooking class, late 1920s (Esther Goldberg, *first from right*). Private collection of Esther Goldberg.

recipes prepared by the students in the late 1930s: spinach borscht, vegetable soup, fish steamed with vegetables, eggs shaped like mushrooms, potato pie, deviled eggs, spinach pudding (made with bread, butter, eggs, and cheese), green bean and tomato stew, stuffed zucchinis or tomatoes, fruit salad, prune soup, and nut cake with chocolate frosting, among others. The majority of recipes are for vegetables, fruit, and eggs, while very few are for meat and fish.[48]

The school lunch program grew rapidly, aided by funds from the Yishuv itself, but in 1945 Hadassah's National Board recommended separating the feeding aspect in the programs from the teaching and transferring a major part of the teaching and education budget to the National Committee (Va'ad Leumi).[49] In the 1950s Hadassah devoted resources to establishing vocational training schools for young olim, highlighting agricultural work (including fishing) for boys and homemaking for girls. The Nutrition Department of the Ministry of Education and Culture took over the Hadassah program in the 1950s and was headed by Dr. Sarah Bavly, a long-time Hadassah member active in this field. The department was responsible not only for serving school lunches but also for operating a college for training home economics and nutrition teachers, as well as teaching these subjects to seventh and eighth graders.[50] According to Yehudit Hitron, one of the first ministry supervisors for nutrition studies and Bavly's replacement, Bavly was very particular about the teachers she employed and their education and continued studies. In fact, when they joined the Ministry of Education they were considered to be the best-trained and most professional teachers of any sector.[51]

### Textbooks in Nutrition and Home Economics

One of Bavly's other major contributions to nutrition studies in Israel was a textbook she wrote on the subject for use in the seventh and eighth grades. *Tzunatenu* (Our nutrition) was published in 1939, when Bavly was still running Hadassah's Restaurant Fund (the school lunch program), and it was approved by the National Union's Education Department as a textbook for the study of nutrition. This was the main text for the teaching of nutrition well into the 1960s. One of the central characteristics that distinguish the book, as well as the entire approach to nutrition studies in Israel's early years, was its clear affiliation with the natural sciences. In his introduction to the book, Dr. E. Rigger writes: "Man's nutrition is now part of the study of biology . . . and will be studied as an organic part of the science of biology. In fact, it appears to me that this subject can be used as a lever to improve the study of the sciences of biology in general."[52] Only in the early 1960s did the subject of home economics begin to replace that of "scientific" nutrition studies. This particular affiliation dictated a focus on physiological processes and a scientific analysis of food products and their functions, as well as scientific experiments in class (more than actual cooking). The scientific approach also helped build teachers' self-esteem and confidence, but nutrition studies were still considered mostly a secondary topic, not as prestigious as "science."[53]

The objective scientific approach coexisted with a national agenda. Rigger discusses the fact that traditional Jewish dishes from the Diaspora were slowly disappearing in Israel, since they were inappropriate to the local climate and produce: "It is therefore essential to determine a new form of national diet for the Hebrew Yishuv in Israel. *A national kitchen is part of the national way of life* [my emphasis]. . . . The nutritional science studied in the Hebrew school in Israel fulfills a public educational duty: through the school the public learns bit by bit the new national nutrition and adapts to it according to the demands of science, climate, and the national and private economy."[54] Rigger ends his introductory remarks by stressing the great responsibility the author of this book had: "In our primary state in the land [of Israel] such a book could have a normative function to a great extent. . . . [I]t is particularly important now, while we are laying the foundations of our material culture in this land."[55]

In the chapter on spices and other "taste givers," Bavly details the "most commonly used" herbs and spices. Her list includes bay leaves, capers, cloves, cumin (whole, "used for adding flavor to bread, cakes, . . . soups, cabbage salad"), nutmeg, paprika, pepper, vanilla, mustard, ginger, horseradish, cinnamon, parsley, celery, and spring onion.[56] Despite the variety, this list offers a very limited picture, ignoring many spices and herbs commonly used by immigrants from Middle Eastern countries or by the Arab population. In fact, Bavly states later in the chapter that there are other "less popular" herbs, such as mint and basil.[57] Because the book does not specify discussing a particular diet, the question that comes to mind is, Popular with whom? The book was written in the late 1930s and as such addressed a population very different from the one inhabiting Israel after independence (and even then ignoring Arab food habits). It mirrors the trends, illustrated earlier, of the European bias of women's organizations, propaganda for local products (such as promoting the local dairy industry), and the attempt to create a homogeneous diet as a tool for unification. By the 1960s, however, Bavly's book gave a distorted picture of the Israeli diet, ignoring a significant part of the population.

### The School Curriculum for Nutritional Education

After examining the school curriculum in the Israeli state's early years, Shimon Reshef concludes that it indicated "a naïve faith in the ability of unified education and a single curriculum expressing a national consensus to develop common national patterns of life."[58] This approach by the state was later amended with the realization (following tests administered to eighth graders) that children from different ethnic backgrounds differed greatly in their achievements, causing many children from "Afro-Asian" backgrounds to drop out of school.[59]

By the early 1960s, nutrition and, later, home economics curriculum dictated by the Ministry of Education still focused on the scientific side of nutrition. The curriculum for both public (*mamlakhti*) and religious public (*mamlakhti-dati*) schools included topics such as how to make beef kosher, the law prohibiting mixing meat and dairy, and the law regarding a drop of blood in an egg.[60]

The curriculum statement from 1963 opened with some remarks on the goals of nutritional study in elementary school. These goals included supplying children with knowledge about the influence of food on human health, proper meal composition, and good table manners. In addition, the curriculum aimed to "awaken in the children the wish to . . . improve the[ir] family's food" and to improve "the understanding of the need to increase local production and the use of local products."[61] These two later objectives serve to remind us that the national agenda, that is, creating a unified diet and promoting *totzeret ha-aretz* products, had not been forgotten. The eighth-grade lessons, however, also include a discussion of foods of the different ethnic groups in Israel.

Unlike the scientific approach to nutrition studies, the later development of home economics took a much more "practical" slant. Its general objective was "to awaken in the [female] student the wish to acquire knowledge and experience in running her home, so that she might develop into a productive personality in her home and society."[62] But while feminism seems to move backward in Israeli history, the approach to ethnic diversity has been more accepting and open-minded: the curriculum attempted to "awaken students' awareness that each ethnic group in its special culture and ways of life can contribute to achieving the same goal."[63]

The main body of practical work in conjunction with the theoretical study of nutrition was done in schools that had a school cafeteria. Those generally served lunch or a late breakfast cooked by the students with teacher supervision. The time in class was thus not spent on learning recipes; instead, students gained hands-on knowledge through practical daily work. Yehudit Hitron remembers that the kitchen was also a place for her to learn more about the children and their homes. She says recipes were adapted and adopted according to stated preferences and actual consumption, and certain changes were made to suit different (ethnic) tastes and to "lure" certain groups toward certain foods.[64] Both school kitchens and educational kitchens in the ma'abarot came under the Ministry of Education and Culture's supervision in the early 1950s. In these kitchens, different ethnic food preferences presented issues to be contended with. Hitron said that the Polish immigrants, for example, did not want to eat "grass," that is, greens, so vegetables had to be incorporated into other foods. Iraqi immigrants, on the other hand, would only eat cheese if served sweet, as a dessert. Another method used by the nutrition teachers to ensure that every child had something to eat was to serve smaller but more varied portions. Hitron also emphasized that teachers made an effort to address children's preferences as much as possible, inquiring into cases where an entire group did not eat a certain dish, learning from children's mothers, and holding shows of different ethnic foods that would be cooked by the children's families. Hitron felt that teachers have in fact contributed greatly to interethnic relations through their treatment of this subject in the kitchen and class.[65]

Negotiating the various ethnic origins of the students was one of the main challenges of the Israeli school system and a constant dilemma for Israeli educators. Despite the fact that the orientation in schools remained distinctly Western (European), the Ministry of Education adopted a policy of encouraging students of African and Middle Eastern descent to maintain their connection with their cultural background. The guiding ideology behind programs such as the one for nutrition studies described above was to appreciate the variations among the different cultures of origin of the immigrants to Israel.[66]

All schools offered basically kosher food through the simple (and economical) solution of not serving any meat or poultry. The abundant use of dairy products was both an efficient and economical solution and an educational goal. Hitron is certain that the reason cheese and dairy products are so popular in Israel today has much to do with the educational kitchens. Some of the recipes offered in school cafeterias included cheese pancakes, cheese dumplings, cheese dough (with different fillings), eggplant and cheese pie, eggplant and cheese salad, cheese dressing, and cheesecake. Most of these utilize fresh, soft cheese.[67]

The school cafeterias worked to make the "national" diet a feature of every student's life, supplementing the ideology offered in the classroom and the textbook. In his seminal work on nationalism, Eric J. Hobsbawm suggested that deliberate propaganda is not as effective at "preaching" nationalism as is the ability of the media to make national symbols part of the life of every individual.[68] Israel provides a case study for Hobsbawm's suggestion. The state created informal methods of education such as children's magazines and popular songs to supplement the school setting, providing an effective connection between ideology and everyday life for its next generation. The examination of food practices suggests that the very use of food in establishing national affiliation exemplifies the idea Hobsbawm raised: making national symbols part of everyday life, or rather making everyday life into national symbols. Hobsbawm argues that this practice breaks down the division between the private and public (national) spheres, allowing national ideology to be standardized and homogenized.[69] Examining food in such a government-controlled setting as school lunches and nutritional education demonstrates the influence of the national ideology in Israel on everyday life and the private sphere.

### THE INGATHERING OF EXILES IN THE KITCHEN

In 1964 the Ministry of Education published the results of a survey of eating habits in Israel. This survey focused mainly on the changes in eating habits of new immigrants in the first, second, and third generations. The families that were questioned were divided into four groups according to the continent of origin of the first generation: Europe, North Africa, the Near East, and native Israelis. The results listed the different elements that affect eating habits and possibly cause changes in those habits: the husband is from a different ethnic background, the wife works outside the home, a child receives nutrition lessons at school, a child receives lunch at school, the wife receives nutritional instruction, the wife reads The Women's Corner column in the paper, the wife listens to *The Women's Corner* show on the radio, she writes down the recipes from the radio.[70] All these elements influence eating habits to some degree, though their effect changes from generation to generation and from one ethnic group to the next. The influence of children receiving lessons or meals at school seems particularly great, but it is important to note the possible bias of the author and conductor of the survey, Sarah Bavly, a long-time Hadassah member and head of the school lunch program for many years.

The survey focused particularly on the adoption of new dishes into the homemaker's repertoire. The two most influential elements from the list above include the husband's background and the children's schooling. It is interesting to note that Bavly claimed that in the European group, school lunches had less and less significance, probably because the dishes served to the children at school are not new to them.[71] In other words, despite the growing pluralistic attitude, the dominant kitchen in public/national ventures is still mostly European at this point in time. An additional element not mentioned before but significant to the issue of new dishes is "new products in the market and eye-catching packaging." This element was influential in the second and third generations and seemed related to the changes in shopping habits and growing buying power mentioned earlier. A great many of the products mentioned in this category were ready-made mixes or canned goods.[72] The types of products that were most resistant to change were fats and oils and bread. Both these products, as well as spices, seem to occupy a very conservative realm in the kitchen. Other than reducing the amount of spices used from one generation to the next, each ethnic group tended to stay loyal to the spices it was familiar with and to resist experimentation. Finally, the survey examined the degree of nostalgia for traditional dishes. Apparently, there was very little nostalgia compared with what was expected. There was some longing for complicated traditional dishes that the younger housewives could not find the time or patience to make, but this, as well as longing for foods that were readily available in the countries of origin, was mostly restricted to the first generation of immigrants.[73] Generally, traditional foods fell into the same category as all other remnants of the Diaspora and were often shunned in favor of the new foods and culture of Israel.

Bavly had been engaged in conducting and analyzing such surveys several times in the past. The survey described above, however, was very different from her other published works. In the surveys from 1946, 1951, and 1956–57, the analysis focused on the consumption of basic food products and their nutritional value, as well as on the differences between economic levels in the country.[74] The differences between ethnic groups came into play to a small degree but were not examined closely. The 1964 survey, on the other hand, was completely unconcerned with the nutritional value and the adequacy of the diet of the families questioned. It focused on cooked dishes instead of ingredients, already transforming the nature of the survey radically and giving it a more "cultural" flavor. The analysis of the results examined cultural and social behavior as well, and not chemical composition of foodstuffs or the "average" standard of living. This last survey was conducted not for the Central Statistics Bureau, as were most of its predecessors, but for the Ministry of Education and Culture, within which Nutrition and Home Economics was a separate department. This new "home" influenced the change in focus to social and cultural questions. Previous surveys were concerned with finding ways to improve the local diet or influence eating habits to increase consumption of inexpensive sources of protein or better sources of iron, while this one suggested the need to preserve traditional recipes so they did not disappear.[75] This new attitude toward food and eating habits transformed them from elements necessary for survival to cultural products. Despite the concern with the reasons for changes in eating habits, there was more openness to difference; in fact, exchange of information and a certain degree of traditionalism were respected and even encouraged.

## THE QUEEN OF THE KITCHEN

In 1964 Tadmor, a school for hotel management, with the aid of several governmental bodies, held the first Parade of Israeli Delicacies (Mitza'ad Mat'amei Israel), whose central event was the competition for Malkat ha-Mitbah (Queen of the Kitchen). This contest called homemakers and amateur cooks to submit their best recipes to a panel of experts. The annual affair was accompanied by the publication of a corresponding cookbook. The name alone, with its reference to royalty, indicates the changed social and ideological climate in Israel at this time. Reading the introduction to the cookbook accompanying the second contest reveals the organizers' objectives as a mixture of familiar Zionist ideology and newer, more materialistic ideas. Their first goal was to "create and strengthen Israeli culinary awareness and to vary and improve the Israeli menu." This goal merged the wish to create and enhance national products with a newer respect for culinary creations as cultural products. The focus on quality and variety was also more modern, as was the assumption that an Israeli menu already existed, even though it needed improving. The second goal was to "progress toward creating a national Israeli dish."[76] Here, the old "melting pot" ideal reappeared: the wish to create a new "Israeli" product out of a multitude of ethnic influences. The third aim was to increase and encourage the use of local products. This too was a familiar objective: the organizers specified that Israeli products such as chicken, fish, vegetables, fruit, and dairy were internationally famous and that the organizers wished to make those products just as popular in Israel.

The final two objectives of the competition's organizers were new and more modern in feel: to create more "service awareness," particularly in the hospitality field, and to recruit workers to the hospitality industry.[77] These two goals reveal that at this stage some of the glamour of the self-sufficient, proud, and assertive new Jewish persona that was created in Israel by the Zionist movement was wearing off. The famous Tzabar coarseness could be a hindrance to a successful tourist industry, which was becoming central to Israel's economy. A second introduction, written by Tadmor, repeats the contest's goals. Tadmor's objectives were to "awaken and rarefy the Israeli diner's palate," to "better the Israeli kitchen with new culinary inventions, . . . seasonal ingredients, and local products," and to encourage in the Israeli home an awareness of the variety of possibilities that local products afforded ("instead of copying foreign menus"). The final goal was "to rescue Israeli fish and chicken from the boredom of routine and to raise them to the honorable gastronomic position the Arabs have given lamb, the French gave duck, the Italians dough, and the Indians spices."[78] This final objective is interesting because it situates food products in a national context and shows the Israeli desire to create a "national" culinary product of its own in order to be a nation among nations.

The public submitted 1,916 recipes to the contest, out of which 1,706 were found eligible. One of the qualities that could disqualify a recipe was not adhering to the rules of kashrut (Jewish dietary laws). This remains an important quality for any formal national venture. The organizers commented on the originality and creativity of the submissions and gave as an example the variety of chicken recipes, which included coffee-coated chicken, chicken in tea sauce, chicken in banana foam, chicken stuffed with quinces in orange sauce, chicken with honey, with wine and mushrooms, with apricot and apples, covered in sesame and peanuts, or stuffed with avocado.[79] The most popular vegetable recipes utilized eggplant or zucchini (the heavy campaigning by wizo and Hadassah had done its part), and the most popular fruit recipes included citrus.[80] The score for each dish was based on the "Israeli nature" of the dish (20 points), taste (25), appearance (10), convenience and cooking time (10), use of local products (10), and special qualities (25).[81] It is gratifying to see that taste ranked with the elusive "special qualities," but the declared goals of the organizers emerged in the judging, which awarded a hefty 30 combined points to the elements of "Israeliness" and the use of local products.

The winning recipe that year was "Baked Fish in Pomegranate Juice and Wine" by Ruth Richter: "Take one whole fish (about 1½ kg), clean, score, salt, and then wash. Put the fish in an oiled baking dish and sprinkle with pine nuts and breadcrumbs mixed with crushed garlic and parsley. Pour a mixture of white wine [Hok, a local producer], pomegranate juice, and white vermouth over the fish and decorate with slices of onion. Dot with margarine and bake in a hot oven for forty-five minutes while basting periodically with the pan juices."[82]

The use of wine or other alcoholic beverages in the book's recipes is striking compared to earlier periods. There was also greater use of spices such as cardamom, cinnamon, cumin, and nutmeg. Several recipes had notes indicating their ethnic origin (Moroccan, Sephardic, Syrian from

Haleb, German, and American, among others) or were described as a "family tradition." The book has the distinct flavor of a community cookbook, and, in fact, the contest's unstated goal seems to have been to encourage the creation of a culinary community in Israel.

Among the recipes attributed to different participants from around the country are several that were contributed by the supporting official bodies, such as the Council for Chicken and Related Products and the Council for the Improvement of Fish Distribution. The fish recipes contributed by the council appear to be mostly ones using ground fish—good uses for leftovers and less-than-perfect fish, such as fish "moussaka," fish "chopped liver," fish balls in sauce, and fish pie. The Chicken Council's contributions seem more original and unique in their choice of products and techniques: chicken with kumquat and cold marinated chicken with curry. These recipes demonstrate the relentless attempt to influence or educate the Israeli public and to promote certain products and culinary approaches. The contest is also a good example, however, of the new approach to forging a unified Israeli society, an approach that allowed for a wide range of ethnic contributions. This contest also attempted to promote a more sophisticated diner, a potential client for a developing restaurant industry. Even though the contest seemed to focus on home cooking, it in fact promoted professional cooking and the development of a tourist industry.

# 4

# THE VIRTUAL KITCHEN

## *Making Room for Pleasure*

*We ask that the industrious housewife refrain from reading our*
*book. It is not for her. She will not find in it any recipe for utilizing*
*leftover beets from yesterday's borscht, combined with the remains of*
*the cooked carrots from the previous day's soup, together with Yossi's*
*unfinished yogurt, all shaped into a pancake. No. We do not want you*
*here, housewife. Get yourself another book, please. Our book is for the*
*frivolous and superficial woman, . . . the woman who not only secretly*
*wishes for a lover but has already found one. . . . Our book is for the*
*man . . . who doesn't always remember his wife's birthday, . . .*
*a greedy, generous, flippant man with a lust for life.*

—Amos Keinan, *Sefer ha-Ta'anugot*

This excerpt from *Sefer ha-Ta'anugot* (The book of pleasures) by Amos Keinan, published in 1970, offers a condensed version of the dramatic transformation the Israeli kitchen went through over the few preceding decades from the early beginning of an ascetic and utilitarian approach by the early halutzim, through the efficient and didactic approach of the women's organizations and the committed nature of state institutions' kitchens, to a discovery of the joy of cooking, along with other bourgeois evils, in the late 1960s.

This chapter tells the story of virtual kitchen instruction: professional instruction for domestic or amateur cooks in a virtual setting (not in person), beginning with the most elementary form, cookbooks, and continuing with radio programs, cooking shows on television, and, finally, the Internet.

This chapter begins with the first cookbook published for a Jewish audience in Israel, its publication coinciding with the realization, discussed in previous chapters, that food and cooking can serve as powerful tools for transmitting Zionist ideology. A close reading of several of the most influential cookbooks published in Palestine and Israel since then reflects the story of the transformation in the cultural and social climate and values in Israeli society and the relationship between the national movement and its various ethnic segments.

This chapter also showcases the growing power of the media as a tool for transmitting both knowledge and ideology. As the status of food in Israel rose alongside the standard of living, the focus shifted from transmitting a message and educating to entertainment. Despite this change, the national agenda is still apparent in modern-day cooking shows and on Internet sites. Unlike the certitude that characterized earlier times, today's culinary shows often serve as a place of exploration, an attempt at defining and shaping an Israeli cuisine. As the existence of an Israeli nation becomes an established fact, the time seems ripe for recruiting cultural products, among them food, to question and explore what this nation will become. Food offers a tool for rethinking Israeli national identity and how it might adopt and adapt to new immigration waves, political and economic changes, and global influences.

Each of the categories discussed here merits a much deeper investigation: cooking shows on television and online cooking forums and blogs are rich sites and constantly changing and evolving sources, making a fixed analysis outdated as soon as it is committed to the page. I therefore refrain from trying to include a comprehensive survey but rather offer some examples that illustrate broader trends and speak to the representation of national identity and a negotiation between unifying national forces and multiple ethnic variations.

## THE WRITTEN KITCHEN

### How to Cook in the Land of Israel?
Once the Zionist movement realized that food could be a tool for transmitting national ideology, cookbooks were quick to follow. In 1935 Dr. Erna Meyer published a cookbook titled *Eikh le-Vashel be-Eretz Israel?* (*How to Cook in*

*Palestine?* as translated in the original publication), sponsored by WIZO.[1] The book stresses the central position of local products in the kitchen both for health reasons and because of their "economic-national importance." It is a prime example of a cookbook as a national manifesto and seems to be the first complete cookbook published in Palestine for a Jewish audience. According to Meyer, housewives had to make a conscious effort to abandon the European kitchen they were used to and adopt a kitchen that was *eretz Israeli* (of the land of Israel) and healthy. "This is one of the most important means to establishing our roots in our old-new homeland," she claimed.[2] The book was written in three languages (Hebrew, English, and German), which demonstrates its didactic approach. It not only offered the housewife recipes but also attempted to teach her the "right" way of cooking in Palestine. In fact, it tried to establish one single way of cooking in order to develop a unified local cuisine. The book was published in three languages not only in order to reach a larger immigrant audience but also in order to establish and teach a basic vocabulary of everyday Hebrew. The use of German and English is perhaps more indicative of the origin of the book's author's background and that of the WIZO guides she worked with (mostly from Central Europe, Germany in particular, where nutritional science was quite developed) than of the origins of the immigrants she addresses.

Meyer unapologetically presents her efforts to introduce the housewife to local products and to create a kitchen that was "fitting to the land of Israel." She assumes her readers wished to learn about new ingredients and techniques that would help them strengthen their bond with the land. She also appeals to concerns about health, economy, and efficiency to encourage the use of these local products in her readers' kitchens. Meyer highlights some of the book's characteristics in her introduction: in the attempt to create a cookbook that is appropriate to Palestine's climate, she focuses on recipes using vegetables and fruit. Since many housewives have difficulties with some of the vegetables grown in Palestine, the book answers not only the question "What shall I cook?" but also "How shall I cook it?" Here Meyer refers to immigrants from Eastern and Central Europe, for whom eggplants and zucchini were foreign. Finally, the book deals with the techniques suited to the Palestinian climate, mostly items requiring simple, quick cooking

12. The cover of Erna Meyer's *Aikh Levashel be-Erez-Israel?* (How to cook in the land of Israel?) (Tel Aviv: WIZO, 1935).

"to save the housewife from the heat and from the noise of the primus." A three-legged gas burner and icon of low-budget cookery in Palestine, the primus appears on the book's jacket.

The recipes in the book reveal Meyer's efforts to keep the promises made in her introduction. The book is indeed geared toward introducing unfamiliar products and techniques, but the approach is different from someone writing an exotic cookbook today. She does not highlight the mystique of the ingredients, their unique and new flavor or aroma, or how they can contribute greater variety to the reader's cooking. Rather, Meyer attempts to make these foreign ingredients seem familiar or at least highly beneficial in order to reduce the "risk" of trying them. Learning to use these foreign products is not a new adventure but a challenge in overcoming resistance. A recipe for a salad of eggplant and eggs begins: "[This recipe is] for those that cannot stand the typical taste of eggplants." The recipe calls for cooking a third of the eggplants in salted boiling water with vinegar and bay leaves, frying another third of the eggplants in oil, and grilling the last third. Finally, everything is ground together in a meat grinder with some boiled eggs and onions and then mixed with mayonnaise.[3] Another example is a comment in the appetizer section regarding the use of olives: "One learns to eat olives quite easily when they are used as a spread on bread."[4]

### Cookbooks and Cooking Manuals during the British Mandate

In 1942 Lillian Cornfeld published a cookbook entitled *Keitzad Mevashlim bi-Yemei Milhama?* (How can we cook in times of war?) (following the publication of several wartime-related columns in *Olam ha-Isha* in 1941 and 1942) with an introduction by the British food controller, J. Walsh.[5] The food controller was involved in several publications on cooking during the war. By helping fund them, the food controller promoted the British government's agenda, for example, endorsing certain products imported from England. In his introduction, Walsh wrote of the importance of the public's help in keeping prices under control in "these difficult days."[6] He stressed the importance of the housewife's role in this project and the significance of her initiative, imagination, and open-mindedness to the creation of low-cost yet nutritional meals for her family. Walsh claimed that in Cornfeld's book the housewife would find advice on balancing her household budget by substituting expensive foods with cheaper alternatives.[7] These alternatives were often products imported by the British, such as powdered eggs and powdered milk. The publishers (*Olam ha-Isha*, sponsored by Hadassah) added their own words, highlighting the significant role of the housewife in times of war: "The housewife . . . has the difficult role of nourishing her family—she stands in the first row of the home front, since sufficient nutrition . . . is a crucial element in fortifying the will of the people to active and passive defense."[8] The Zionist organization had its own message; it was less concerned with sound economy but rather more with promoting food's role as an instrument of unification for the Yishuv. These agendas coexist in all such publications during the war years. What both bodies have in common is the appeal to the housewife: positioning her as an important and politically influential figure.

Cornfeld's book offers "cheap menu" suggestions, general nutritional information, and many recipes, including ones using leftovers and substitutions. The list of dessert recipes can be found in the index divided into the following headings: "Cold [Desserts] with No Eggs," "Desserts without Sugar," and "Desserts with One Egg." The majority of recipes are for vegetable dishes, but there are also many for grains, legumes, and dairy products. The chapter dealing with meat is titled "Cheap Meat Dishes" and includes such dishes as eggless meatballs, cabbage leaves with lungs, stew of kidneys or heart with cabbage and rice, stuffed spleen, and mock chopped liver (made with kidneys). There are also several suggestions for "stretching" a meat portion, using leftovers and some "local" or "Oriental" options like *shishlik* (shish kebab) or rice pilaf. The recipe for shish kebab calls for the use of lamb or mutton in small pieces threaded on a skewer and roasted over a fire. It ends by saying, "Fixing this dish is easy, and it is very comfortably digested." A section on butter substitutions deals not only with butter's functions in cooking but also with replacing its nutritional content, offering such solutions as margarine, olives, peanuts, mayonnaise, avocado, fish oil, and tahini.[9] These suggestions show the author's own agenda: Cornfeld tries to introduce "Oriental" (i.e., Middle Eastern) dishes to her readers and offers a wealth of nutritional information, sometimes using the latter to encourage openness to the former, as in the suggestion of shish kebab or tahini mentioned above. These two objectives, educating the housewife about proper nutrition and introducing her to local dishes and ingredients, will characterize all of Cornfeld's books. She often uses Arab cooking as one of the models for creating a nutritionally sound, local, Jewish cuisine.

Another example of a "joint venture" of the food controller and Zionist women's organizations was a brochure entitled *Recipes of the Season*, published in June 1945 in English.[10] The name may have conjured images of fresh seasonal fruit and vegetables or perhaps heartier meals suited for wintertime versus salads and light dishes for the summer. The cover image, however, indicates that the publishers of this booklet had something else in mind: the cover is divided into sixteen squares, each one featuring a drawing of a chicken or a potato stick, with the repeating respective captions reading "dried egg" and "dried potato." The brochure begins with instructions on how to reconstitute dried egg and dried potatoes and then goes on to give recipes for various types of mayonnaise, yeast cakes, and other cakes and sweets, all using egg powder instead of eggs. The main incentive for the British government in this particular project appears to have been to encourage sales of the dried eggs and dried potatoes it was importing to Palestine at the time.[11]

*The Cookbook*

In 1948 WIZO published a cookbook based on the recipes that appeared in the organization's pamphlets and brochures created for its various courses. Instead of having a single author, the book is by "WIZO's Instruction Department." The book, titled simply *Sefer ha-Bishul* (The cookbook) in the early editions, was supposed to cover WIZO's instructors' twenty years of experience in "teaching and guiding the Hebrew Yishuv in Israel."[12] According to the short introduction by the department's management, the instructors perfected the recipes over the years to finally settle on their current forms, which "best [suit] the . . . Yishuv's taste and living conditions."[13] The introduction goes on to describe what is unique to this book in comparison with foreign cookbooks: mainly, that the chapter on meat dishes is short because meat is expensive and that the book's recipes accommodate the country's warm climate. The chapters on vegetables, dairy, and eggs (totzeret ha-aretz, of course!) describe these items as reasonably priced and "nutritionally important and easy to digest."[14] The authors' stated aim is to create in Israel "unified Israeli food habits, based on proper nutritional regulations," to replace those "different and bad eating habits" that were brought "from the *gola* [Diaspora]."[15]

The book's revised edition, published in 1960, repeated the organization's commitment to correcting the "corrupted eating habits" brought from the gola by the majority of immigrants in favor of correct and, "as much as possible, unified" nutritional habits.[16] The qualifying "as much as possible" appearing at the end of the 1950s indicates perhaps WIZO's growing frustration with the task of unification when encountering people not so eager to shed their "corrupt" habits in favor of WIZO's suggestions. In the book's new title, the addition of *Kakh Nevashel* (<u>So</u> we shall cook) before the old title, with the "So" underlined for emphasis, suggests, however, the authors' strong convictions and almost stubborn belief in the ideal of unified eating habits and one "right" way.[17]

### The 1960s: Dining In / Looking Out

The greater exposure to the outside world and the growing tolerance toward individual pleasure were accompanied by greater openness to cultural diversity within Israeli society. Allowing for ethnic contributions from non-Western sources was perhaps most visible in the realm of food. In the early 1960s cookbooks made this greater accommodation of ethnic influences most evident compared to other cultural spheres. Despite the greater prestige of kitchen work compared to previous decades, food was still far from being perceived as an important cultural sphere. As such, it was one of the first realms to allow for contributions from non-Western sources. During the 1960s the voices of immigrants from the Middle East and North Africa began infiltrating mainstream Israeli society in literature and music, but at a slower pace. Despite the fact that European recipes still dominated, dishes from the Middle East and North Africa were no longer exiled to a separate chapter under the heading "Oriental" dishes but were incorporated into different, appropriate chapters (although a separate index entry might appear for them). Even though the term "Oriental" is still sometimes used to indicate dishes originating in Arab countries, there were more instances of a specific indication of the source (i.e., Turkey, Syria, etc.) or "nationalizing" a dish, making it part of the Israeli repertoire with no special indication of its origins, whether it is schnitzel or falafel. There was also greater ethnic diversity in the recipe sources in general: Moroccan, Iraqi, and Yemenite dishes appear in addition to German, Russian, and Balkan contributions. Lillian Cornfeld divided her book *Israeli Cookery* into chapters according to the ethnic origin of the recipes: Near and Far East (Yemen, Iraq, Bukhara, Persia, and Kurdistan), Middle East, North Africa, Bulgaria and the Balkans, Eastern Europe, Central and Western Europe, and finally some chapters on Sabra (native Israeli) foods. The Sabra recipes are based on either typical local ingredients or what Cornfeld calls "adaptations of Ingathering of Exiles," so they include quite a variety, from lasagna to blintzes. Cornfeld also acknowledges the contribution of Arabic cooking to Israeli eating habits, referring to them diplomatically as "the local people."[18]

Unlike the sparse offerings in previous decades of Israel's history, the 1960s began with a publishing flurry of cookbooks that accompanied the official end of the rationing program in early 1959. A close examination of these cookbooks shows some of the trends that had been established in earlier times, as well as some changes that would develop further with the economic prosperity following the Six-Day War in 1967. This was a time of transformation: habits that had been established during the period of the Yishuv and the difficult times of the country's early years were altered by the new social and ideological environment that has characterized Israel from 1967 to the present. Lillian Cornfeld published the cookbook *Ha-Mitbah ha-Meshubah: Ha-Bishul be-Yameinu* (The superb kitchen: Cooking in our time) in 1960, and it became a "must-have" for every young bride in Israel. Soon after, in 1962, she published another cookbook, *Israeli Cookery*, this time in English—an attempt to describe and define Israeli cooking to an American audience. Thiya Bat-Oren published a cookbook in 1961 titled *365 Shulhanot Arukhim* (365 set tables) based on her cooking program on the radio, *The Women's Corner*. In 1963 Ilana Tzukerman published her book *Ha-Bishul ve-Meshek ha-Bayit* (Cooking and home economics), and

Molly Bar-David published in English *The Israeli Cookbook* as part of the International Cookbook series in 1964. The publishing of these books so close together is indicative of a growing interest in food and entertainment, a higher standard of living, and a higher percentage of Hebrew readers. Devices such as food shows were neglected in favor of cookbooks and newspaper and magazine articles in a society that included more Hebrew speakers and readers than new immigrants and more money to spend on luxuries such as cookbooks, women's magazines, and more sophisticated ingredients.

Cornfeld begins her cookbook by saying that this book has been updated "according to the phenomenal changes that have occurred in the world of cooking in recent years, mainly regarding time saving in the cooking process." She gives as examples of this progress inventions such as the pressure cooker, freezing of precooked food, soup powders, self-rising flour, frozen vegetables, canned corn, and instant coffee.[19] Cornfeld ends her opening remarks by saying, "My ambition [is] to encourage and raise the cooking standards in the home, the institution, and the restaurant."[20] This last remark represents the main difference between the above-mentioned books and earlier examples. The main intention of the authors here is to raise existing standards, teach more sophisticated cooking, and offer greater variety in ingredients and techniques. They are not aiming to introduce their readers to a new land or to help them survive in times of crisis. Bat-Oren begins her introduction by saying: "I hope you like to eat and like to cook—since you are, in fact, the one determining the joy of life of your family."[21] In other words, despite their practical nature these cookbooks deal more with the pleasure of cooking and of food than with food as a necessity for survival. Examples of this new attitude can be seen in Cornfeld's book in the inclusion of a chapter on alcoholic drinks and wines, her suggestion of a menu for "a successful cocktail party," and her opening to the hors d'oeuvres and appetizers chapter: "Opulence to the eye and mouth transforms eating from merely a necessity to joy and pleasure."[22] Some of the recipes she offers in the book demonstrate a similar attitude, as well as the greater buying power of her readers, like a discussion of caviar or a recipe for stuffed beef filet braised in wine.

The more practical side of these publications addressed the fact that a large percentage of their readers worked outside the home. Many women in Israel joined the workforce because a second income was (and still is) necessary for most families. Wives taking on employment had a serious impact on the food habits of many new immigrants. The Kitchen column in *La-Isha*, dedicated to the "working mother," discussed various ready-made products available in the market. The column mentions prepared hummus in a jar, falafel powder mix, powdered soups, ice cream, chocolate syrup, and filo dough and offers quick menus using these products.[23] The modern innovations in ready-made products and the existence of new technology (refrigerators, washing machines, etc.) helped many working women. Cornfeld includes a special section in her 1960 cookbook titled "Quick Cooking for the Working Woman." She details appropriate recipes from other chapters in the book and gives general advice on time saving, cooking for "two days," and the use of leftovers. Her advice includes ways to improve the taste of canned foods, how to make one-pot meals, and how to use a pressure cooker.[24] Thiya Bat-Oren's cookbook offers similar advice and pays particular attention to matters of time saving and efficiency in cooking.

Many food-related articles and columns from this time began by saying, "With the end of the rationing of food products . . ." or "At the end of the bitter period of rationing . . ."and went on to offer recipes for meat dishes or to suggest new products.[25] Partly due to the improved economic situation and the rise in the standard of living, Israeli citizens were now significantly more aware of the world around them. Due to both the ambivalent relationship with the Diaspora and the immediate economic, social, and security concerns that troubled the Yishuv and the young state, Israeli society was surprisingly introverted for a country of immigrants up to the late 1950s. Only when the threat to their existence seemed to be at bay and the economic situation improved did Israeli citizens begin to travel more and look outward for models of culinary behavior.

Amos Keinan concludes his 1970 cookbook *Sefer ha-Taʻanugot* (The book of pleasures) with the following thoughts:

One day in the month of June 1967 the author returned, like everyone else, from the war. He sat at home and began to think how beautiful

תושבי פריס

נהנים בלי יוצא מן הכלל ממרק הבצל,
המוגש במסעדה הידועה בפריס:
"LE CHIEN QUI FUME"

תושבי ישראל,

גם אתם יכולים ליהנות ממרק הבצל החדש
של ויטה, שהוכן לפי מתכונת צרפתית
טהורה. — נסו עוד היום ותיווכחו

מחיר 36 אג׳, 4—6 מנות

ויטה

כשר — פרווה

מרק ויטה - בכל ארוחה

13. "Citizens of Paris enjoy onion soup served at the famous Paris restaurant
Le Chien Qui Fume. Israeli citizens, you too can enjoy Vita's new onion soup,
prepared according to a pure French recipe—try it today and see for yourself."
Advertisement for Vita soup mix in Lillian Cornfeld, *Ha-Mitbah ha-Meshubah*
(The superb kitchen) (Tel Aviv: Published by the author, 1960).

life is, really, and had an idea: why not write a book about the beautiful life and about the most beautiful thing of all, pleasures. . . . It occurred to the author that he went to war so that he might stay alive . . . and staying alive is worthwhile, since then you can enjoy good wine, hot soup, music on the beach, a woman, and a fish in the oven.

The effects of the 1967 Six-Day War on Israeli society were numerous and varied, but this quote is typical in one sense: it appears that for many Jewish Israelis this war was life affirming.

Keinan's *Sefer ha-Ta'anugot* is, perhaps, the most striking departure from previous cooking publications. The very word "pleasures" in the title indicates that this is no longer WIZO territory. Efficiency, practicality, and housewives are not this book's concern. The author is a man, indicating the growing prestige of the cookbook genre; and even though Keinan is not a professional cook, the 1970s would usher in a growing professionalism in cooking and with it more male cookbook authors. The recipes, as the book's title implies, are not practical or sensible; they are not everyday fare for the family or suitable for any particular holiday or social function. These recipes, like the rest of the book, are just for fun. They are an indulgence. They assume a readership that cooks not because it must but because cooking is enjoyable. The recipes are interspersed with ruminations on the author's travels abroad (particularly to Europe) and the foods he had tasted and enjoyed on his travels, like fried fish in Genoa's port, roast ox in Yugoslavia, and gazpacho in Barcelona. He also reflects on other corporeal pleasures, from washing in the sea to sex. Discussing the pleasures of sex and the body were just as great a taboo among the early halutzim as nonkosher foods were in the public domain of the Jewish state. The author proceeds to break both prohibitions in this book, indicating a change in the moral climate of Israel.

Keinan locates Israel in the Mediterranean, not the Middle East. He focuses on the seashore, on small plates of meze, on the foods of Italy and the South of France. His culinary roots are French, and he offers basic French sauces, compound butters, and a variety of French recipes from *bœuf bourguignon* to escargot, but he also mentions and exalts other cuisines, from

Romanian to Chinese. Keinan does spend some time on the advantages and flavor of lamb and mutton, admonishing the Ashkenazi population for its ignorance and encouraging them to demand it from their butchers. He has no complaints when it comes to salads, though, writing: "It is somewhat of an insult to explain to an Israeli reader how to prepare salad. Salad is the national food of Israel." He does offer a short list of possible additions to the basic vegetable salad such as tahini, sour cream, ham, fennel, olives, and nuts, to name just a few. He ends with: "Putting together a salad is a kind of creation that bestows pleasure. See the kibbutz member with a large pile of fresh vegetables in front of him: slowly, with great conviction, he puts together his personal salad, a corner of individualism in the heart of the commune."[26]

### The (In)visibility of Nonkosher Food

The first recipes in Keinan's book are for seafood dishes. This is another break with previous cookbooks and will remain a rare phenomenon in Israeli cookbooks for the next three decades. Seafood recipes are nonkosher, and that is the first reason for their rare appearance in Israeli cookbooks: including nonkosher products and recipes guarantees a book will lose a large percentage of its potential readership in a market that is small to begin with. Keinan laments the linguistic limitations on seafood in Hebrew. One word describes a whole slew of related creatures, such as *hasilonim* (shrimp) for *crevette grises*, *bouquets* (prawns), and langoustines (small lobsters) or an unspecified "filet" for any number of different fish. He proceeds to offer seven recipes for shrimp, calamari, crab, and lobster. Keinan comments on the fact that most of these delicacies are extremely cheap in Israel (if you know where to find them), since there is no demand for them.

It is significant, however, that when it comes to recipes for pork the book appears "shy." Unlike other products in the book whose recipes are accompanied by illustrations depicting the source in a realist manner (such as sheep, cows, chickens, and the seafood mentioned above), the pork recipes are accompanied by illustrations of jovial men and women or their parts (women's legs for a recipe for pork leg). Pork might be the most "loaded" of the nonkosher products; the sense of taboo and the cultural

רגל בשר לבן — נוסח סאן מאנולד

14. "White Meat Leg à
la San Manold." Amos
Keinan, *Sefer ha-Ta'anugot*
(The book of pleasures)
(Tel Aviv: A. Levin-Apstein,
1970), 105.

connotations are deeply embedded. This "unobtrusive" approach to pork recipes in particular will change significantly by the 1990s and is a perfect example of the transitional nature of the 1970s in terms of culinary openness and experimentation.

*Burda Sefer ha-Bishul* (1974), originally published in German as *Burda-Kochbuch* (Verlag Aenne Burda, Offenburg), is another example of "invisible" nonkosher food. This book was translated and adapted for the kosher kitchen by a local publisher, but no credit is given to a translator or editor. It was not originally a kosher cookbook, so it is interesting to note its adaptation to the Israeli kitchen. The book includes color photographs for every recipe (one recipe per page). These photographs were unique at the time, when most cookbooks were still accompanied solely by illustrations. They also enabled an attentive reader to decipher the kosher version of the recipes. For example, "Swedish Platter" included a number of small dishes, including a plate of mussels; however, the text describes it as "smoked fish."[27] The butter served with a "[beef] filet with compound margarine" cannot be seen but can be surmised; a Yule log–shaped cake (translated into "fruitcake") or "Nicolas flakes" might be kosher but may raise other questions. The book is obviously rooted in a different culture, but the Israeli publisher seemed to think that there was a market for such a book. The choice to make it into a kosher book is also understandable in view of the increased market, but this particular method of "translation" assumes either an uneducated reader or that the *kashrut* here is one of appearances more than substance. This is another example of the transition into greater openness to outside influences while still filtering them through a nationalistic prism.

In 1989 chef Israel Aharoni joined forces with Shaul Evron to publish his second cookbook, on Italian cooking. The major significance of this cookbook was its nonkosher status. It was the first of its kind since Keinan's book twenty years prior. It resembles Aharoni's first (Chinese) cookbook in its high production standards, employing the same photographer and shooting the photographs "on location" in various sites in Tuscany. The book includes recipes for tripe salad, stuffed calamari, grilled shrimp kebabs, and shrimp in a spicy tomato sauce. The meat chapter opens with a photograph of row upon row of hanging slabs of prosciutto. This photograph is a clear indication of the change Israeli society had gone through in the time span between Keinan's book (1970) and the late 1980s. In addition to the recipes, Aharoni offers a chapter on wine and an Italian restaurant guide. This book suggests a growing degree of sophistication, greater buying power (the glossy photographs and higher price tag for this album format), and the ability to travel (a restaurant guide and the attention to authentic details). Aharoni's readership is assumed to be interested in getting to know new places through their cuisine, interested in the context of a recipe and particular ingredients, and not particularly troubled by kosher restrictions. It targets an upper-middle-class population, pointing to a growing chasm within Israeli society, both economically and ideologically. Like Keinan, Aharoni and Evron envisioned a readership of Israelis for whom buying power, cooking as a leisure activity, and disregard for kashrut go hand in hand to compose an image of greater worldliness and liberation.[28]

## From the Kitchen with Love

In 1975 Ruth Sirkis published what many consider to be the "Bible" of Israeli cooking, or at least the book no newlyweds should live without (usurping Cornfeld's 1960 supremacy). This cookbook, *From the Kitchen with Love*, is strictly kosher, which resulted in some interesting interpretations of non-kosher classics such as moussaka with a white sauce made with margarine and water instead of butter and milk and beef stroganoff with nondairy cream substitute. It is also, somewhat in the spirit of Cornfeld and the WIZO cookbooks that preceded it, practical and instructional in nature. However, it differs from these books in other ways: Sirkis's book is specifically designed for entertainment, for the hostess, not for the housewife or the working mother. This in itself is a testament to the rise in the standard of living and improved economic situation, as well as to the greater emphasis on food as a source of pleasure and a leisure activity.

In 1982, when Ruth Sirkis published a follow-up to *From the Kitchen with Love* titled *Me-Hamitbah be-Hana'a* (From the kitchen with delight), she returned to the focus on cooking instruction for the working woman (and man). In the introduction she explains the need she perceived for the new book seven years after the first one: "During these years there were developments in [available] ingredients [in Israel], in kitchen appliances, and in the attitude toward food and cooking. This book reflects these developments. The interest in food and cooking has grown, and we dare to taste more of others' dishes. . . . We attribute great importance to the joys of eating and preparing food. . . . The recipes have been adapted to the needs of busy people, . . . today's fast pace, . . . [and] a chronic lack of time."[29] The later book is framed, much like the 1960s books, as practical and efficient, situating many recipes similar to the ones in the earlier books in daily life rather than special occasions. Sirkis's books serve as an example of the way these culinary trends emerged in Israel in the 1960s, developed in the 1970s, and matured in the 1980s. The pleasure and importance of cooking for the family and the openness to new and varied influences appeared in the 1960s, but the focus was still very practical, and most influences were those of different ethnic groups within Israeli society, not faraway exotic cuisines. *From the Kitchen with Love* demonstrates openness to international influences on a grander scale, as well as room for cooking as a leisure activity (the focus is on entertainment and special occasions). By the 1980s the same attitude of cooking as a leisure activity and the incorporation of multiple international influences could be applied to everyday cooking for the family and not reserved for special occasions. By 1982 Sirkis assumed that, despite a shortage of time, her audience was interested in making and eating varied, tasty food.

Sirkis was inspired by her extended stay in the United States with her husband on two separate occasions; she was greatly influenced by American and other international cookbooks. These in turn prompted her to travel more extensively to experience other cuisines in their original settings. Before publishing *From the Kitchen with Love*, Sirkis published two English-language books in the United States: *Gourmet Food from Israel* and *Taste of Tradition*, both in 1972. She later began writing a column for the women's magazine *Āt* (You, in the female form) and to present a segment on the radio show *Kan ba-Bayit* (Here at home). Many of the recipes in the book are based on this previous experience and her familiarity with her audience. Her didactic approach is stated plainly in the introduction: "I was introduced to the American method of cooking instruction, an efficient, clear method that does not require a sixth sense, natural talent, or luck. It is sufficient to follow the clearly stated and tried recipe—and the dish will always succeed."[30] Sirkis explained that she chose basic recipes that represent the main cooking and baking techniques and that the recipes are presented simply and clearly according to "logical, easy-to-follow steps."[31] She detailed possible reasons for success or failure and often offered tips on the recipe's background and what the finished dish should look and taste like.

In the back of the book, Sirkis provides appendixes on spices and their uses, weights and measurements, cooking and serving implements, and cooking terms. This final section is particularly interesting in that it made a great contribution to the creation of a common Hebrew vocabulary. Words such as *livzok* (to sprinkle), *lehashhim* (to brown), *mirkam* (texture), and *mitbal* (dip) needed to be created and circulated, and Sirkis's cookbook followed in the steps of the early food shows in instilling this linguistic knowledge.

The rise in the standard of living at the time Sirkis's book was published is apparent in the inclusion of ingredients that were unavailable, uncommon, or unfamiliar in earlier cookbooks: Sirkis calls for the use of olive oil in "Israeli Salad" and not simply "oil"; she discusses a variety of cheese types, including Roquefort and *kashkaval* (a Bulgarian cheese made from cow's or sheep's milk or from a mixture of both), and not just hard cheese or soft (fresh) cheese; and desserts as well as savory pies call for butter instead of margarine.

Eastern European cuisine is still very much present through dishes such as pickled tongue, jellied calves' feet, and pirogi, but shish kebab, *bourekas* (savory stuffed pastries), and a wide variety of eggplant dishes, as well as hummus and tahini, also play an important part. Dishes from a variety of cuisines are represented, from cheese fondue to lasagna, hamburgers to goulash, "Chinese-style" chicken with almonds to "Hawaiian-style" chicken with pineapple. The 1982 book adds Mexican, Indian, Creole, and Indonesian dishes to the international mix of recipes, demonstrating the development of this trend. More ambitious dishes, such as soufflés, crepes, whole fish, and homemade bread, are also represented in the later book, presuming a more accomplished and knowledgeable cook.

In an interview with Aviad Kleinberg in 2005, Sirkis said she never consciously tried to create or shape an Israeli kitchen but rather wished to include in her cookbook dishes that she and her friends liked. In putting the book together, she had in mind the people whom she knew, her social circle. It is obvious from the book itself, as well as from the interview, that the public Sirkis addressed was firmly located in the upper middle class of Israeli society. Notably, her 1982 cookbook addressed a larger audience, as its focus on daily cooking for working parents implied. In the interview, Sirkis also commented on her wish to write a thorough "master's dissertation": a compilation of all her knowledge on the subject up to that point, reviewing the subject from different angles in an organized manner.[32] She emphasized the importance of the didactic approach, of clear instructions, of repeatedly trying recipes, and of educating and enlightening the Israeli public as to the culinary possibilities of the world around them. Kleinberg, the interviewer, brought up the cookbook's popularity as a gift for newlyweds. It became a household name. The Israeli market was ready for just such a cookbook: the combination of clear, simple instructions based on available ingredients with recipes that were familiar enough yet also had an international flavor and a whiff of sophistication proved to be a winning formula. The fact that the book was produced, unlike previous cookbooks, in a large format with color photographs helped it attain popularity as a worthy wedding gift: it was elegant yet practical.[33]

The book's title also calls for a comment about the role of cooking within the family. With most women working outside the home and with the greater availability of convenience food, the nature of cooking for the family as an act of love and caring had become more pronounced. The title also highlights the importance of the family in Israel at this period of time (in contrast to the days of the early halutzim). Bob Ashley and colleagues, in their study of British foodways, comment on grocery shopping in modern times as an act of care for the family.[34] This approach to cooking and food shopping became even more apparent in the 1980s as supermarkets proliferated and new appliances and equipment became available to home cooks in Israel, as Sirkis's later book demonstrates. The 1982 book also differs from its predecessors in addressing its audience in the male rather than the female form. This change does not speak so much to an equality of the sexes as it does to the greater professionalism of cooking.

The greater variety of ingredients and new technological innovations combined in the 1980s with a political legitimization of capitalist ideology to allow for a flourishing culinary scene. The shift from the Labor Party to the Likud after decades in power, from socialism to capitalism as the governing ideology, had significant effects on the Israeli economy, but the changes in Israeli society and dominant ideology were already in place prior to the actual political shift and in fact enabled it.

## Aharoni's Chinese Cooking

In the mid-1980s Israel Aharoni rose as another important and influential figure in the Israeli culinary scene. His cookbook *Ha-Bishul ha-Sini shel Aharoni* (Aharoni's Chinese cooking) was published in 1986 as part of a series edited by Nira Russo (the title appears in English within the book as *The Kosher Chinese Gourmet*). In his introduction Aharoni describes his culinary background: he fell in love with Chinese food through an Israeli friend and after ten years of experimenting as an amateur decided to go to Taiwan to study professional cooking. During his study and with the aid of his teachers, he was able to work as an intern in several restaurants. Upon his return to Israel (he does not specify the length of his stay in Taiwan), he opened a Chinese restaurant in Tel Aviv. Aharoni comments on the ease of adapting Chinese cooking to the kosher kitchen because it seldom includes any dairy. Dan Daor cowrote the book, offering general background information on Chinese cuisine. Daor describes typical ingredients, basic philosophy, and the distinctions between different regions within China. He also includes quotes from Chinese poetry and literature that describe food and feasts. The book describes the structure of a Chinese meal, its aesthetics and presentation, basic ingredients and their possible substitutions, utensils and cooking implements, and basic techniques. Aharoni's book was groundbreaking in the world of Israeli cookbook publishing in its high production values and in its focus on and in-depth study of one cuisine, again demonstrating the rising interest in cooking as a leisure activity and in the world outside Israel's borders.

### The Audible Kitchen

The radio station Kol Yerushalayim (Voice of Jerusalem) began operating in 1936 with the blessing of the British Mandate due to its definition as "binational and trilingual" and to the fact that Jewish agencies financed it. It was, however, intended by its creators to be an instrument of Zionist national propaganda, a way to circumvent British censorship. In 1945 the station changed its name to Kol Yisrael (Voice of Israel) and broadened the scope of its broadcasts.[35]

The Zionist agenda found its way into the programming of the British-operated Palestinian Broadcasting Company as well. In the 1944 annual report of the Nutrition Department of Hadassah, Sarah Bavly, the department's head, discussed, among other matters, the nutritional broadcasts undertaken by Hadassah with the encouragement of the food controller. The initiative for the project came from the food controller, who requested Hadassah's help in the preparation of a weekly nutritional radio program. Bavly stated in the report that the program had become one of the most popular shows of the Palestinian Broadcasting Company, judging from the fan mail, which averaged some thirty letters a week—"a record here."[36] Radio programs from 1944 and 1945 demonstrate both the British influence and Hadassah's attempt to use the programs to promote Zionist ideology. The programs began with "Eat More Potatoes" (30 May 1944), continued with "Tea Sandwiches" (18 July 1944) and "Something about Mutton" (8

August 1944), and then moved on to deal with egg powder with various accompaniments in the next four shows (22and 29 August, 5 September, and 3 October).[37] Before the program returned once again to egg powder and milk powder on its fifteenth show, it devoted seven programs to the topic "How to Eat in Palestine." The controller tried to promote the use of government-imported dried foods, while Hadassah encouraged mutual learning between different ethnic groups. Both bodies tried to enhance listeners' use of local products, but with different motives.

### "How to Eat in Palestine"

Throughout the months of October and November 1944 the radio show examined the foods eaten in Palestine by different ethnic groups, Sephardic, Yemenite, Kurdish, Bukharian, Persian, and Ashkenazic, concluding with "Vegetables of the Season." The programs examined the pros and cons of each ethnic group's eating habits. The series began with some general comments on good nutrition and the importance of eating a diet that was right for a particular climate. It then went on to discuss the tendency of each group to hold on to cooking and eating habits brought from its country of origin and claimed that these practices might not always be the best for life in Palestine and should be adjusted accordingly. Generally, it advocated eating a large amount of fruits and vegetables, reducing cooking time in order to preserve nutritional value, limited deep-frying, and reducing meat consumption while increasing that of dairy and fish. This series of programs was specifically structured for wartime. One of the strategies for dealing with the limited quantities of imported products and their higher cost during the war was to encourage the public to use more local products. Therefore, Hadassah's focus on local products in these talks seemed quite appropriate for the time. In this way, Hadassah was able to use the cooking shows to promote a Zionist ideology: the campaign for the use of local products benefited the war effort, but at the same time it was in line with the Zionist ideology of promoting totzeret ha-aretz products. Unlike the shows of previous decades, these shows acknowledged a variety of ethnic influences, even though the ideal was still one of obliterating old ways in favor of a new, unified culture and cuisine. The discussion of Yemenite practices, for example, begins with a promise to point out "those dishes which we shall call Diaspora dishes, meaning that this particular dish is, so to speak, in exile, uprooted from another climate and from another country and therefore wholly unsuitable for Palestinian conditions."[38] The final program of the series begins by saying that trying to improve feeding conditions is a worldwide project, but in Palestine it appears easier, since "when introducing new dishes we do so on national grounds. We are obliterating a [D]iaspora, a [D]iaspora of food, and are trying to suggest food that will not possess an assembly of characteristics but will have a national character."[39] This is definitely a clear case of Hadassah's agenda and not that of the British government. Hadassah used the hard economic reality to promote the ideal of self-reliance, a new Jew and a new Jewish people different in every way from the ones in the Diaspora. The broadcast demonstrated a wish to create a more united community and achieve a more homogeneous character in a very diverse immigrant society.

## "The Sephardim" (16 October 1944)

The miniseries "How to Eat in Palestine" began with an introductory talk followed by a program about Sephardic eating habits. The show explained that the Jewish community was comprised of the Sephardim, who had been living in Palestine long before the arrival of the first Zionists (according to the program, since the year 1267). They were also distinguished from the Ashkenazi Orthodox community, whose members lived off donations from abroad (haluka) and were intentionally isolated, while the Sephardim lived among their Arab neighbors and interacted with them. The broadcast distinguished between the Sephardim and the "natives of the country" but stated that the Sephardim are "the most deeply rooted in Palestine." It highlighted the Sephardic use of seasonal fruits and vegetables, claiming that this should serve as an example for other ethnic groups: "The Sephardic woman knows how to make use of every kind of vegetable grown in Palestine, and she uses it mostly when it comes into season."[40] The discussion of vegetables was prefaced by the observation that green vegetables have great nutritive value, "especially during wartime, when we find it difficult to obtain eggs and milk products."[41] In this fashion the program was tied to the larger objective of the series: coping with wartime food management.

The program on Sephardic habits continued by discussing some of the most popular methods for preparing vegetables: usually "braising" the vegetables first (in this case, braising meant deep-frying) and then cooking them in a sour sauce (e.g., water with lemon juice). The Hadassah host commented, "This is not very commendable, as exaggerated braising in itself is not very wholesome for the stomach [again, referring to deep-frying], and . . . vegetables will in the course of boiling lose much of their nutritive value, . . . [so] the amount of work put into the preparation of vegetables does not pay."[42] As an example, the program offered a recipe for cauliflower: blanched in boiling water, dipped in a flour-and-egg batter, "braised" in hot fat, and then cooked for two to three hours in some water with lemon or tomato juice. The Sephardic use of seasonal vegetables is therefore commended but not the cooking methods, which do not correspond to the ideal of short cooking times (both for retaining nutritive value and for economic reasons, such as saving fuel). Another labor-intensive way of preparing vegetables in the Sephardic community was stuffing them with meat, eggs, or hard cheese combined with rice or bulgur. The same stuffing was also used in pastry dishes. This method was described as requiring a lot of work but "worthwhile," since the meat or cheese in the filling created a "nourishing and tasty" dish. This method of preparation conformed with Hadassah's idea of what was suitable for the climate in Palestine, as it allowed "stretching" meat: "There is no exaggerated consumption of meat, this being very suitable to the climate of the country and its economic conditions."[43]

The Sephardic use of plenty of hard cheese was applauded, while their practice of using milk only rarely (usually as an addition to coffee) was "worth altering." Toward the end of the program a few sentences were devoted to spices: the Sephardic food was considered to be sharp and spicy. The main "spices" used were pine nuts, green, red, and black pepper, cumin, and cinnamon. The program also listed parsley, lemon, and salt among the common spices. Finally, the program ended with a call to women to send in their favorite recipes to extend the collection of recipes already available and to correct existing recipes if necessary. Suitable recipes would be shared with listeners in future talks. This final comment helped frame the radio shows as a community product. It authenticated the recipes from different communities and situated itself as an instrument for a dialogue between them instead of as dictated from above. The programs demonstrated a more flexible approach and openness to diverse influences, but a paternalistic note tempered this apparent tolerance: one practice was commendable, another one was not; this was suitable, that was not. Certain methods, techniques, and ingredients from each ethnic community were accepted, while others were discouraged. The guidelines determining the distinction between the two were set by Hadassah nutritionists. The recipes seemed to be valued according to practical considerations: whether they were healthy, economical, or difficult to make. Taste was a secondary consideration. Each community was encouraged to learn from others, to adopt "beneficial" practices while discarding others, so the openness to multiple influences was actually aimed at diminishing differences.

A list of program topics was included as part of the material submitted to Hadassah members in the United States describing the success of the radio shows. It is interesting to note that one program was missing from that list: a talk titled "The Arab Food" (5 December 1944). Perhaps Hadassah felt that prospective Jewish donors would not appreciate it. This talk was situated between one on dried eggs and milk powder and one dedicated to Hanukkah dishes using dried potatoes. The program began: "I am unable to approach the Arab foods critically, as I have done with the foods of the other communities, for they have one positive characteristic, they are based on natural, seasonal products of the country."[44] The program went on to say that there were faults here too but that they were generally the result of economic conditions. It stated that the show referred specifically to the food of the lower classes, that of the Arab *fallah* (small-time farmer). It gave as examples pita bread, "baked very primitively in an oven called *tabun*," hummus, *libnah* (soft yogurt cheese), and shish kebab, among others. This program, like other examples described in previous chapters, held the local Arab figure as a role model, on the one hand, while consistently describing him as primitive, on the other.

The radio shows are an example of the growing attention to food as a "practical tool" that characterized this period. A wealth of food-related articles appeared in print as well. The majority of these pieces deal with wartime rationing, but their very existence indicates a new approach to food and cooking, a realization that cooking and eating habits can be harnessed to promote the national project and its agenda.

## "The Women's Corner"

One of the important elements indicated in Sarah Bavly's 1964 survey, mentioned in chapter 3, as influential in changing immigrants' eating habits is the radio program *The Women's Corner*. The media became increasingly important in influencing eating habits over the next few decades. It also became increasingly influential as a site for displaying the "nation."

Thiya Bat-Oren, whose cookbook was mentioned earlier, presented *The Women's Corner* from 1948 to the late 1960s. In an interview she raised one problem new to the 1950s and 1960s: her constant conflict as a woman with presenting this "kitchen corner" while trying to escape the actual kitchen and create a "real" career for herself as a writer and artist.[45] She appeared conflicted over this show, as well as over the cookbook and newspaper column she wrote in its wake. On the one hand, she was proud of the popularity of the show and her writing; she felt that they fulfilled a real need and that she was able to promote important issues through them. On the other hand, she felt she should apologize for this "trivial" area of expertise and wished to put that period of her life behind her. Bat-Oren said that her friends would joke and imitate her and did not value this career choice. She was very concerned with feminist issues but said that her efforts to promote such an agenda were squashed by the administration. *The Women's Corner* was broadcast in the morning between 9:00 and 10:00 a.m., so it was obviously intended for women who were at home during the morning hours and thus excluded working women and men from the potential audience and, as a result, from the kitchen. Her sense was that the radio and magazines did not want to help women leave the home; rather, they encouraged them to be full-time housewives—an interesting reappearance of the dilemmas of women during the Second Aliya discussed earlier.

Bat-Oren said that there was great demand for the radio show, since women really needed the advice she offered. It was meant more for native Israelis than new immigrants (another example of the change Israeli society had undergone) and was treated like an oracle, since her generation was completely ignorant about cooking—"We considered it beneath us." The important elements in both the radio show and the newspaper column included practicality and efficiency: saving time and money through the use of leftovers, cooking meals for two days at once, and similar techniques. Bat-Oren insisted, however, that presentation and table manners not be neglected. She dealt with simple, practical home cooking, "not Chinese food," and with matters of wise consumerism (e.g., "go shopping with a list"). Her attitude, particularly by the early 1960s, became direct and friendly, sharing her own experiences with women like herself and using humor instead of the "all-knowing" authoritative tone favored by WIZO and Hadassah instructors in previous decades.

### THE VISUAL KITCHEN

In the past few decades, the role of radio and printed journals in providing cooking instruction and advice has largely been taken over by television. Just like the early radio broadcasts, early cooking programming on Israeli television was presented in short segments for the housewife. Unlike the radio, the very first shows did not address new immigrants or established housewives; this time, the first target audience was Arabic housewives. Television broadcasts began in Israel in 1968. One government-controlled channel offered black-and-white programming three times a week. Initially, much of the programming targeted the Arab population in Israel and in the neighboring Arab countries in an attempt to improve Jewish-Arab relations following the Six Day War. Also, since Israel had only just acquired the new technology, very few families in Israel actually owned television sets; they were more common in the Arab population, which already had access to television programming from neighboring countries.

In 1971 Israeli television began broadcasting a "cooking corner" program. It was five to seven minutes long and was presented, along with other advice for housewives, once a month in the evening hours.[46] The "cooking corner" was presented by Tova Aran, a teacher by profession who wrote a cooking column for *Āt* (*You*) magazine, with a simultaneous translation in Arabic by Lilith Nagar. The content was decided on by the producer and editor along with Aran, after which Aran would "do her homework" on the chosen topic and prior to the show would cook everything in her home kitchen and bring it to the studio in Jerusalem by taxi at 4:00 a.m. During the filming she would pretend to cook on a painted set with a mock oven and mock cabinets.[47]

The program covered everyday basic recipes such as vegetable soup and meatloaf. It offered basic advice on peeling, using knives, and nutritional value, as well as many tips on saving and stretching food and using leftovers. The show featured European food but targeted a mostly Arab audience, which influenced some of the content choices: the show on ground beef, for example, featured a recipe for meatloaf (known as *klops* in its Eastern European version, which includes whole hard-boiled eggs in the center of the loaf), chosen by Aran over meatballs, which she assumed her audience was already familiar with. Aran served the klops like a cake, cut into triangular slices. She recalled this as being a big success and quite a revelation for her audience.[48] The approach to content was very much like the one displayed by women's organizations toward new immigrants from the Middle East: it used Central European home economic practices that stressed efficiency and nutritional value in the kitchen. When approaching a mostly Arab audience, the Israeli team chose to represent itself as "Western" and European and as the bearers of efficiency and scientific knowledge (i.e., modernity and the West).

Aran recalls the production as being clumsy and lumbering: a four-minute segment could take up to five or six hours of shooting time (including the electrician's coffee break, the soundman's lunch break, etc.). Like Bat-Oren, Aran arrived at her culinary profession without formal nutritional or culinary education. After she left the show, the "cooking corner" was presented for a while by professional chefs. About a year later it began airing once a week in Hebrew but soon thereafter was canceled.

During the late 1970s and 1980s, food and cooking appeared on Israeli television in the form of short segments in magazine-style shows devoted to other topics. Aran, who went on to work with Tnuva, the largest dairy manufacturer in Israel, said that during her tenure with Tnuva she repeatedly tried to interest the broadcasting company in producing a cooking show but always encountered a complete lack of interest (despite her offers of corporate sponsorship) and responses such as "Who would be interested in a cooking show?"[49] This situation had changed drastically by the late 1990s.

The first full-length cooking shows appeared on Israeli television with cable television imports from European channels (such as the British program *The Two Fat Ladies*). The first locally produced cooking show was *Teʻamim* (Flavors) in 1996. It was the brainchild of Eugene Wolf, who produced and edited it. Hila Alpert, a food writer, was the first presenter, but after the first season both the format and the presenter were changed. The show then began with a segment on one international cuisine that was filmed abroad on location. It was followed by a couple of segments presented by chef Zachi Bookshtater that were based on interpretations of that week's featured cuisine and that ended with a segment by a guest chef or restaurant owner who was also related to the same cuisine. According to Wolf, he, as the producer and editor, was responsible for the material and recipes featured on the show, while the chef's input was only in the form of suggestions and comments on the material.[50] Wolf said that he changed the recipes to fit the Israeli palette and temperament. According to Wolf, Israel is "an impatient country": a single recipe cannot require more than fifteen to twenty minutes of preparation. Other examples are the popularity of chicken as the main ingredient (far exceeding beef) and the reluctance to use interior parts or to see a whole animal on the plate. He said that he did try to educate the public to a degree, promoting the use of fresh (as opposed to frozen) beef, for example, or advocating olive oil or sheep's milk cheeses, but he appeared very cautious in such attempts—his first goal was to gain and keep viewers.

Wolf said he was able to "sell" the idea to the network because of his previous success as the producer of a long-running and very popular film magazine. He attempted to create a popular show with broad appeal; thus, one of his choices was to restrict the recipes to kosher ones, offering kosher adaptations of various recipes and creating "Israeli" interpretations based on local ingredients. The idea was that a show featuring kosher recipes would be more inclusive in a country like Israel, where a large percentage of the population keeps kosher to some degree. The same approach was utilized in his choice of locations abroad, targeting destinations that appealed to a broad segment of the Israeli population (not, for example, three-star restaurants in France). His approach was apparently successful, as the show remained very popular for several years, with a 12–14 percent rating of the original broadcast and 3–5 percent in the two reruns presented during the week.[51]

Following the success of *Te'amim*, there began a slow surge in local cooking programs of varying approaches and formats. The first one to be produced by a major network was *Shum, Pilpel, ve-Shemen-Zayit* (Garlic, pepper, and olive oil) in 1997. Produced and created by Eylon Goyten and presented by Gil Hovav and Ayelet Latovitch, the show focused on Mediterranean cooking ("very 'hip' at the time," according to Hovav), which allowed them to concentrate on local ingredients and incorporate a variety of ethnic influences (Sephardic, Middle Eastern, and North African) while introducing their audience to some classic French techniques and terms.[52] In an interview, Goyten said that the idea of concentrating on Mediterranean cooking evolved while he was trying to interest the network in the program: Rashut ha-Shidur (the national broadcasting system) was not inclined to find a timeslot or funding for the project, but at the time there was a separate division for programs in Arabic that was allotted two hours each day and a larger time block on Saturdays.[53] Goyten approached the Arabic program director and proposed the cooking show to him for the Saturday time frame. He suggested focusing on Mediterranean cooking so the show would be relevant to the Arab viewers as well. The ingredients and techniques would be of interest to all the viewers living in the region.

As work on the show progressed and presenters were chosen after participating in a screen test, the general program director began to take an interest in the show and, after viewing the screen test, assured Goyten they would find a timeslot for it within the regular programming in prime time. Funding was still an issue, and Goyten had to solicit outside contributions. Since Rashut ha-Shidur was a government-run venture, he could only approach public bodies and so eventually received funding from the boards of different local products—the Fruit Board, the Dairy Board, the Vegetable Board, and so on. He promised them all that the show would deal with fresh, locally grown food and that it would be Mediterranean and local and thus support their products. He showed the screen test and succeeded in committing each public board to an equal contribution, promising that they would all get some exposure in each program. The producer, presenters, and a culinary consultant (Dalia Pan-Lerner, a food writer and cookbook author) worked as a team to choose the recipes.[54] They would choose a theme or subject and then pass it on to two researchers, who would gather recipes and information to add some context and background. All the information was then given to a screenwriter, who would forge a loose structure—a basic format and suggestions for transitions between topics. Hovav and Latovitch would use the script as a base and would add to it on camera, Hovav mostly adding stories and context, as well as asking questions of Latovitch, who did more demonstrating and added professional tips and information.[55]

Every program included four or five recipes, each one taking up about five minutes of screen time and no more than twenty minutes of actual preparation time. This seemed to Goyten most appropriate to prime-time television. The early shows were framed as complete meals: the show on eggplant, for example, included a discussion on choosing and buying eggplant and recipes for eggplant soup, stuffed eggplant, and eggplant jam, among others, so they could be put together at the end to form a meal with an appetizer, main dish, and dessert. The shows included some basic techniques, such as how to sharpen a knife and how to work with yeast, as well as introductions to some ingredients and encouragement to use the best ones available ("Buy the most expensive olive oil you can afford," for example).[56]

The show was essentially kosher: it did not include pork or seafood recipes and did not mix dairy and meat dishes in the same program. This was mainly the producer's decision so as not to offend or alienate anyone. Although meat and dairy were not mixed on the show, the host would occasionally say that it was possible to do so at home: "If you wish, you can sauté the meat in butter." A related consideration was how to frame the programs so they would be both relevant and inoffensive in reruns. As the season's entire batch of programs went into reruns, Goyten said he was concerned that the bread program, for example, would appear around Passover. For this reason the show tried to stay away from ingredients that have a very restricted season.[57]

After two seasons the host changed to chef Haim Cohen, then the chef of one of Israel's top French restaurants, Keren, in Tel Aviv. Cohen's appearance on this show coincided with a shift in Keren's menu to include more local influences and dishes inspired by Cohen's family heritage and his mother's cooking—a mixture of Turkish, Kurdish, and Syrian traditional influences.[58] In more recent years, particularly since the closing of Keren in 2003, Cohen has used the television program as a sort of culinary laboratory: he has a team that helps him collect traditional recipes and track unique cooks, and he then creates his own versions of these recipes, simplifying them for home cooking. In fact, Cohen's partner in the restaurant, Irit Shenkar, claimed that the wish to do more television-related work was one of the reasons behind the closing of Keren—the television program required Cohen's absence from the restaurant, which he saw as a problem and an either-or choice.[59]

A newspaper article lamenting Keren's closing speculates that one of the reasons for Cohen's cooking show's success is his personality: he is warm, direct, and amiable. He would take calls at the restaurant from viewers, answering at length questions about the details of a recipe or why it went wrong at home.[60] Gil Hovav, in an interview, said he has no professional background in cooking, but, in his opinion, success on a cooking show has more to do with the host's personality and ease in front of the camera than with his knife skills. Television is an intimate medium: close-ups are common, and the people who appear on television, admitted into our homes on a regular basis, acquire a sense of familiarity: "I think I know her."[61] The more personal and informal attitude of television hosts is in tune with changes already made in radio shows: from cooking as a vehicle of propaganda, to an all-knowing tone delivering didactic information, to practical and later even friendly advice. Cooking shows are slowly approaching the realm of entertainment.

Today there are no fewer than ten original productions about food and cooking on Israeli television; you can watch an original cooking show almost every day of the week, mostly during prime time. Even the few that are still instructional in nature (i.e., they demonstrate the preparation of recipes) employ celebrities or use exotic locations to enhance their entertainment value and draw a wider audience. Despite the shows' clearer framing as entertainment, some trends remain similar: Israel as a country of immigrants, a nation comprised of a multitude of ethnic groups, is a recurring theme, as is openness to the outside world and a wish to be sophisticated citizens of this world. This greater sophistication and a view of food as part of a broader cultural system, entwined with other social and cultural themes, can be seen in several shows as well.

When chef Haim Cohen cooks on *Shum, Pilpel, ve-Shemen-Zayit*, on the National channel (the Israeli Broadcasting Authority) during prime time, he shares with the viewers his search for an Israeli cuisine. He creates food based on local ingredients, based in the Middle East, on the shores of the Mediterranean Sea. The show features visits to various food-related locations around the country, helping situate it in a specific geographical location. Cohen regularly invites a wide variety of guests to join him, bringing into the kitchen and the television studio a cross section of Israeli society, grounding it in the wider Israeli culinary scene, as well as helping to create a common knowledge and a shared culinary language. Despite Cohen's more direct approach to investigating and shaping an Israeli cuisine, other shows contribute to the same cause. By mirroring different elements of Israeli society and culture, reflected through a culinary lens in a public forum, they become part of the national project to define and shape Israeli national identity.

## THE DIGITAL KITCHEN

When I began my research on Israeli cuisine, the Internet was of small significance as a medium for culinary knowledge. Today, it is the primary site for finding and sharing recipes, restaurant reviews, and other culinary information. I will not attempt to cover the full range of Internet sites and blogs devoted to food and cooking in Israel today, but I do want to touch on some of them in relation to their place in the story of Israeli nationalism and cuisine.

One of the earlier contributions of the Internet was its effect on the structure of culinary shows on television: by supplying detailed recipes and exact quantities online, cooking shows were released of the burden of actually cooking the recipe for their viewers. They no longer needed to devote time to the full recipe or allow time for viewers to jot down quantities while following the presenters' actions on the screen. By creating websites for specific shows, producers were able to expand past the actual show time to offer additional information, products for sale, a place for viewers' questions and comments, and online communities (forums).

In conjunction with these sites, other culinary websites began to develop, some sponsored by food corporations (such as Bishulim.co.il, sponsored by Osem), some by culinary magazines (such as hashulchan.co.il, sponsored by *Al ha-Shulchan* magazine), some by individual chefs (such as www .Mevashlim.com, with chef Haim Cohen and Dr. Eli Landau), and some as sections within larger lifestyle sites (such as Ynet Food, Tapuz Food, and Whallah Food). Another development was the appearance of an Israeli website as a resource for food professionals (chef.co.il, no longer active), including biographical information and short interviews with a great number of Israeli chefs; links to suppliers of restaurant equipment, food products, and professional development resources; and a forum for food professionals that includes, among many other topics, job announcements.

Despite being a more recent phenomenon, these sites are clearly linked to Israeli culinary history. An abundance of cake and baking recipes supported by a multitude of specialized forums and blogs on baking and cake decoration reflects similar trends in earlier cookbooks. A strong interest in cooking with and for children reflects the constant importance of children and the family in Israeli society in recent decades, as well as the "practical" side of everyday cooking. Forums and recipe categories for kosher cooking remind us of both the large segment of the population cooking kosher food and the fact that it is not necessarily the national norm. The overwhelming number of poultry recipes compared to any other protein continues to be an Israeli characteristic. There are also a significant number of dairy recipes. The enormous diversity in recipe sources and the wide variety of ingredients, cooking implements, and techniques from international sources highlight Israel's continued fascination with and openness to the outside world and to immigrant groups within it (a trend that was established after the 1967 war and that has since grown rapidly). Finally, the very existence of these sites, with the wealth of cooking information and the restaurant guides and reviews they offer, reflects the recent embrace, rising status, and growing professionalism of all food and cooking in Israeli society. It also reflects the greater buying power, consumerism, and pursuit of pleasure that characterize Israeli society today.

In addition to the more established websites, there is a growing number of Israeli food-related blogs. Some are authored by professional chefs and reflect their culinary explorations and inventions and often the most up-to-date culinary information from around the world, such as chefilan.com/blog, which in February 2009 included a discussion of the Spanish chef and "father" of "molecular gastronomy" Ferran Adria in addition to chef Ilan's own recipes and photographs. Other blogs are by experienced housewives who wish to share their knowledge, tips, and successful recipes gathered over years of cooking for family and friends with a wider audience (in lieu of writing a cookbook). Some blogs are by younger amateur cooks, combining recipes with restaurant reviews and travel stories. Often such blogs attempt to bring news and information from abroad to an Israeli audience while also keeping in mind an international readership and including Israeli cultural products (music and art) among their recipe offerings.

Blogs such as *My Mom's Recipes and More* (momsrecipesandmore.blogspot.com) and *Baroness Tapuzina* (no longer active) were conscious of the Internet as an international forum. Many offer both Hebrew and English versions, but some blogs have a particular message for an international audience, using their blogs as windows to Israeli culture in general. In February 2009 *My Mom's Recipes and More* described itself as the first English-Hebrew blog in Israel, and it is unique in having both languages on the same page (rather than separate pages for Hebrew and for the English translation). It was created in 2005 by Chanit and Ran, two enthusiastic amateur cooks/bakers, and offers Israelis food-related news from abroad. It also showcases Israeli music and art for viewers from abroad, in addition to a wealth of recipes and food photographs. Chanit defines her blog as an "Israeli food blog," stating that it includes (among other things) childhood recipes and "mother's and grandmother's recipes" made simple. The author states her dedication to home cooking, on the one hand, but repeats her commitment to professionalism and precision in both the photographs and the recipes, on the other hand, stressing in this way the distinction between her work and that of an experienced housewife. Given these definitions, accompanied by the awareness of being a window into Israeli culture for "outsiders," part of this blog's project is defining an "Israeli cuisine."

Many of the blogs and websites also attempt to create or define an Israeli cuisine either as part of their stated agenda or as a "side effect." Some approaches are more subtle: in February 2009 Haim Cohen, on his website Mevashlim (Cooking, www.mevashlim.com), offered web surfers the opportunity to create their own "culinary family trees" online by building a structure for family recipes that have been passed within the family from one generation to the next. This is a great way of compiling a culinary heritage with the possibility of displaying it in a public forum. It is an artificial or accelerated way of constructing a traditional, national cuisine. This particular website has an incredibly large recipe collection and a very comprehensive index and search engine. One of the many possible search categories is "seasons and holidays." It is interesting to note that the list of holidays includes, in addition to the traditional Jewish holidays, Christmas, Ramadan, and Hag Ha-Korban. By including these recipes, this website clearly includes Christian and Moslem communities as part of its intended audience, and since the recipes are offered in Hebrew with no distinction from other categories, it in essence includes them as part of its definition of Israeli cuisine. This is a major departure from earlier "holiday" recipes in Israeli cookbooks, and it reflects both a greater degree of confidence and the influence of the more recent immigrant groups to Israel, with their larger component of non-Jewish immigrants.

These blogs and websites often provide links to each other that, if followed, can provide a current, encompassing picture of the Israeli kitchen. None of them really stands alone; rather, they offer a complete network of culinary information covering many aspects of Israeli society. Some of the blogs use the international status of the Internet and the links device to convey a political or ideological message: in Baroness Tapuzina's blog in February 2009, for example, viewers could find links to a variety of blogs discussing specific international cuisines, among them Saudi Arabian and Jordanian food blogs (in addition to Swiss, French, and others). The blogs and Internet sites that are directly linked to each other create virtual maps of affiliation and alliance.

Finally, the Internet provides a space for community building by offering a site for specialized forums that replace community cookbooks in creating a shared repertoire and a common language. Besides its much grander scale and access to a much larger community than traditional community cookbooks, the Internet offers a presence in real time. There is no time lag; the information is the most current and up-to-date. The community can grow and change constantly because of the interactive mode of participation. Because of Israel's small size, virtual forums can also be translated easily into meetings in the real world that strengthen the community further. The public discourse of various topics of culinary interest helps to paint a picture of Israeli cooking and eating that reflects the actual cooks and eaters. For the most part, a single author, a women's organization, the government, or any other interest group does not mediate these forums, so they reflect, in the most direct way, the voices and the kitchens of Israel today.

### The Next Frontier

Kinetic Art is an Israeli start-up that has developed a platform for culinary apps for the iPad (and later other platforms). Its first product was a cookbook app for Israeli chef Meir Adoni titled Look & Cook, with photographs by Dan Peretz (released in August 2012). Adoni is one of Israel's premier chefs: he owns and operates a fine-dining restaurant, Catit, and three other restaurants in Tel Aviv, and he recently began hosting a television show, cementing his superstar status in Israel. The app included fifty-two recipes from Adoni's repertoire adapted for home cooks. The project illustrates a culmination of several current trends mentioned earlier. The recipes include numerous international influences and inspirations: *tom yam* soup, gnocchi, barbecued spareribs, crêpes suzette, green papaya salad, tuna sashimi, and *poyke* beef, to name but a few. More than a quarter of the recipes are nonkosher, including lobster, pork chops, and oysters, all illustrated with beautiful, detailed photographs. Two out of the seven sections in the app are devoted to outdoor cooking ("Barbecue" and "Picnic"). Several recipes represent ethnic groups within Israel, such as *shakshuka* (North

Africa), *kubaneh* bread (Yemenite), pickled herring (Polish and German) and spaetzle (Hungarian), and some recipes are inspired by the Arab kitchen, like tabouleh salad and grilled lamb chops. Some recipes call for a special ingredient—*yuzu* juice, red miso paste, or squid ink—or special equipment—a poyke (a cast-iron pot used for outdoor cooking), a pasta machine, or a blowtorch—all treated as fairly common and accessible. This signals greater buying power and disposable income, as well as the higher status of food and cooking, worthy of an extra expense. This last point is exhibited in the status of chef Adoni as an Israeli celebrity as much as in the recipes themselves. The app reflects the current sophistication of the Israeli home cook, the familiarity with world cuisines and with local, ethnic variations, and the growing influence of a secular (nonkosher) audience.

The app was originally released in English, targeting a mostly American audience, with a Hebrew version following it. A few months following its release, the app was featured in an Apple ad campaign in the United States and Japan, a fact that received much positive attention in the Israeli press. The common sentiment was pride in receiving Apple's stamp of approval and a sense of the "little Israeli app that could," as well as positive support for the entrepreneurial spirit and vision of the founders. The press coverage signals a view of start-ups as pioneering, visionary enterprises and as ambassadors of Israel abroad. The app demonstrates the power of technological innovation as the premier Israeli export, as well as a growing international market for recipes from the "New Israeli Kitchen." The word "new" is significant in demonstrating a recent attempt to rescue Israeli food culture from its earlier bad reputation, a necessary component for maintaining a strong tourist industry. It is also a reflection of a new attitude within Israeli society: taking pride in its cuisine as a cultural product and in its ethnic diversity as a source of inspiration.

Perhaps most significant in this context, the recent developments and examples of Israeli cuisine in international settings and forums reflect a greater confidence and security in Israel's national "legitimacy." This more mature performance of Israel through its cuisine can be generous about including both difference from within and inspiration from without, less concerned with proving authenticity and more with exploring identity.

# 5

# THE PROFESSIONAL KITCHEN

## *Articulating a National Cuisine*

Professional cooking covers a wide variety of sites and settings, from restaurants and hotels through special events and institutions. It seems natural that a chef who works for a national venture such as the Israeli airline or one representing the country of Israel in an international competition would be influenced by a national agenda and adapt his or her cooking style to represent the country in some way. Chefs working in other professional settings, though, often find themselves in the service of the nation as well, representing their country to outsiders (e.g., tourists) or creating cultural products in a public setting for their fellow citizens, helping to articulate a national cuisine as part of the national culture.

The restaurant scene in Israel has blossomed, particularly since the 1990s, and it is tempting to describe here all the wonderful chefs and restaurants and their individual contributions to the local culinary landscape. Elegant Continental restaurants, small bars, innovative local chefs working with new ingredients and techniques, foreign chefs creating ethnic cuisines adapted to local tastes, Israeli-Arab chefs, kosher restaurants, dairy restaurants run by artisanal cheese producers, pastry shops, street-food stalls . . .

Since this book lacks the space and scope for such a survey, I decided to refrain from an extended discussion of restaurants in Israel and concentrate instead on a few other professional cooking sites that speak to the relationship between cooking and the nation. This chapter mostly focuses on hotel dining, a venue that, even more than restaurants, speaks to outsiders, to visitors to Israel, and that serves food as part of a larger package of the "Israeli experience." The chapter also focuses on the semiprofessional and most adamantly national army cooking, which caters almost exclusively to Israeli citizens. The kitchens of both contribute to the definition and construction of Israeli cuisine, but they approach it from opposite ends. What they do have in common, a trait that sets them apart from most restaurant cooking in Israel, is that they both insist on kosher cooking, though they do so for different reasons. Since *kashrut* is a significant marker of Jewish religion, it often serves as a sign for Jewish nationalism, reflecting the struggle to articulate a secular Jewish national identity.

## INSTITUTIONAL COOKING:
## A NOTE ON A HOTEL PRECURSOR

Eating in cooperative kitchens, Histadrut (the Israeli workers' union) hospitals and convalescent homes, and college cafeterias was popular with a large part of the Israeli population and influential in shaping eating habits in Israel in the 1950s and early 1960s. These might be seen as the first professional kitchens, but in fact they were perceived as supplying the necessary service of substituting for home cooking and not as a leisure activity. The overwhelming majority of institutional kitchens employed female cooks, and many of these kitchens were operated by women's organizations. A typical menu from the cooperative kitchen in Beit-Brener (the workers' union headquarters) in Tel Aviv appeared in Cornfeld's *Israeli Cookery* as part of her survey of dining establishments in Israel at the time (from the late 1950s to the early 1960s). The menu included herring salad, chopped liver, jellied calves' feet, "filled fish," noodle pudding, and cold or hot borscht in the appetizer section. The main dishes included stewed carp, goulash of lungs, boiled, stewed, or pickled beef, breast or leg of chicken (the cooking method is not specified and is probably boiled), schnitzel of beef or chicken, and *shishlik* (shish kebab) and grilled liver.[1] The (dis)proportion between Middle Eastern and European influences is quite obvious. The work in these kitchens did not carry the (rising) prestige of professional cooking in a restaurant setting and can be seen as an extension of home cooking done in a public setting (like the kibbutz communal kitchen). I wanted to acknowledge here these institutional kitchens and their contribution to and influence on the Israeli dining scene, but they stand apart from the professional hotel-dining category.

## HOTEL DINING

The Hilton Hotel in Tel Aviv serves a most sumptuous breakfast buffet. It offers a range of salads, cheese and yogurt, fresh fruits and vegetables, pastries, made-to-order omelets, and more. I remember it as a very special treat from my childhood, reserved for birthdays and very important guests. The Hilton breakfast, based on fine fresh local products, is perhaps the most luxurious example of the famous "Israeli breakfast," a meal noted by many tourists to be the most memorable culinary experience of their visit to Israel (until the 1990s). Whether tourists were visiting a kibbutz or a big city, they knew breakfast would be reliably delicious. A meal based on fresh dairy and eggs and including an abundance of raw vegetables and freshly baked bread was a perfect example of all the best features of the Israeli diet. Granted, this meal requires a minimum amount of actual cooking, relying instead on the quality of the basic ingredients. Hotel chefs have been trying to create other meals that would measure up to this famous breakfast in providing a noteworthy Israeli dining experience.

The nature of hotel dining has changed radically over the past few decades not only in Israel but the world over. Whereas in the past hotels offered a standard, familiar, often quite average Continental fine-dining experience, today they more often rely on local ingredients and techniques, providing part of the package of visiting an exotic location. In her work on "culinary tourism," folklorist Lucy Long highlights the role of dining as part of the tourist experience of "otherness." Through food consumption the tourist can engage with another culture on a physical level, utilizing all the senses and truly participating, rather than observing, another culture. Long emphasizes that a key to understanding tourism is in seeing it as a voluntary activity, a matter of choice, therefore implying an openness to the other and the new.[2] In contrast, culinary tourism to Israel often results from a search for a sense of belonging. Even though some tourists do visit Israel as an exotic location and Israel, especially in recent years, strives to supply them with a unique experience, a large percentage of visitors are

Jewish tourists who come to Israel in search of familiarity, roots, and a common identity rather than an experience of the exotic. This approach is reflected in what they are offered in the dining rooms of Israeli hotels. As the perception of what constitutes Jewish cooking changed to include a larger percentage of Middle Eastern influences, so did the selection in the dining rooms of Israeli hotels.

Eastern and Central European cooking did not influence hotel and restaurant menus as much as it did the institutional kitchens. Classic French cooking was the predominant influence in high-end dining establishments, but, particularly in the hotels, it was adapted to a kosher kitchen. A sample recipe for quiche Lorraine from chef Miller at the Dan Hotel in Tel Aviv included cheese, milk, and eggs but no ham or any other meat; similarly, at the Sheraton Hotel chef Steiner's recipe for beef Stroganoff included no cream.[3] Hotel dining was one of the first venues for professional experimentation in creating a new local cuisine. Lillian Cornfeld's collection of some of these early recipes (published in 1962) includes chef Miller's version of crêpes suzette accompanied by *arak* and orange sauce and chef Steiner's recipe for chicken à la Sabra made with orange juice and olives.[4] Sometimes this "localization" involved only the dish's name, such as "Sauce Yehudit" from Ramat-Aviv Hotel's chef, Joseph Rabinowitz, which is, in fact, a hollandaise sauce. Hotels that were a little more "down-market" offered menus similar to those of the institutional kitchens in the sense that they combined a heavy dose of Eastern and Central European influences with a smattering of Middle Eastern dishes, mostly salads or shish kebab. This highlights the difference between hotels that targeted primarily local tourists and those that catered to tourists from abroad and therefore tried to supply a local cuisine to complete the total experience of visiting the land of Israel. Today, the menus at both types of hotels have changed dramatically from these 1960s examples.

Tourism has been an important source of income for the Israeli economy since its early days. Tadmor, the Central School of Hospitality, was opened as a governmental venture in 1962, demonstrating the importance the Israeli government placed on developing the hospitality industry. The growing prestige and professionalism of cooking in Israel during the 1960s was closely tied to the development of the tourist industry and to the status of hotel chefs. These chefs were initially trained abroad in Switzerland, France, or Italy and brought with them to Israel not only techniques and recipes but also a higher status and a growing professionalism that gave them greater influence over the fashioning of a local Israeli cuisine.

One example of the change in attitude toward professional chefs (particularly in the hotel setting) is apparent from a new line of advertisements from the late 1950s and 1960s for Telma food products. One example reads: "Follow the lead of the chefs of the leading hotels. Use Telma Genuine Mayonnaise." In the background, behind the silhouette of a professional chef, appear signs for these leading hotels: the King David Hotel, the Dan Hotel, the Megido Hotel, the Dagon Hotel, and ZOA (Zionist Organization of America) House. These ads denote a status and an authority new to the Israeli culinary profession.

## The King David Hotel

The King David Hotel in Jerusalem has played host to many tourists and to formal state functions since its opening in 1931. It remains the hotel of choice for visiting dignitaries and celebrities to Jerusalem. As such, it serves as a good case study for high-end hotel dining in Israel as a venue for articulating a national cuisine for visitors. The King David was built during the British Mandate, which improved roads, railways, and ports in Palestine, thus encouraging tourism. The hotel was designed to "evoke, by reminiscence, the ancient Semitic style and the ambiance of the glorious period of King David."[5] Its Swiss designer used pillars, heavy potted plants, and Egyptian, Assyrian, Phoenician, and Greek-Syrian motifs to "produce the unique and exotic Middle East flavor." The Star of David, pomegranates, grapevines, and the Shield of Solomon were other motifs in the hotel's décor that are still visible today.[6] The food in the hotel came mainly from Egypt, by daily train from Cairo. The hotel management was Swiss, the chefs Italian, and the majority of service staff were Berbers. Very few Jews or Arabs were on the staff. The hotel was an island of foreign "occupancy."

By the 1960s the influences on the hotel's service style and cuisine remained foreign, but the management and staff were now Israeli citizens

15. "Genuine Mayonnaise." Hildhaimer Archive A 449-52, 1954, Central Zionist Archives.

(both Jews and Arabs). The senior staff was mostly comprised of Jews from Central Europe (Germany and Czechoslovakia), while the majority of the service people were Arabic. The Federman family, owners of the Dan Hotel chain, bought the hotel and made substantial renovations in the mid-1950s. According to Avraham Weiner, retired director of food and beverages, under the Federmans' ownership the hotel's kitchen was transformed to adhere to the laws of kashrut in 1958. This last change also resulted in a change of the executive chef and senior kitchen staff to Jewish personnel.[7]

Its high standard of service placed the King David as host to many visiting dignitaries. The dining room menus from the early 1960s serve as examples not only of high-end dining available to tourists but also of what was offered formally to other heads of state. Unlike the décor, which made a point of invoking the "mystique of the Orient," the dining room menus reflected French haute cuisine almost exclusively, but it was a kosher version of French cuisine.[8] Certain adaptations and substitutions were made to the original French recipes in order to conform to the laws of kashrut. Items such as "Filet de Boeuf Grillé Maître d'Hôtel," "Consommé Chaud ou Froid," "Entrecôte Minute Grillée Sauce Béarnaise," "Pommes Mignonettes Dorées," and "Tranche de Saumon Poche au Court Bouillon" are some examples of dishes served at the hotel in 1965.[9] Certain concessions were also made for traditional Central and Eastern European Jewish fare, like chopped liver or the gefilte fish served regularly as part of Friday night's dinner and especially prepared by elderly Polish women hired for this purpose.[10] This particular meal carried cultural significance, but in this high-end hotel serving Western European food, the Sabbath meal was represented solely by Eastern European fare. This choice most likely reflects the attitude of the Ashkenazi hotel management toward non-Ashkenazi cultural products and influences at this time and their perceived low status.

## Chef Yizhak Nicolai

Yizhak Nikolai, the executive chef in the hotel from 1959 to 1961, was one of the most influential figures on the Israeli culinary scene at the time. He published a series of cookbooks in the late 1960s and early 1970s (the last one was published posthumously), attempting to simplify and teach classic

French techniques to the Israeli public. Nicolai went on to be one of the founders and administrators of Tadmor, the Central School of Hospitality, and was one of the judges in the "Queen of the Kitchen" competition. He not only spent time thinking and developing a distinct Israeli cuisine but positioned himself to bridge the gap between professional and home cooks in Israel, working to raise the status of cooking throughout Israeli society.

Nikolai was of German origin and trained in Europe. He was particularly known for elaborately presented, buffet-style dishes. Weiner claims that Nikolai transformed the presentation at the King David Hotel's dining room. He says that the food was already at a high standard of professionalism, but with the arrival of chef Nikolai the presentation became much more elegant and sophisticated, particularly for formal events.[11] Some of the recipes attributed to Nikolai are "Israeli Pancakes" (a version of crêpes suzette with fresh and dried fruit), "Mediterranean Fish" (fish filets simmered in fish stock, covered in tahini sauce, and then broiled), and sautéed turkey slices with a brandy-mushroom pan sauce, as well as "Liver Pâté in Chaudfroid" and "Pickled Ox Tongue in Aspic Garnished with Asparagus and Covered with Truffles."[12] His kitchen was characterized by an attempt to create an Israeli cuisine based on local ingredients and Middle Eastern influences using French techniques, with French haute cuisine dishes and some Italian and Central European additions as the foundation.

The series of cookbooks published by chef Nikolai around 1970 (there is no publication date in the volumes) was coauthored by Hanan Efraim. Titled Madrich le-Omanut ha-Bishul (A guide to the art of cooking), it was geared toward professional chefs and cooks, though it crossed over to the general public to a limited degree and served as a marker for the growing professionalism of the dining scene in Israel. The president of the Cooks' Union claims in his introductory note to the first volume that the series is the first professional guide of its kind in Hebrew and would be valuable for "the young generation."[13] The series includes the titles *The Cold Kitchen*; *Beef, Chicken, Fish, Sauces*; *Soups, Egg Dishes, Vegetables*; and *Cakes, Desserts, Ice Cream*. All of the volumes are firmly grounded in classic French technique. Each dish is accompanied by its French name. Mother sauces are followed by all their derivatives and variations with appropriate names in

French and Hebrew. Spices and herbs are listed accompanied by appropriate drawings, names in Latin and French, description, and uses. Vegetables are listed alphabetically, with several preparation methods most suited for each of them. Beef cuts and parts include detailed drawings of their place within the body of the cow and how they appear at the butcher's in addition to the best preparation methods for each one. It is important to note that the books are kosher and therefore omit some classic recipes and amend others. They do not include seafood or mention pork products. The almost scientific organization of Nikolai's books and the heavy reliance on charts and tables emphasize the professional aspect, locating the books farther from the home kitchen and closer to the laboratory. Another significant contribution to the professional attitude of these books is that, unlike most other cookbooks from this period, they do not address the reader in the female form. Beyond a more familiar attempt to adapt French cooking techniques to a local kitchen, Nicolai's books show an effort at reconciling classic French cooking, seen as the gold standard of professional cooking at the time, with the unique needs of the Jewish state's kitchen, namely, kosher restrictions.

### The Kosher Conundrum

Shula Hirsch, an American housewife, published a book in 1962 describing her life and impressions from a summer spent in Tel Aviv. She and her husband were most surprised by the trouble they had finding a kosher restaurant in Israel, though she does mention that in the end they discovered that the hotels offered kosher meals.[14]

Ha-Casba restaurant and nightclub in Tel Aviv (opened in 1961 and closed in the 1990s) could be compared to the King David Hotel in status and price. Despite its name and a décor inspired by "Moorish influences," the menu is comprised of French and Italian dishes such as steak tartare, "Steak Entrecôte with Sauce Chasseur," shrimp bisque, and "Cannelloni Casba" (stuffed with meat and tomato sauce and covered in béchamel sauce).[15] The main difference between the offerings at the Casba restaurant and at the King David Hotel is the disregard for the laws of kashrut. This is a fairly typical division between hotels and fine-dining restaurants in Israel to this day.

Although there are, of course, kosher restaurants, they comprise only about 25 percent of the total number of restaurants in Israel, possibly reflecting the secular orientation of a significant part of the Israeli restaurant-going population.[16] However, kosher food is seen as essential to a hotel restaurant. This anomaly is due both to the large number of kosher-keeping tourists to Israel (who comprised about 90 percent of hotel occupants in the early 1960s) and to the fact that any culinary venture that officially represents Israel to the rest of the world tends to serve kosher food (e.g., El Al, the national airline). The food that tourists consume in hotels is part of an Israeli "package," like a visit to the Wailing Wall, a kibbutz, or the beach. It does not necessarily represent Israeli food eaten by the local population but rather food that matches the image the state of Israel wishes to project. This image includes kosher food as a sign of "Jewishness."

Recently, new high-end kosher restaurants have been opened in two hotels by renowned Israeli chefs: celebrity chef Yonathan Roshfeld opened a kosher branch of his Herbert Samuel Restaurant at the Ritz-Carlton Hotel in Hertzeliya (2013), and chef Meir Adoni opened Blue Sky (which serves dairy but not meat, 2013) and Lumina (which serves meat but not dairy, 2014) at the Carlton Hotel in Tel Aviv. These chef-restaurants display both the rising level of hotel dining in general and the wider audience for high-end kosher dining in Israel. The kosher menus created by these high-profile chefs show their attempt to articulate an inclusive Israeli cuisine grounded in local ingredients yet drawing inspiration from Asia, Italy, and the Middle East and even reclaiming traditional Eastern European Jewish dishes. Both ethnic influences and local purveyors are mentioned in their menus. Their menu choices allow for the creation of kosher dishes without compromise (e.g., no need for nondairy substitutions). They are aided by the fact that French cuisine is no longer viewed as the only option for a fine-dining establishment, thus providing these chefs with other cuisines to draw on, ones that lend themselves well to a separation of dairy and meat.

This new approach is indicative of a change in the global culinary scene that is different from the one described by chef Uri Guttman, who has represented Israel in many international culinary competitions over the years. In a 1999 interview, he said that he would sometimes have to use nonkosher techniques in order to compete on an equal footing with other chefs (such as finishing sauces for meat with butter or cream), but he stated that, as a representative of Israel, he would never prepare something that was overtly nonkosher, such as pork or seafood. The nonkosher element had to be "invisible" to a casual observer.[17]

The culinary image Israel wished to present during the 1960s can be described as a "united front." Despite some changes, Israel played down the culinary (and other cultural) contributions of various ethnic groups, focusing on Western/European cuisine in all formal or international settings and events. The influence of Arab cuisine was also minimized. When elements adopted from Arab cuisine came into play in Israeli cuisine, they were often presented as the influence of the ancient (biblical) Hebrews or minimized in some other way. In addition to the idea of a national "pride in authenticity," this reflects both the ambivalence many Jewish immigrants felt toward the Arab population and the national agenda, which attempted to present Israel as occupying an empty and desolate land, playing down the presence of any previous local inhabitants.

Looking at the King David Hotel's culinary offerings today presents a new perspective: the hotel advertises its main restaurant, La Regence, with phrases such as "creative menu highlighted by superb local ingredients and subtle Middle East spices and herbs," featuring dishes like "Israeli Lamb Chops in Charcoal Grill" and "Israeli Trout Escabèche, smoked Salmon." The Garden Restaurant boasts a "modern, intensely flavorful dining experience . . . a dairy, fish, and vegetarian menu that reflects Israel's ethnic diversity," featuring both gefilte fish and "Jerusalem Hummus."[18] The hotel still serves kosher food, offering a more formal meat restaurant, as well as a more casual dairy one. It attempts to lure its target audience of tourists from abroad with "superb local ingredients," "ethnic diversity," and local, exotic spices and flavors. The "united front" has been replaced with a highlighting of ethnic diversity, and although classic French techniques are still the norm in this kitchen, the dishes offered reflect pride in local ingredients and a clear geographical location in the Middle East.

## A COUNTRY MARCHES ON ITS STOMACH:
## THE ISRAELI DEFENSE FORCES

While Israeli hotels try to create a local Israeli cuisine for visitors to the country, the Israeli Defense Forces (IDF) must create an Israeli cuisine to serve Israeli citizens. Here, the creation of a local cuisine should have been a by-product of the necessity of feeding the variety of ethnic groups and factions that compose the army. In reality, during the country's early years, a conscious attempt to create and shape a unified Israeli cuisine characterized the army diet as well.

The IDF is one of the most important socializing agents for new immigrants to Israel. Because of the ongoing threat to the country's survival, security has been a central concern for Israel since its inception. Due to the national consensus regarding this threat and compulsory service in the army throughout the years, the army has become "a staple of the Israeli experience and a key to the Israeli-Jewish identity."[19] The army often provided new immigrants their first encounter with a "common" Israeli culture and with each other; it also offered a setting for the creation of a shared cultural base. Education and aid for immigrant absorption were, according to Israel's first prime minister, David Ben-Gurion, among the IDF's primary tasks: "Extensive and rapid mass immigration is a primary element of our security, unequaled by war and security efforts."[20] Ben-Gurion saw the IDF as an instrument of education and unification, uniting the people of Israel around a state and central in defining the new Jewish identity.[21] Psychologist Micha Popper claimed the army was the most important socializing body in Israel, giving as an example the fact that in addition to their security tasks, soldiers were busy teaching Hebrew and establishing housing for the multitudes of immigrants arriving in Israel during the 1950s.[22]

Not only is service in the IDF mandatory, it also involves a large portion of the population through the Reserves and the care provided for family members of soldiers. It is an army of the people in the most literal sense. As such, it serves as both a reflection of socioeconomic changes and, often, their instigator. In the realm of food, as in other spheres of day-to-day army life, soldiers were presented with choices dictated from above, exposing them to often unfamiliar foodstuffs. Thus, a common diet, mostly oblivious to ethnic differences and preferences, was created.

In August 1948 the newspaper *Davar* published a short item titled "*Sten* [a type of firearm] Accompanied by Cooking Pot." The piece described an intensive cooking course offered by WIZO to young female soldiers. After two months of both practical and theoretical study, these women would return to their units and implement their knowledge: "After the war we will return to our kibbutzim, and there too this knowledge will be useful."[23] This is an early example of the very direct influence of cooking in the military on cooking and eating habits in civilian society. As the IDF grew in size and evolved in structure, so did its influence on the society at large.

Ze'ev Kline wrote in *IDF: Encyclopedia for Army and Security* in the early 1980s that the IDF's influence on creating an "authentic Israeli kitchen" was greater than that of any other element in Israeli society.[24] He claimed that the food in the army was "universal" and represented the entire ethnic spectrum in Israel: "Few are the soldiers, whether from Russian or Moroccan origins, that finish lunch hungry or dissatisfied."[25] Kline wrote that, according to various recent surveys, the young Israeli-born generation generally preferred a Mediterranean diet and dishes from the "Oriental" kitchen. By that Kline apparently meant Arab street foods such as hummus and falafel, which are the "Oriental food" examples that he offered.[26] This inclusion of Middle Eastern dishes is one example of the change the army diet has gone through since the 1950s. This change reflects several changes in Israeli policy and society: Israeli authorities have adopted a more pluralistic approach toward various ethnic influences, giving up the attempt at homogenization, and they have paid greater attention to soldiers' (individuals') personal preferences. This demonstrates the other face of the Israeli army, not only influencing Israeli society but also reflecting its changing nature.

Before Operation Nahshon in April 1948, a month prior to Israel's independence, fighting units suffered a lack of food, often relying on sandwiches alone for sustenance due to the absence of an administrative and logistical infrastructure. During Operation Nahshon the logistics of supplying the needs of a large task force encountered several problems, including waste of products and equipment (unfamiliar products, such as condensed milk, were thrown away), lack of trained cooks familiar with field conditions, and lack of attention to nutrition by commanders in the field.[27] The army was in fact established during a war, which contributed to the lack of infrastructure and waste. In July 1948 the Supply Service was established. Its responsibilities included improving food rations, varying menus, updating cooking methods, improving storage facilities, supervising consumption, and extending the education system. The service included a cooking school, three supply bases in the large cities, three area bases, mobile supply units, a meat supply unit, a butchering section, and army bakeries. The service employed both army personnel and civilian professionals such as cooks, inspectors, and butchers. The addition of civilian professionals contributed greatly to the improvement of the army diet.[28]

During the early 1950s the economic situation in Israel was difficult, and food supplies were limited. At the same time, the situation in the army was aggravated due to problems with infrastructure and transportation. Two soldiers from the Fifty-First Regiment wrote Prime Minister Ben-Gurion complaining about the food. They detailed the daily menu:

Breakfast:   a piece of bread (100 gm), margarine, jam, a cup of tea
Lunch:       a piece of bread, some noodles, a fish filet or a piece of meat, eggplant, a glass of juice
Supper:      a piece of bread, a small portion of noodles, a cup of tea, a piece of radish[29]

Other examples show that the food supply was indeed very uneven in the early years and that the situation in each base depended not only on food availability and the location of the base but also on the wit, willingness, and experience of the cook.

In 1948 an order for one day's worth of supplies for a regiment included dry biscuits, sardines, canned meat, hard cheese, chocolate, tomato puree, instant pudding, milk, flour, sugar, beans, corn flour, tea, dates, oatmeal, noodles, barley, salt, garlic, onion, dried fruit, olives, canned carrot, and oil.[30] By 1952 the list of available ingredients had expanded but was still very limited. It included eggs and egg powder, potatoes and potato powder, both dried and fresh vegetables and onions, meat (unspecified), fish filet, herring, sardines, rice, noodles, *ptitim* (Israeli couscous), cheese, olives, legumes, and sausages, as well as some other basic ingredients.[31]

*Ba-Mahane*, IDF's weekly magazine, dealt with questions of food and nutrition fairly often, as apparently food, or lack thereof, was a constant concern for soldiers. In 1995 the magazine published a special issue devoted to the history of army food. In this issue Nir Cohen summarizes army food from the 1950s and 1960s: "The army kitchen [in those years] tended toward Eastern Europe. The majority of cooks were Hungarians, certified in the boiled chicken department."[32] The food, according to Cohen, included mostly milk powder, rye soup, fried kippers, spinach pancakes, and *maʾakhal ahid* ("common dish," meaning a stew made of all manner of leftovers such as vegetables, legumes, and meat), and for dessert, apple-flavored strained zucchini or bread pudding.[33]

In addition to the limitations dictated by the economic situation in the early 1950s, as well as those imposed by conditions in the field and lack of trained personnel, army cooking has been influenced by the decision to keep all kitchens kosher. Like other national institutions in Israel, the army uses only kosher meat, keeps dairy and meat products and utensils separate, and employs inspectors who supervise the upholding of the laws of kashrut. It appears that this rule was accepted with no arguments, since it allowed the recruitment of observant soldiers and was seen as befitting the army of the Jewish state.

### All You Need Is Luf

A unique addition to army rations in the 1950s was Luf (canned chopped meat, similar to Spam, but kosher, not made of pork). Richard Levi, a butcher who opened a factory for meat products, invented this product in 1955 following a request by the food division of the IDF.[34] Luf, a mispronunciation of "loaf" (as in meatloaf), became part of Israeli army mythology and has been the subject of countless jokes, as well as recipes that attempt to improve it under field conditions. One example calls for opening a can of Luf, slicing it, and frying the pieces in a pan on an open fire, then adding a can of strained peas to the pan. A more sophisticated 1990s version of the

16. An army kitchen. The pots in the front are marked "dairy," and the ones in the background are marked "meat." No. 48126, IDF Archive.

same dish suggests that cooks finish it with a generous helping of freshly ground pepper, basil, tarragon, and herbes de Provence.[35] The 1979 cookbook *Bishul la-Gever ha-Meshuhrar* (Cooking for the liberated man) includes several recipes for Luf in its chapter "Cooking in the Field." The authors preface these recipes by saying: "There are many variations on cooking the infamous Luf and turning it into a dish worthy of human consumption. Some people claim that Luf is tasty, but then again there is no accounting for taste. What we can all agree on is that certain adaptations in preparing Luf improve its taste and further the soldier's ability to tolerate it for extended periods."[36] One of the recipes they offer is for "Lufgania Shakshuka" (Luf with eggs and tomatoes):

*1 green pepper*
*1 onion*
*1 tomato*
*2–3 eggs*

*1 can Luf*
*Margarine for frying*

*Chop the onion and pepper and sauté in margarine until golden brown.*
*Add Luf in small diced pieces and lightly brown. Dice the tomato and*
*add it to the pan. When the vegetables have softened, add the eggs, stir*
*until curds form, and serve.*[37]

Despite constant complaints, Luf became synonymous with army food. In
fact, a plate with three slices of Luf arranged in a small pool of red sauce and
garnished delicately with two canned grapefruit sections and a few small
canned carrot cubes and canned peas graced the cover of *Ba-Mahane*'s
special issue on the history of army cuisine.

In one of the articles in this special issue of *Ba-Mahane*, several Israeli
celebrities reminisced about mess hall food. Impressions of Luf appeared
in several accounts: "I don't know why Luf has such a bad reputation," said
a popular singer. "After all, many contractors use it as a substitute for white
plaster!" Another recounts, "I love Luf in any form. To this day I take it
with me on any outing, even when I travel abroad. You could even make a
dessert from Luf: you dip it in sugar, add whipped cream on top, and fry.
It comes out sweet, quite a delicacy."[38] An Israeli did not need to actually
consume Luf to understand its cultural meaning and context. Luf spoke
of a shared experience and conjured up a shared meaning for all Israelis.

### From Cooking Manuals to Cookbooks

The publication of the first official army cooking manual in 1962 by the chief
supply officer can be seen as an indication of the growing professionalism
of army cooking. Prior to this publication, written recipes were available
only on single sheets of paper. This cookbook, titled *Cooking and Nutrition
in the IDF*, was created with the aid of food writer Dalia Lamdani and is
adorned with many small illustrations. The opening states that the author's
intention is "to assist kitchen and storeroom staff in their daily work. At
times let your commanders consult this book too, so they could learn what
can be prepared from the food products that are supplied [to them]."[39]

The book is very thorough, including basic guidelines for proper nutrition,

במחנה
עיתון חיילי ישראל
גיליון 39 ■ בי"ב בסיון התשנ"ה ■ 31.5.95 ■ 6 שקלים

47 שנות מאבק
תולדות האוכל הצבאי

גיליון מיוחד

17. Cover of *Ba-Mahane*, no. 39, 31 May 1995.

cooking methods, guidelines for menu planning (based on the number of soldiers, available equipment, nutritional needs, variety, climate, and use of leftovers), hygiene and sanitation, and, of course, recipes. It also includes a very detailed explanation of the regulations for keeping army kitchens kosher.[40]

Examining the recipes in the book reveals an obvious predominance of European-influenced dishes with a few Middle Eastern contributions such as cumin soup, shish kebab, and several eggplant recipes. The recipes also reflect the influence of the Zena (rationing program) on Israeli eating habits, incorporating such dishes as "Chopped-Liver-Flavored Eggplant" and "Vegetarian Brain" (made from zucchini), several recipes using herring and the notorious "fish filet," and quite a few recipes featuring fresh cheese and eggs to compensate for having relatively few meat dishes. The largest section is the one devoted to vegetables. If this book is indeed an indication of the sort of food most soldiers experienced during their army service, it seems clear that many of them would have had to learn to eat new things or go hungry. Borscht, goulash, Viennese schnitzel, carp in congealed sauce, pickled, fried, or baked herring, cooked carrots with sugar, raw carrots with sugar, and semolina porridge were but a few of the dishes soldiers from a non-European background encountered for the first time.[41]

The problem of catering to an ethnically diverse population was apparently a familiar one to army authorities. The IDF Archives hold a few letters of complaint and correspondence between different army officials dealing with this problem (usually in reply to soldiers' complaints). A letter addressed to the chief of staff from the head of the Afsana'ut (Storage) Branch in one of the large training camps from 1952 reads: "The ethnic makeup problem is a general problem that may, from time to time, cause certain suffering. From one time to the next, temporary measures are taken to overcome these difficulties by way of supplying alternatives to the dishes."[42] Another letter from 1952 deals with the same problem, this time from the head of the Nutrition Division, who was trying to understand the reason for soldiers' complaints: "Due to the fact that the ethnic makeup of the unit's soldiers is very diverse and that not all ethnic groups are accustomed to all the dishes, it is possible that not all prepared food is eaten by all the soldiers."[43] The writer also suggests that the soldiers' young age, the sudden change from the home environment to the army, and the rigorous training might cause the large number of complaints in basic training camps.

Articles dealing with this problem make a point of saying that the army diet was changing and that new "Oriental" dishes had been added to the old repertoire. "One example, the introduction of hummus and tahini to the army kitchens—dishes that those coming from Oriental countries are used to—was also well received by those born in the country and immigrants from the West," writes Avraham Meron in 1958.[44] "The Oriental dish is slowly penetrating the army menu—tahini and halva are common in the IDF menu, in addition to a good portion of hot spices!," exalts Eli Sahaf in 1961.[45]

The next version of an official IDF cooking manual appeared in 1976. *Cooking in the IDF* was published by the chief maintenance officer. Unlike its predecessor, this manual is not illustrated and has a very "efficient" appearance. In addition to recipes, it has a very short section on nutrition, a description of cooking methods, some professional terms, and a survey of utensils and serving dishes. The sections on kosher cooking, herbs and spices, cooking in the field, hygiene, and menu composition that were included in the previous publication have all been dropped. The recipes now include greater ethnic variety, with dishes like stuffed peppers or zucchini, *moussaka*, "Oriental" bean soup, eggplant salad with *tahini*, and "Oriental-flavored" carp. There are also more sophisticated recipes, such as deviled eggs, blintzes, and stuffed carp. Finally, we can see some new popular ingredients, such as turkey and mayonnaise.[46]

Another interesting change by 1976 is the fact that this publication received a review in *Ba-Mahane*. Despite the fact that the previous publication was much "friendlier" and more appealing and seemed to be aimed at a larger audience, while this one seemed to be aimed mostly, if not exclusively, at army cooks, it received a glowing review. The reviewer, Ali Mohar, was surprised by the fact that there were strict rules that governed the army cook's actions (probably because of the gap between his own experience and the material he encountered in the book). This "single certified official recipe book . . . [is] stimulating, exciting, and often fascinating. . . . I particularly liked the parts on 'egg-salad with potatoes,' 'chicken fricassee,' 'pickled herring,' 'potato soup' (most interesting!) . . . and much, much more. . . . It is an interesting, suspenseful book, rich with information."[47] It is apparent that food and cooking merited more serious consideration in the 1970s than they had been given in Israel's formative years.[48] The relative security and economic prosperity following the 1967 war allowed for more attention to matters of personal comfort. The immediate threat to Israel's existence was alleviated for a time, allowing its citizens to concentrate on improving their standard of living.

### Army Cooks

Building the infrastructure for supplying soldiers with food took time. Before the army established official army kitchens and training programs, women volunteers did most of the army cooking. Yehudit Klienman described how several women from the Union for Working Mothers (Irgun Imahot Ovdot) became involved in cooking for the army.[49] According to her story, these women were appalled to hear that the soldiers survived on canned and dried food; they approached the army authorities, offering to prepare cooked dishes, fruits, and fresh vegetables for the same budget. From an initial number of 150 soldiers, the operation grew to feed thousands of soldiers. Klienman states that the main motivation for the many volunteers who took part in this work was the feeling that they were taking part in the war effort. Since many of them were mothers of soldiers, they saw the work as a direct contribution to the soldiers' well-being, as well as a way to alleviate their own stress and worry about their sons at the front. Klienman claims that the Union for Working Mothers was the founder of this program but adds that other women's organizations joined the effort soon thereafter and that all these women volunteers were considered recruits by the army authorities.[50]

Molly Bar-David wrote an article on Hadassah's work in turning the Haganna organization (one of the Jewish paramilitary organizations in Palestine during the British Mandate) into an army. She claimed that the problem with supplying food to many soldiers was not only the actual cooking but also the teaching of mass cooking to volunteers who were most likely only familiar with home cooking. She compared the new kitchens established by Hadassah volunteers with the previous British kitchens: cleanliness and efficiency were the top priorities in the new kitchens, using what was available to create smaller portions but with greater variety. According to Bar-David, a "before" (British) menu included barley soup, barley cereal, and barley pudding, while an "after" (Hadassah) typical menu was composed of vegetable soup, fried sausage, mashed potatoes, eggplant in tomato sauce, fruit salad, bread with margarine, and tea. Bar-David ended by repeating the main problem faced by Hadassah's workers and the cause for the often low quality of food: the dependence on well-meaning yet inexperienced volunteers who either could not cook at all or did not know how to cook for a large group of people.[51]

The Israeli public saw the army and the war effort during Israel's formative years as essential for national survival. Since the issue of security was so dominant in Israeli society, involvement with the army through the kitchen allowed many women to take an active part in public life and play a role in a field seen as central to Israeli life yet also distinctly masculine.[52] WIZO was one of the other organizations that was actively involved in feeding soldiers and in helping the army establish the infrastructure necessary for future operation of its kitchens. A report on WIZO's activities during the war detailed the establishment of training courses for women soldiers who would take over army kitchens, as well as for female managers and storage officers for the army camps. The other food-related field that WIZO was involved in was the establishment of army canteens and clubs. Due to the limitations of army cuisine, many soldiers turned to the canteens for "nutritional supplements" in the form of candy bars and soft drinks.

In later years, army cooking became an exclusively male domain due in part to the simple fact of the growing numbers of soldiers and the resulting need for large quantities of food and very large pots, turning army cooking into a very physically challenging task. An article from 1958 demonstrates that the transition from kitchens operated by friendly women volunteers to ones managed by army-trained men had not gone smoothly. The article examined the reasons for soldiers' complaints about army food and offered several explanations, including the selection of cooks. It described a caricature that portrayed a soldier who, having failed at the tasks of gatekeeping and sanitation (the lowliest of army jobs), was sentenced to jail and finally sent by his commanding officer as a last resort to the army cooking school. A commander questioned about this cartoon admitted he would not send his best men to be cooks—he needed them in the field. He also said that soldiers sent to the cooking program had usually served for a year by the time they got to the course. After several months of training as cooks they only had a year of service left, and only by its end had these soldiers acquired enough experience to really be good at the job. Other problems the article raised were the bad image—and therefore ridicule—army cooks suffered, as well as the low standard of education and lack of motivation of most cooking school candidates in the army.[53]

The type of soldier sent to the army cooking courses is often cited as a cause of the problems with army food. Ze'ev Kline wrote in 1983 that the soldier population that arrives at the army's cooking courses is mostly "problematic, lacking motivation, and has a multitude of social, economic, and family problems."[54] During my own army service as commander in charge of service conditions (*mashakit tash*) in 1985 and 1986, I served in a camp of basic training for soldiers with "difficult" home situations within a special army program designed to recruit and assist these soldiers on their way to a better civilian life in the future (Na'arei Raful). The majority of these soldiers were not fit for combat service, and so the idea behind the program was that the army was the last opportunity for them to learn professions that could serve them later on in life and help them become "useful members of society." One position remained as a last resort for the most difficult cases: a cooking course. The army cooking course was seen not as learning a profession but as a solution for soldiers who otherwise would not be able to serve at all. All army cooks uniquely serve in a structure of alternating weeks, spending a week in the army and the following week at home and so on throughout their service. This enables soldiers with particularly difficult situations at home to hold a civilian job in addition to their army service. This made the cook's position a coveted one among many soldiers who were looking for extra money or as little to do with the army as possible, but this structure did not contribute to the image and self-esteem of army cooks.

In recent years, as the status of food and food-related professions rose in Israeli society, so did, to a lesser degree, the quality of army food and the status of those preparing it. Though many large army bases still offer uninspiring fare prepared by reluctant cooks, some benefit from enthusiastic

18. An army kitchen. The size of these pots alone can be daunting. No. 4314/15, IDF Archive.

cooks and a larger variety of available products (particularly dairy products for breakfast and supper). Occasional cooking competitions and surprise visits and meals cooked by professional chefs aim at promoting better cooking and a higher status for army cooks.

A cursory search of a variety of current IDF publications, websites, and Facebook pages reveals that army food is still largely characterized by monotony (chicken, mostly breaded and fried, and rice, with salad and hummus on the side), limited quantities, and a disproportion of canned foods (particularly in field rations for obvious reasons), as well as a prevalence of lackluster cooking by overtired cooks. However, there are some significant changes reflecting changes in Israeli society at large. Most glaring perhaps is that even though complaints about the food abound, Facebook and related online sources allow soldiers to offer each other advice and create solutions beyond those offered through the official channels. Several examples offer tips and ideas for possible improvements on army field rations.[55] Others offer advice on healthy solutions to the standard deep-fried lunch offering.[56] Another approach can be seen in a recent survey and critique of soldiers' favorite take-out pizza places near their army bases throughout Israel.[57] These offer a handy supplement to the army diet and reflect a changing landscape of fast-food eateries in Israel. All these examples demonstrate the growing sophistication of the soldiers themselves as informed and educated eaters.

A more significant overhaul and centralization of the food system in the army might be under consideration but is still far in the future. The IDF menu today is much more reflective of Israel as a multiethnic society: boiled chicken has been replaced with fried cutlets, potatoes have been replaced with rice, and hummus, eggplant, and chopped vegetable salads round off the core dishes of the main meal (lunch). But the shift in the importance placed on food and the rise in the cooks' status have had an interesting side effect: the increasingly important role of food in Israeli society and the improvement in cooking and restaurants have resulted in more educated and demanding consumers. Israeli soldiers' complaints today are different from the complaints of the past. They revolve around health concerns and monotony, but they seem to be an essential part of army life regardless of the relative improvement in army kitchens and dining rooms.

# 6

# NO TABLE REQUIRED

## *Consumption and the Public Sphere*

*Of all the days I love Friday the most, because it comes right
before Saturday and because of the food. . . . It is the day of
chicken soup, the food I love most of all. I fill up the bowl and
wait for Rivka, who is passing out shkedei marak [miniature
soup croutons], to reach me. Chicken soup without shkedei-marak
is worthless. . . . After lunch we return to the "children's house."
On Friday each one of us gets four chocolate squares. . . . In
summer we get lemon popsicles too, and we all sit and eat
our popsicles in class and watch Zehu-Ze on TV.*

—**Naama Orbach,** *Eich Ossa Yalda* (What a girl does)

In the conversation about national cuisine, we tend to concentrate on home-cooked dishes or natural products; the processed foods, the odd treats that make up childhood memories, are often forgotten. Artist Naama Orbach's account of childhood on a kibbutz mentions two of these typically Israeli products, foodstuffs that for many Israelis are inseparable from their early memories: *shkedei marak*, or soup croutons, are tiny, golden nuggets of crispy dough; and lemon-flavored popsicles, which were "immortalized" by the 1978 Israeli cult film *Eskimo Limon* (Lemon popsicle). This list also includes Bamba (a puffed peanut snack), Crembo (a chocolate-covered fluffy egg-white cream), and chocolate spread (similar to Nutella). These are some of the food products Israelis seek out when they live abroad and would trek to faraway grocery stores to purchase. These foods trigger nostalgia as effectively as a mother's cooking might.

Consumption often happens away from a kitchen or a table. The fact that these snack foods, as well as other casual eating events, play such a central role in Israeli cuisine is not incidental. Most food cultures have a wide array of street foods as part of their cuisine, but how many of these cultures hold these foods up as their national emblem? I would like to focus here on a few other dining occasions that are central to Israeli culture but that share falafel's context: consumption away from an actual table.

In the Hasidic *tish* ("table" in Yiddish), described by Barbara Kirshenblatt-Gimblett, the community leader (the *rebe*) presides over a festive meal that includes a variety of songs, dance, and discourse. Even though the tish is structured as a meal around a table, the food "is present not to satisfy a physical hunger but rather in the interest of commensality."[1] The word "table" is used here in a broader sense: to refer to the total event rather than the actual object. The dining room in the Israeli kibbutz, established by early halutzim bent on eradicating the old, Diasporic Jewish traditions, ironically follows the same logic, as this chapter will demonstrate.

The *kumzits*, or outdoor eating, is another tableless dining event central to Israeli culture. It grew out of the kibbutz and youth movement culture to metamorphose and spread throughout Israeli society. The changes in the kumzits reflect broader changes in Israeli culture and summarize much of what has been discussed in previous chapters. This chapter also includes a short study of the Mimouna celebration as one example of the transformation and negotiation of a specific ethnic tradition within the national consensus. This celebration offers an opportunity to examine reciprocal relationship between a particular immigrant group and the dominant Israeli culture and the changes in this relationship over time. The Mimouna offers a way of reflecting on the tensions within the dominant national culture and a single immigrant group through a single case study. This chapter is mostly about change, about the evolution and transformation of Israel's culinary scene. It reflects socioeconomic changes in Israeli society at large and highlights the tenuous nature of any attempt at fixed definitions.

## THE KIBBUTZ DINING ROOM;
## OR, WHAT'S FOOD GOT TO DO WITH IT?

In celebration of the opening of the new dining room in 1950, Kibbutz Kfar Giladi dedicated an entire issue of its local newsletter, *Al ha-Giva'a,* to the saga of the new building's inception, the progress of its construction, and a farewell to the old dining room.[2] The issue included a collection of previously published materials and minutes of meetings. It brings to light several issues central to the question of the communal dining room. While the newsletter took a joking look at the many faults of the small, old dining room (a building that could accommodate 80 eaters and was still used when the kibbutz community numbered 350), it included a nostalgic note, lamenting the possible loss of the former dining room's finer qualities. These qualities included a sense of intimacy and a tightly knit community, a center of culture and social interaction more than a place for consuming food.

Other descriptions of dining rooms and "workers' kitchens" from this earlier period highlight their social and cultural role as a place for gathering, singing and dancing, and ideological debates. B. Z. Kolman wrote: "The workers' kitchen was not only an 'earthly' place where one comes in order to eat, like a regular restaurant. It was a place to meet friends, arrange work, and have political debates."[3] In his "Words of Farewell from the Old Dining Room," Tzvi Vardi describes everything that happened in the old dining room used by Kibbutz Merchavia for twelve years. The list includes ideological struggles, discussions about shaping society, sharing complaints, dealing with disaster, receiving good news, having parties, dancing, and singing—the only glaring omission is eating.[4]

Many of the memories regarding Kfar Giladi's old dining room revolve around the difficulty of food shortages and overcoming them. The tough economic situation contributed to the greater importance of these other activities in the dining room. They helped take the edge off the hunger and the difficult conditions, making them seem a worthwhile sacrifice (as in Manya Shohat's story described in the first chapter).

Much like the Hasidic tish, the meal in the kibbutz dining room revolved around commensality and spiritual satisfaction. Even though these halutzim from Eastern Europe have forgone the rebe (leader) figure in favor of a community of equals, religion in favor of Zionism, they have retained the idea of community building and spiritual satisfaction as the central components of gathering around the table, of song, dance, and commensality as aids in combating a difficult reality.

## The Question of Service

Much like communal cooking, the service in the dining room raised conflicting emotions: it tried to reconcile a need for efficiency in accommodating a large group of diners while also making them feel comfortable and welcome (replacing the role of the home-cooked meal). Before establishing self-service, kibbutz members were assigned to serve the food in the dining room and clear the tables. One server lamented her inability to do the work properly. She wrote that one night she was particularly proud of herself because she had been able to serve everyone reasonably quickly without neglecting or forgetting anyone. But her triumph was dampened when a member complained that she was too hurried and too much like a professional waitress. He said she should serve slowly and calmly while stopping for a moment to chat with each member. She ended her piece by asking, "Do *you* know how to serve 250 different portions, including substitutions and special additions, in 120 minutes between 7 and 9 p.m., calmly and pleasantly and with clever conversations with the members?"[5]

Gidon Keich's caricatures from kibbutz life comment on the service in the dining room as well. The practice of table service was a constant source of complaints as this caricature, showing kibbutz members asleep around dining room tables, demonstrates (fig. 19).

The alternative option was self-service, which was eventually established as the preferred method in all kibbutzim. Despite initial hesitations, this method offered the closest approximation to dining at home in a casual, warm atmosphere for growing kibbutz communities. The kibbutz dining room did not replace a restaurant. It did not simply solve the technical problem of a place to feed a large group of people. Rather, it replaced the family table: it was a place that served not just nourishment but also comfort, warmth, and

19. "I guess some servers are missing again." Gidi Keikh, *Efshar le-Hitpake'a! Karika-turot me-Hayey ha-Kibbutz* (You could burst! Caricatures of kibbutz life) (Tel Aviv: Mifalei Tarbut ve-Hinukh Ltd., 1966).

spiritual and emotional sustenance. This complex role was negotiated and experimented with in different ways. Eventually, it was found lacking, and slowly most kibbutzim have turned back to family meals in the members' private quarters, reserving the dining room for functional meals during the workday (cafeteria style) or for festive holiday meals, when the entire community gathers together like an extended family or a Hasidic *tish*.

### "Privatizing" Cooking in the Communal Settlements

Perhaps the clearest site for the transformation in the attitude toward cooking and consumption can be seen in the communal settlements: originally offering the most profound break from the traditional family structure and roles, the communal kitchens of the kibbutzim went through further transformation in the second half of the twentieth century.

After World War II the standard of living in the country as a whole rose, creating greater demand for a similar rise within kibbutz society. Members

20. "I am only 'rag'! I am only . . . 'soup'!" Hik, Kfar Giladi newsletter, 1956. Published with the permission and aid of Gidon Barkani.

of the kibbutz who served in the British army during the war were accustomed to a certain level of personal comfort. With the demobilization of the military system, these members brought back to their private rooms in the kibbutz certain objects that were not provided to the entire community, such as paraffin stoves and electric kettles. Some kibbutzim elected to solve the problem by "leveling" these possessions: once a significant number of members acquired a certain item, the kibbutz purchased and distributed a similar item to the rest of the community. This process was known as the "electric kettle syndrome."[6] It is plain that in accord with the rise in the standard of living after World War II, the attention to individual needs and comforts grew as well.

The fact that this syndrome was named after the electric kettle signifies the importance of the afternoon tea ritual in kibbutz society. In a brochure published in honor of Kibbutz Geva's seventieth anniversary (1991), the editor, Bina Peleg, wrote: "In the beginning there was the kettle. . . . [M]any claim that from that fatal assembly decision appeared the first cracks in the absolute kibbutz unity." She continued to illustrate the transition from the communal dining room to the members' private quarters: "When I arrived in Geva in the early 1960s there were still remnants of the 'four o'clock meal,' which was served in the dining room for the entire public returning from the field. Later there was a distribution of cookies, sugar, coffee, and tea to the members, and the kitchen was available to the women, who would come in the evenings and bake delicacies for the family."[7]

By the late 1950s (the exact time varies from kibbutz to kibbutz), not only was afternoon tea commonly taken in members' private rooms, but most of the baking for tea was performed there too. Generally, baking was done just before the end of the week, prior to the Shabbat. Cakes would be served to children, who would typically spend the afternoon with their parents in their private rooms, as well as to guests. Given the limited space and facilities in the private quarters, most of the personal baking was done initially in a *seer peleh* (wonder pot), a circular pan with a hole in its center (it resembles a Bundt pan and includes a lid). Initially this pan was placed on top of the primus (a small oil burner) and later became a freestanding electrical appliance (allowing baking without the aid of an oven). Providing an opportunity for displaying personal creativity as well as maternal care and good housekeeping skills in the best bourgeois fashion, baking became quite popular in the kibbutzim. By the 1960s several kibbutzim took to publishing a community cookbook of such personal recipes, mostly devoted to cakes and cookies (replacing the oral transmission of these recipes).

Sheli Ganiel began her cookbook of cake recipes from her kibbutz with the question: "Why are we not satisfied with the cake—right for all tastes and preferences—that the kibbutz kitchen distributes?" She continues: "The debate regarding the downfall of the general cake in favor of the rise of the private cake we will leave as material for academic discussions."[8] For the academic discussion at hand, this is a question worth examining. It appears that cakes and cookies baked at home offered an occasion for an individual touch within the communal structure. Their popularity demonstrates the power of cooking (or in this case, baking) as a symbol of the family and the home. Kibbutz women, having been released from the necessity of putting dinner on the table, still turned to baking as part of the ritual of the family unit. As the ideological climate in the kibbutz changed from marginalizing to embracing the family, private cake baking became more popular. It supplied kibbutz women with the opportunity to feed their families, since most other cooking was still done in the communal kitchen.

A caricature from this time shows a woman hard at work through many stages of preparing a cake, the final one being throwing the finished product into the trash. For his inspiration, the artist, Gidon Keich, quotes from the kibbutz newsletter: "The *hatzran* [caretaker] suggests holding a cake-baking course—he finds too many of them in the trash cans."[9] This caricature demonstrates the popularity of cake baking in the kibbutz, the waste that a better economic situation allows, and the dedication kibbutz women applied to the task. Despite the cynical treatment, it is obvious that cake baking is accepted as a common practice in the kibbutz regardless of its "frivolous" nature.

Private baking developed in many kibbutzim to eventually include preparing supper and the afternoon meal. Kibbutz Sha'ar ha-Golan published a brochure titled *Matkonim ba-Sha'ar: Recipes from the Private Kitchens of the Members of Kibbutz Sha'ar ha-Golan* in 2000.[10] This extensive collection of recipes demonstrates how far kibbutz cooking has come since its early days, ideologically as well as substantively. A small sample includes gefilte fish, liver pâté (with bacon and sour cream), eggplant and pomegranate salad, cherry tomato and basil salad, bean sprouts and rice noodle salad, pickled olives, pizza, stuffed peppers, chicken with dried fruit, chicken with whole garlic cloves, Chinese-style ribs, and a variety of other fish, chicken, rice, and vegetable recipes, in addition to several cake and dessert recipes. Each recipe is presented with the name of its creator, and readers are encouraged to call that person should anything go wrong while attempting the recipe. This collection is meant mostly for the kibbutz members and describes itself as a "collective local creation."

Such community cookbooks became popular in the kibbutzim in the late 1970s and 1980s. Kibbutz communities grew, making the oral exchange of recipes more difficult; they also opened up to trends in Israeli society at large, as well as to the world beyond Israel's borders. The variety of recipes indicates the greater diversity within the kibbutz community in addition to multiple outside influences. Most cookbooks still include an overwhelming majority of cake recipes. Some versions were even published and distributed to the general public, but most of these collections were meant for internal distribution only. The recipes might not be shared in the communal dining room, but the sense of a close-knit community remains.

Geva's recipe collection offers a few words in the prelude to most recipes: "For the grandchildren's birthday Yona labors to make something special"; "In Neomi Viesman's family Thursdays are devoted to baking"; and "From their last tour in the Far East the Dotan couple brought a delicacy that became a local hit."[11] These remarks assume a common knowledge of the recipes' authors and evoke the sense of an intimate community, as does the use in many of these collections of first names only for both contributors and editors. The comments are also another indication of kibbutz members' broadening horizons: they travel abroad and are much more exposed to outside influences than they were in the 1940s and 1950s.

Sha'ar ha-Golan's collection is unique among other such kibbutz community publications in that it includes, in addition to recipes, historical material. The book includes archival photographs from the kibbutz kitchen and dining rooms and nostalgic recipes that are no longer in use, such as pumpkin with raisins, noodles with cabbage, mushroom-flavored eggplant, zucchini pudding, and half(!) a hard-boiled egg.[12] The book also includes a "local dictionary" for food-related terms, such as "four o'clock meal," *bimkom* (instead), *haluka* (distribution), and *marak-da'isa* (soup-porridge), among others. Most of these terms were common in many kibbutzim. Bimkom (instead) refers to the option for a substitution to the main course, as in the sentence "What is there 'bimkom' today?" Haluka means the distribution of supplements to the family afternoon meal (the four o'clock meal), such as eggs or cheese. *Kolboynic* (catchall) is the name of the bowl that stood in the center of each table in the dining room and was meant for trash. *Marak-da'isa* was the server of soup and porridge in the dining room before the days of self-service.

The fact that Sha'ar ha-Golan's members saw the need for such a dictionary may indicate the diminishing use of these terms, with the central dining room losing ground to the private kitchens. Tamar Katriel studied language as "an instrument for constructing social reality through public display." Examining food and cooking terms unique to kibbutz culture can offer a "key" to the change in the social reality of the kibbutz over this time period. Katriel argues that certain "key words" are used in "constructing social boundaries" that distinguish "us" from "others" and display power struggles and social status.[13] Words such as *kolboynic* and *bimkom* were

21. "Today there is no bimkom!" Hik, Kfar Giladi newsletter, 1956. Published with the permission and aid of Gidon Barkani.

unique to kibbutz members. They were needed to describe a special dining arrangement and used with pride as markers of difference between kibbutz members and outsiders. With the rising improvement in the standard of living and the growing importance of the nuclear family, the communal dining room lost its central position in kibbutz society, and the specialized language became archaic—a nostalgic remainder of a different era.

## THE KUMZITS

The origin and nature of outdoor cooking and eating in Israel follow closely that of the kibbutz dining room, going through a similar transformation. Sociologist Oz Almog described the origins of the word *kumzits* from the Yiddish *kum zits* (come sit), meaning "come and have fun / make merriment."[14] This expression was apparently only used in this context in Palestine and Israel. The origins of the kumzits—gathering around the fire to eat, drink coffee, and sing songs—can be traced back to the time of the halutzim of the Second Aliya and the coffee ritual adopted by members of Ha-Shomer (The watchman) organization from the local Bedouins around the first decade of the twentieth century. The heyday of the kumzits, however, was sometime later as it became a popular practice with the youth movements and the legendary Palmach (the paramilitary organization that preceded the Israeli army). The Palmach, beginning with its training camps in the early 1940s, was the force that transformed the kumzits into a rite of youth and togetherness, a symbol of the *tzabar* (Israel-born Jew) way of life and an icon of youth culture in Palestine and, later, Israel.[15] The kumzits, or outdoor cooking, remains an important phenomenon in Israeli popular culture. It has gone through many changes over time yet remains a constant feature of Israeli popular culture to this day.

As stated earlier, Zionist ideology was concerned with creating a connection between new Jewish immigrants and the land of Israel. Putting down roots through acquiring an intimate knowledge of the land was an ideal that was enforced in several ways. One of the reasons for the success and resonance of the kumzits is its unique compatibility with this particular ideology: outdoor cooking and eating are intrinsically closer to nature, and, in the case of the kumzits in particular, the food is emphatically found food and locally grown food, either from local orchards and fields or from the wild. The act of sitting on the ground in a circle of equals around the fire is an additional advantage for a socialist ideology.

### Around the Fire

The prominent Israeli poet Nathan Alterman wrote a poem in 1948 in celebration of seven years of the Palmach organization. The poem is titled "Misaviv la-Medura" (Around the fire). The title itself exemplifies the centrality of gathering around a fire as a hallmark of the Palmach and later of the youth movements and youth culture in Israel in general. In Alterman's poem a group of young Palmach members sits close together around a fire eating olives and dates, drinking from crumpled aluminum cups.

Another song written in 1948, "The Finjan Song," became part of the canon of Israeli folk songs typically sung during the kumzits:

*The cool wind lightly blows.*
*Let's add another twig to the fire,*
*thus in scarlet arms,*
*like a sacrifice, to be consumed by the flames.*
*The fire flickers, the singing blossoms,*
*the finjan turns around and around.*[16]

In a more recent song, "Ha-Stav Biladav" (Fall without him), written in memory of Prime Minister Itzhak Rabin, the poet Nathan Yonathan refers to "The Finjan Song" to conjure up Rabin's place in Israeli history as a quintessential tzabar, commander in the Palmach and, later, the Israeli army:

*A cool wind blows again,*
*so he sang as the battles' fire departed. . . .*
*Shall we add another twig to the fire?*
*How time passed without him.*

This is a testament to the associative power "The Finjan Song" carries in Israeli society and the iconic status of both the song and the event it describes.

The members of the Second Aliya's Ha-Shomer organization adopted the Bedouin "coffee ritual," which formed the basis of the kumzits. This practice involved cooking and then sharing Turkish or Arabic coffee in a small pot, called a *finjan* by the Israelis, on the fire (an art requiring great precision). Men were generally responsible for coffee making and for other forms of cooking in the kumzits setting. This was part of the attempt to adopt certain Bedouin practices as behavioral models for the new immigrants. It is interesting to note, however, that in Arabic the word *finjan* is in fact the name of the small cups in which the coffee is drunk, while the word *bakraj* is used for the pot.[17] This indicates that the halutzim's enthusiasm for Bedouin culture was often ambivalent and that precise details seemed less important than a certain romantic aura.

The early Jewish settlers adopted many dishes and ingredients from their Arab neighbors but often had a difficult time adjusting to the new flavors. Several ingredients were embraced in the kumzits setting but not in the daily diet, pita bread and coffee being the prime examples—tea and

European-style bread remained the mainstays of the settlers' diet in the "civilized" dining room setting. Another Arab habit that was only adopted within the kumzits setting was that of gathering wild plants and herbs. Even though the settlers knew that certain wild plants, such as *hubeiza*, were edible and used them in times of crisis and extreme hunger, these plants never entered the regular diet outside the kumzits, placing the Arab influence firmly in the realm of nature and tradition (i.e., not culture and modernity, which were perceived as the European settlers' domain).

During the early 1940s, prior to Israel's independence, the Palmach organization and the youth movements continued the kumzits tradition, developing and enhancing it. In her work on patterns of communication and social rituals in Israel, Tamar Katriel writes of the centrality of the ethos of the youth movements in forging the symbols of Israeli secular culture. She specifically discusses the importance of fire as a powerful, multifaceted symbol of solidarity, purity, and power that was popular with youth movements in Europe around the turn of the previous century. Youth movements in Israel adopted the ritual of gathering around the fire from the European models. According to Katriel, the use of fire also echoed traditional elements in Jewish culture—fire as mediator between God and man, manifested in modern times in the lighting of candles or torches on different occasions. As such, fire became a powerful, multifaceted symbol in Israeli society: inspired by both European and Jewish tradition, yet manifested in a new and vital form.[18]

Gaston Bachelard has contemplated the poetics of fire. He examined fire as a potent universal symbol, a "privileged phenomenon" that lends itself to a variety of applications and treatments. Bachelard comments on the nature of fire as a "social reality" rather than a "natural reality," explaining that respect for fire is a respect that has been taught: the social prohibition preceded the discovery of fire's ability to burn/hurt.[19] Bachelard's point can illuminate the role of fire within the kumzits setting: it was employed in the construction of a social bond between those gathering around it. Fire's utility in providing warmth or cooking food was secondary. So despite food's appearance as a central element of the kumzits, the alleged purpose of the gathering around the fire, it was but an excuse for conviviality and not an end in its own right (much like the communal dining room).

A kumzits most often involved "found" or gathered food, like "snitched" chickens, most often not roasted over the fire but rather boiled in a pot(!), as was the practice in the kitchens these youths had been exposed to, water-melons, potatoes, and other products from the kibbutz fields and orchards. Alterman's poem mentions olives and dates, both local foods that do not require any additional cooking (they also have the added advantage of being among the seven types of foods the land of milk and honey was said to be blessed with in the Bible). The setting of the kibbutz in a rural area was perfect for developing the kumzits tradition, since the existence of fields, orchards, and chicken coops made these foodstuffs available for the taking. Helping yourself to common products had a romantic, mischievous aura; it was not "stealing." As their knowledge of the land grew, young kumzits makers could rely more on native wild plants and herbs. This is part of the allure of the kumzits: advocating communion with nature and the land, as well as with fellow group members. It promoted socialist ideology because of its affordable nature, as well as through the act of equals gathering together in a circle around the fire. Relying on "found" products and focusing on self-reliance helped situate the kumzits as an antithesis to bourgeois habits and to entertainment options in the city. Gathering around a fire was also a practical option for entertainment in a rural setting, as well as in a poor country with limited economic possibilities.[20]

The 1940s were a time of high prestige for kibbutz culture and all that was associated with it. The Palmach and the youth movements were seen as Israel's future, as those who would shape the nation and create a new and vital cultural framework to replace the old European models of Jewish society. By association, the kumzits enjoyed the same high status and romantic aura.

## Around the Mangal

By the late 1960s, the climate of greater security and prosperity had been combined with a more ethnically varied society to promote urban culture at the expense of kibbutz culture and its symbols. The kumzits was still popular with the youth movements, and the open fire remains an essential fixture of Lag ba-Omer celebrations, but a new phenomenon became per-vasive in Israeli society: the picnic.[21] A variation on the kumzits, the Israeli picnic involved, as a rule, a fire of some kind, but a basic coal grill now often replaced the open fire. Instead of the group of peers gathering around the flames, the grill was part of a family outing and was in line with a different hierarchy: not a gathering of equals but a different division of labor in which the men would typically tend to the fire while the women would prepare the rest of the meal in advance and look after the children. A picnic could be a single family event, but often several families would come together to have one. The picnic retained the kumzits's association with nature, indicating a trip to a forest or the shore, unlike the American barbeque, held in the backyard. This is also an indication of the greater urbanization of Israeli society, requiring a trip to reach "nature," not living in close proximity to it, as on a kibbutz or a *moshav* (a socialist settlement). My father, Amiram Raviv, and Asher Shaham wrote in their 1979 cookbook, *Bishul la-Gever ha-Meshuhrar* (Cooking for the liberated man): "Cooking in nature is one of the hallmarks of Israeli culture. . . . The combination of coal grill + table + pack of cards and ten tots is a familiar experience, and while we are doing it, we grumble against the rest of Israeli society crowding around us on the shores of Lake Kinneret."[22] It is obvious that any romantic aura that might have been associated with the kumzits is long gone. This shift indicates a change in Israeli demographics: not necessarily so much in ethnic makeup as in age. Israel of the 1960s, 1970s, and 1980s was no longer a society of pioneering youths. It was an older society and thus more "normal" or "natural," with more families and a more diverse social structure, including a substantial middle class. The middle-aged, middle-class man with a protruding potbelly had replaced the youthful, muscular kibbutznik as the typical Israeli figure.

By the 1980s the experience of outdoor cooking was even further removed from the original kumzits. The *mangal*, a kind of barbeque typically done on a small, coal-stoked range, had been relocated to a seminatural site, that is, any available stretch of grass in the public domain, such as a public park or even a traffic island. The word *mangal* is traced to Turkish-Balkan or Arabic sources—it exists in different versions in both Farsi and Arabic, even though it is pronounced somewhat differently than in the Israeli variation. In either case, the word relates to a mobile coal grill.[23] The name change is indicative of a change in attitude toward Middle Eastern cultural products and foods and their rising status. In 1996 Askola, a school for design in Tel Aviv, held an exhibition of students' work centered around the mangal theme. The exhibit was accompanied by a catalog that included several scholarly articles contemplating the social history of the mangal phenomenon from various aspects such as gender roles, ethnic affiliation, and historical roots. Several of the contributors mentioned a popular song written by Yair Nitzani in 1986 as an important agent in assimilating the word *mangal* into the Hebrew language. It is titled "Shir ha-Mangal" (The mangal song):

*Yes, we've ventured afar,*
*loaded the car,*
*gone to the picnic—picnic.*

*I prepared the skewers,*
*strapped in the kids,*
*picnic at Mesubim crossroads.*

*The shishlik is burning, the kaboby, bobby.*
*Wash the dishes, honey, bunny.*
*Give me a steak or a skewer, ewer,*
*and we'll sing and dance pootzi, mootzi, pootzi, mootzi. . . .*

*A few last skewers still on the grill.*
*Wave the fan, it's drying out.*
*I want a skewer in a pita—Rita. . . .*

*Every Saturday there is salad and tahini, tahini.*
*The children are burned, where is Dina, Dina?*
*You smell of garlic and onion, onion.*
*I turned out an unbelievable skewer, ewer.*[24]

Initially the mangal was seen as an exclusively Sephardic (non-Ashkenazi, mostly Middle Eastern or North African) phenomenon, but by the late 1980s it had become clear that it surpassed ethnic divisions to become an all-inclusive Israeli phenomenon, as the song above denotes. The song is unique in using the word *mangal* to indicate not the grill itself but the entire event, and it was often used this way beginning at this time. The grilling of meat is just part of the experience, which is clearly described as a family affair and includes some travel, but in this case not to a forest or a shore but rather to a place near a central, busy intersection (Mesubim Junction in Tel Aviv). The song also implies a gender division in which the man is responsible for the grilling while the woman looks after the children and washes the dishes.[25] It offers some indication as to the other foods associated with the mangal, such as pita bread and tahini. These accompaniments indicate the Middle Eastern heritage of the mangal; yet, as food writer Dalia Lamdani points out, unlike the typical Arab grill, which uses fresh lamb, Israelis favor beef and chicken and often use frozen kebabs and steaks.[26]

The centrality of beef is another element that further removes the mangal from its kumzits ancestor. The kumzits thrived in a time of economic hardship and relied, as discussed above, on "found" food, mostly vegetables and fruits. Food was not the kumzits's focus, and meat, a luxury even in the dining room, was not even considered. The mangal, on the other hand, flourished in a time of economic stability that included a higher standard of living and a tolerance of, if not an outright search for, individual pleasures. Meat consumption was one of the ultimate symbols of prosperity and as such became central to the mangal event. Accordingly, the focus was not so much on the quality of the finished product as on the quantity of meat served.

According to Iris Kalka's contribution to the Askola exhibition catalog, the mangal is a middle-class and lower-middle-class phenomenon more than an ethnic one.[27] It was associated with the Sephardic community in Israel partly because it became prominent during the public, outdoor Mimouna celebration. Askola's 1996 exhibit of mangal-related projects is evidence in itself of the rise in status of the mangal in the 1990s and of the non-Ashkenazi ethnic groups and their cultural products within Israeli society.

## Around the Stainless-Steel Frying Pan

In recent years, food has enjoyed a constantly rising status and increased prominence in Israeli society. The abundance of quality restaurants, the vast selection of exotic ingredients, and the proliferation of cooking shows on television reflect the growing interest in cooking and eating and the growing knowledge and sophistication of the Israeli consumer. These manifest themselves in outdoor cooking as well. Rami Gilbo'a's 2004 book, *Salt of the Earth: Outdoor Cooking with the Best Chefs in Israel*, is a perfect example of this trend.[28] The book reflects not only more advanced and complex cooking methods and recipes but also a shift in the setting of the field trip: the long hikes with heavy backpacks or the short drive to an organized picnic area were replaced with excursions into nature in off-road, 4x4 vehicles. These allow the adventurous Israeli family a trip to remote corners accompanied by all the amenities and ingredients necessary for a gourmet meal. Gilbo'a describes a variety of outdoor cooking methods, from cooking over an open fire in the kumzits tradition, the "good old" mangal(!), the *fuyke* (a massive cast-iron pot, also known as a Dutch oven, that weighs around twenty pounds and is carried in a special wooden crate), the *tapaniyaki* (an iron board that also weighs around twenty pounds), and a Thai wok.[29] This variety of equipment and cooking methods indicates an ability to carry heavy equipment into "the wild," diverse international influences on Israeli society, and the full onslaught of unapologetic consumerism.

Gilbo'a's cookbook originated in a magazine column intended for owners of 4x4 vehicles. The magazine's target audience is affluent, with money to spare on exotic ingredients and tools. The cookbook indicates the resurgence in the status of outdoor cooking. This time around, the food itself is central to the experience, and the focus is on quality, not quantity. The author, aided by famous chefs from a variety of well-known restaurants and catering services, offers a dizzying array of recipes, from falafel, lamb chops, and hamburgers to Thai noodles, chicken tikka with chutney, paella, and miso soup with seaweed. In place of the ubiquitous coffee cooked in the nostalgic finjan, Gilbo'a offers methods for brewing espresso or cappuccino to finish off a satisfying meal.[30] These recipes indicate both the shift to a capitalist—consumerist society in which individual pleasures are happily indulged and the openness to a variety of international influences and cultures.

This latest kumzits metamorphosis is significant in the context of a discussion of Zionism because despite the flexible nature of the kumzits phenomenon—its ability to incorporate influences from both within and without—it remains an important marker of Israeli identity. It is prominent during Yom ha-Atzmaut (Independence Day) celebrations and an important part of both youth culture and family life. In all its variations it has remained located in a public, natural setting. This unbreakable link with nature and the land enforces Israelis' ties to the physical land of Israel, thus embodying the Zionist ethos in the most concrete manner.

The centrality of outdoor cooking, as well as the rising status of the Sephardic community in Israel, can be seen from a different angle in the transformation of the Moroccan Mimouna celebration in Israel. The shift in the role and status of the mangal, mentioned above, can be better explained in the context of this larger event.

### THE MIMOUNA CELEBRATION

Until the recent arrival of the FSU immigrants, the Moroccans were the largest Jewish ethnic group in Israel. Most of them arrived during the mass immigration in the 1950s and early 1960s and encountered a difficult situation in a young country that was not equipped to absorb the large numbers of new immigrants, resulting in a housing shortage and unemployment. They also encountered great pressure from the hegemonic, established community to abandon their Diasporic traditions and beliefs in favor of a new, unified (Western and secular) culture.[31]

Negotiating new and old affiliations and identities is complicated for any immigrant. In the case of the Moroccan community in Israel, the bridging of these multiple identities was complicated further by the negative associations projected onto Arabic culture by Jewish-Israeli society, as well as by the assertion that the immigrants had to find more in common with their fellow Ashkenazi Jews than with their former Muslim compatriots. Focusing on the Mimouna celebration and the changes they have undergone offers insight into the changes in perception and attitude of the Moroccan community toward their culture of origin, as well as toward Israeli society. Food plays an important role in the Mimouna. With the transplantation to Israel, both the role of food within the festivities and the actual foodstuffs have gone through some changes that illuminate not only the position of the celebrants themselves but also their status within Israeli society.

The Mimouna—a Moroccan Jewish festival that takes place at the end of the Passover holiday—is a celebration of spring and renewal whose origins are somewhat vague. The Mimouna festivities were restored in Israel as mass celebrations in the mid-1960s with some significant variations on the original customs observed in the Arab country of origin (mostly Morocco, but also to some extent Algeria, Libya, and Tunisia). These celebration have gone through some significant transformations in Israel over the past decades, offering an example of the transmutation of a unique ethnic festivity into a national holiday.

An abundance of sweet delicacies typically greets guests to the Mimouna celebration. Tables are laden with plates of stuffed dates, honey and butter cookies, almond nougat, sweet crepes, fruit, nuts, and jam, a wealth of meticulously presented sweet treats that have taken days to prepare. The women of the house often prepare a great part of this feast in advance of Passover and then freeze and "sell" it to non-Jews to be "bought back" after the holiday at the end of the ban on leavened bread.

The first leavened bread consumed after the Passover holiday and the abstention from all leavened bread products was *mufleta*. One of the central dishes of the Mimouna table, the mufleta is a crepe coated with honey and butter. In one description of Mimouna customs from Israel, displaying yeast on the holiday table is said to symbolize the immigration (*aliya* in Hebrew—literally, "raising") of Moroccan Jews to Israel and the resulting "improvement of their condition."[32] But according to other sources, yeast appeared as one of the symbolic foods of the Mimouna celebration long before immigration to Israel, often in connection with the interaction with Arab neighbors. Claudia Roden writes in *The Book of Jewish Food* that the mufleta invokes Israel by being served with honey, butter, and milk, introducing the connection to the "land of milk and honey," which predates the immigration to Israel and therefore seems more plausible.[33]

Other food products appear on the Mimouna table to symbolize plenty and good fortune in the coming year: live fish in a bowl of water or whole fish on a bed of lettuce, a plate of flour with seven (or five, depending on the source) green bean pods (or green fava beans and/or coins), sheaves of grain, trays of fruit such as oranges and apples, nuts and almonds, milk, and other pastries and dairy foods. All the food is sweet (no salty or sour dishes) to symbolize plenty and happiness in the coming year. Fertility, renewal, and good fortune are some of the central themes of this springtime celebration.

One description of some Mimouna customs in Morocco reads:

> On the last day of the [Passover] holiday, in the afternoon, we go to buy from the Muslims barley stalks, which we wrap around the lamps, mirrors, and clocks in the room. We buy roses and orange blossoms to perfume the table. . . . We visit our relatives and upon entering wish them "May you prosper and be happy." We kiss their hands, and they give us sour or sweet milk and say, "Take this and begin with this (begin the year with luck); you will prosper and be happy." . . . We visit the rabbis, bow to them, and kiss them. They bless us and touch our foreheads with green beans soaked in milk. When we leave, the rabbis give us dates, and we kiss their hands. . . . Those who have a fiancée go that night to her house to eat dumplings with fresh butter, milk, and honey.[34]

Though not mentioned here, it was common to spend the day outdoors at a picnic in a garden, in a wood, or near a spring. Another custom described in several sources is receiving some dairy products and yeast from Muslim neighbors, as well as giving them certain Jewish dishes (one source mentioned egg and meat pie, matzoh, and salad).[35] The gift of yeast enabled the Jews to begin preparing bread immediately following the Passover holiday.

Several theories attempt to explain the origins of this holiday: it is not a religious festival but rather an ancient folk celebration and therefore spawned many variations in the related customs and many interpretations as to the reasons behind them. One of the points all the theories agree on is that the celebration's origins are unclear, and so is its meaning in the social context. Some of the interpretations offered by scholars involve a wish for *geula* (redemption) in the future, an association with a marriage or engagement celebration, or the strengthening of the relationship with the Muslim community. Muslims have a special role in supplying certain products to their Jewish neighbors, and Jews sometimes dress up as Muslims on this holiday.[36]

### The Public Face of the Mimouna

After immigration to Israel, the Moroccan community continued to celebrate the Mimouna in the family setting, but in the mid-1960s the Israeli version seems to have picked up on the custom of going out into nature and picnicking, and it changed from a family event into a community festival. The custom of going to visit private homes and serving visitors sweets still remained, but because of the public nature of the outdoor celebrations, they became the element most clearly associated with the Mimouna for Israelis of other ethnicities. In order to be familiar with the other customs, one had to be invited to a Moroccan home for the holiday. The foods served in the outdoor celebrations were somewhat different, mainly because of the inclusion of barbecued meat and a host of foodstuffs associated with it, whereas what was served in the homes was a variety of sweets, baked goods, and dairy.

All cultural products of non-Ashkenazi descent had suffered from the Israeli Ashkenazi community's Western paternalism and fear of "Levantinization" of their culture. David Ben-Gurion said in 1962: "We do not want Israelis to become Arabs. It is our duty to struggle with the Levantine spirit that corrupts people and societies. We have to preserve the authentic Jewish values crystallized in the Diaspora."[37] In 1965 he said of the Moroccan Jews: "The Jews from Morocco are not educated. Their customs are Arabic. . . . Perhaps in the third generation something different will emerge from the Oriental Jews. But I do not see it happening yet. . . . I don't want to see the Moroccan culture here."[38] Zeev Jabotinski, from the other end of the political spectrum, wrote, "We, the Jews, have nothing in common with the Orient. As long as the untutored masses of our people remain close to the relics of their Oriental past, we must force them away from [it]. . . . [W]e must, today and tomorrow, extirpate from the Jews of Eretz Israel all traces of the Oriental soul."[39] Ella Shohat wrote of the struggle of non-Ashkenazi Jews in Israel to retain any sense of their cultural heritage: "The pervasive notion of 'one people' reunited in their ancient homeland actively disauthorized any affectionate memory of life before the state of Israel."[40] Shohat wrote that the pattern of discrimination against non-Western culture within Israeli society touches on every aspect of life, from immigration policy to governmental food subsidies. She states that the cultural and historical links the Sephardim shared with the Arab world "threatened the conception of a homogeneous nation akin to those on which European nationalist movements were based" and that secular Zionism was trying to promote.[41] The Sephardim were taught in Israel to see the Arabs as the "other" and thus also their own culture and history.[42]

How is this cultural climate reflected in the Mimouna celebration, a distinctly Jewish tradition that is nonetheless also rooted in the Arabic (non-Western/European) Diaspora? In looking at the history of the Mimouna in Israel, several changes are immediately apparent, such as the shift in focus to public, outdoor festivities and Ashkenazi Jews filling the role of Moroccan Arabs.

A newspaper article from 1973 describes the Mimouna celebration under the title "A Picnic called Mimouna": "Immigrants from Morocco will pour tomorrow from all corners of Israel to the Matzleva Valley in Jerusalem to take part in the Mimouna celebrations. . . . [T]here will be delicacies such as only Moroccan descendents can make." The article traces the history of the event, which started eight years earlier. In 1966, the first year of the event, the celebrations took place in Hertzel Forest and included three hundred immigrants from one Moroccan city (Fez). The following year the number of participants rose to five hundred, and it took place in Jerusalem. By its third year the celebrants numbered a thousand, and in 1973 the organizers were expecting about a hundred thousand revelers.[43] A 2015 website claims that in 2005 the celebration in Jerusalem was attended by 250,000 participants, and similar celebrations took place in sixty cities throughout Israel.[44] The public nature of the celebration is described as an attempt to transform it into a national holiday, "to bring the experience of hospitality, a tradition deeply rooted in North African culture, to all the people of Israel. . . . The festivities emphasized friendship and brotherhood among men."[45]

Several special guests were expected to attend the celebration in 1973, among them Israel's president, the minister of education, Jerusalem's mayor, and other dignitaries. These dignitaries became a fixture of these celebrations: as the political power of this community rose within Israeli society, this event became its public celebration par excellence, and political and public figures began to see it as an essential tribute. A more recent article, however, examines the current turn of events and the growing decline of the political power of the Mimouna celebration: the trend it foresees is a return to the Mimouna as a family celebration. One of the celebrants is quoted as saying, "Once, when a prime minister would come, we'd feel he was bringing honor to the Moroccans. Now we know they come for themselves, not for us."[46] The Mimouna celebrations became important as political rallies, for the Likud Party in particular, during the late 1980s. But most recently this trend too has changed, as the power of the Likud Party within this community has declined in favor of other, more extreme or religious political parties, such as Sha'as, and celebrants have become more cynical about the power of such celebrations to bridge cultural divides within Israeli society.

The organizers framed the public celebrations in Israel as a wish to transform the Mimouna into a national holiday "to increase joy, friendship, and camaraderie among all factions of the [Israeli] public."[47] The description of the celebration from the early 1970s includes some explanation about the food served (such as a detailed description of the moufleta) and details the nature of the entertainment offered: various bands, dancing troupes, and choirs, as well as a contest for the most beautiful traditional dress and the best tea set. The "feast" (*hinga*) ended with balloons and fireworks.[48] Descriptions from the 1980s, on the other hand, make a point of mentioning that the celebrations "will not only include singing and dancing but also an art exhibit and bookstalls."[49] The chairman of the organizing committee, Sam Ben-Shitrit, talked to the newspaper about the changes in the content of the Mimouna celebration that transformed it into a "culture and heritage endeavor."[50] In an interview that same month, Ben-Shitrit explained that in the past the celebrations had too many elements of a feast. The attempt that year would be to "showcase . . . [that] we are a grand Jewish *eda* [sect] with wonderful traditions and culture."[51] Ben-Shitrit spoke about the wish to show the Ashkenazi population in particular the nature of the Moroccan celebration and introduce them to the beauty of Moroccan culture. He specifically stated that one of the objectives of the celebration was to rectify the negative image of the North African community in their own eyes, as well as in the eyes of the greater Israeli society.[52] The focus of the celebrations would shift from the food (perceived as "low culture") to other cultural products such as literature and fine art.

## Mimouna in the Private Sphere

Amelia Uzeri immigrated to Israel from Morocco in 1956.[53] These days she usually celebrates the Mimouna at her daughter's house in Be'er-Sheva, where her daughter Tzila and her son-in-law (a chef) help her prepare the food for the celebration. Her other daughter and her family join them (Uzeri's two sons now live abroad). Uzeri has been cooking for the Mimouna for many years. The range of sweet pastries and confections that she has mastered is overwhelming, and her skill in their preparation is astounding: hundreds of uniform, perfectly shaped meringues and almond cookies appear to have come off an assembly line. Her repertoire includes jams and candied fruit and peel, marzipan, a variety of nuts, almond and sesame confections with caramel or chocolate, and a number of different fried dough preparations. Uzeri's mother came to Israel in 1966 and lived with her for fourteen years. She taught her many of the traditional Moroccan dishes, such as *maspan*, a very thinly rolled dough placed in special molds and filled with ground almonds, sugar, egg yolks and whole egg, and a few drops of citrus water; and *mentecaos*, powdered sugar, oil, roasted nuts, and flour shaped into round cookies with cinnamon sprinkled on top. Dates stuffed with colored marzipan and marzipan "sandwiched" by nuts or meringues with or without ground nuts are very popular, as are ground hazelnuts mixed with marzipan and dipped in chocolate or dough triangles filled with grape jam and nuts, which are then dipped in syrup. The list goes on and on.

The visual presentation is as important to Uzeri as the taste. Different nuts are better suited for different preparations, as are different types of dough or jams. For some dishes she prepares her own marzipan, for others she uses store-bought; sometimes she will use food coloring (she prefers light pink and green), and sometimes coffee adds both color and flavor. Another flavoring agent is rum (soaking vanilla beans in a bottle of rum offers additional flavor). Uzeri said that she is very happy her daughter has taken up the tradition and is intent on learning to make the dishes and celebrate the Mimouna in the way it was celebrated in Morocco. For a few years, while Uzeri and her husband lived on a kibbutz, they did not celebrate the holiday. Uzeri said she did not mind, since there were plenty of other celebrations, but when she moved to "her own home" in moshav Even-Menachem close to the northern border of Israel, she took up the practice again, as did other members of the moshav who hail from Morocco. When I asked about her feelings about the public, outdoor celebrations, she said that they are positive events because they make the holiday known to the wider public and that any happy celebration is essentially a good thing. When we talked about the origins of those celebrations, Uzeri and her husband thought they were derived from the Moroccan custom of going out for a picnic on the day following the Mimouna itself.

Uzeri and her husband recounted how, soon after they came to Israel, they went out into the field after a rain shower and brought back snails to cook with butter in the French manner. They stopped this practice later because some of their neighbors were shocked by the consumption of this nonkosher food. The more established population perceived gathering food from the field as "primitive," but the Moroccan culinary repertoire, seen in the Mimouna dishes and in everyday cooking, is much more sophisticated than the common Ashkenazi cooking. Since Moroccan cuisine was shaped by a long tradition of court cuisine and by later French colonial influences, the resulting culinary tradition was far more complex than what developed in Eastern Europe at the same time.

The transformation of the cuisine of the Moroccan community in Israel is similar to the transformation of immigrant cuisines in other countries. Krishnendu Ray, in his study of immigrant labor in fine-dining restaurants in New York, illustrates a relationship between the status of an immigrant group in the United States and the status of their cuisine. He offers Italian cuisine as an example of a cuisine that was seen as marginal and uninspiring in the late nineteenth century, while today, following the establishment of Italian Americans in American society, it is accepted and regarded as equal in status and sophistication to French cuisine.[54] Other scholars examine through a similar lens Chinese and Indian cuisine and their transformation in the West.[55] Only in the past couple of decades has Moroccan cuisine attained greater respect and appreciation in Israeli society, corresponding to the rising socioeconomic status of Moroccan descendants in Israeli society.

In a 2005 article, Hamis Aboulafia hints at what might become an interesting new shift in the "target audience" of the Mimouna celebration. Aboulafia, an Israeli Arab, was invited to the Mimouna celebration at the house of Ami Savir, a Jewish lawyer. This gesture was inspired by the custom, described above, of inviting Muslim neighbors during the Mimouna celebration in Morocco. Aboulafia reflects on this symbolic act as a small step in bringing people closer together and building trust between them.[56] This is not to say that all Mimouna celebrants in Israel have opted to invite Arabs to their homes, but it demonstrates another change in the attitude of the Moroccan community in Israel toward the celebrations: not just greater confidence and pride in their traditions but an openness to personal interpretations, finding inspiration in unique traditions and offering an updated, individual twist on those traditions.

To date, the Mimouna has not been declared an official national holiday by the Israeli government. However, the public celebrations have become more and more pervasive, encompassing not only Moroccan but also other, mostly Sephardic communities. In recent years it was declared an "optional" holiday (*yom behira*), one of several days civic workers could choose to take off (like International Workers' Day on May 1 or the ninth day of Av, the destruction of the Temple). Usually, the Mimouna is described on various Israeli government and tourism sites as a "colorful ethnic celebration," lacking the gravitas and recognition of a formal national holiday.

The shape and content of the Mimouna celebration and its role within Israeli society is an ongoing process and a reflection of the tension and constant negotiation between Israel's dominant culture and diverse ethnic influences. Every immigration wave introduces new practices and traditions that influence Israeli culture. As time passes, these traditions change and evolve as a result of the encounter with mainstream Israeli culture and the new environment. In return, these new products and traditions influence Israeli society and force it to reexamine itself, to question the meaning of the "Jewish state." As new immigrants become more established and more influential within Israeli society and their culture gains more respect, the relationship with their cultural contributions changes as well, creating a dynamic process of revaluation and reformulation, rather than a fixed definition of the nature of Israeli nationalism.

# CONCLUSION

*Nostalgia, like any form of narrative, is always ideological: the past it seeks has never existed except as narrative, and hence always absent.*

—**Susan Stewart,** *On Longing*

I am quite certain that were I living in Israel now I would not take up a research project about Israeli culture. The distance in both time and space created in me a nostalgic wish to revisit, as well as a personal interest in understanding the performance of national affiliations and the process of immigration. Conscious of the problematic nature of nostalgia as a research lens, I was happy to have a firm base in which to ground my work: looking at food in its various stages through concrete evidence offered a solid foundation in juxtaposition to the elusive and changeable signs of the nation.

The notion of immigration has taken on new meanings in the twenty-first century. People retain multiple identifications and affiliations, they travel back and forth, they stay in touch with multiple groups and locations through social media and the Internet. Immigrants sometimes maintain dual (or triple) residences and work globally in several locations, often holding on to a variety of liminal positions (student, tourist, refugee) for extended periods of time before declaring (officially or to themselves), "I am an immigrant." This more fluid identification forces us to reexamine our ideas about national affiliations. In a small country like Israel, where each immigration wave has made such an impact on the established population both materially and ideologically, a country in the process of defining itself as a nation-state, negotiating multiple demands and concerns, this change should have a significant impact, and its repercussions are still unfolding.

When I was younger and an avid science fiction reader, I thought the world would change to leave behind borders and languages in favor of global unity, but despite the intimate links across space we have forged with the aid of new information technologies, that vision seems unlikely now. National divisions seem as strong and meaningful as ever. However, individual relationships to the nation seem to have changed: less dependent on physical proximity, they are more nuanced and complex, allowing for multiple affiliations and individual interpretations. Processes of globalization have spurred scholars to question the usefulness of Nation as a concept, but I believe the past decade has shown that it is still a powerful construct—perhaps one that needs a more nuanced, flexible, process-based view.

I started working on food and foodways in Israel about fifteen years ago. When I started my research, secondary sources were few, original material was difficult to access, and, perhaps most acute, people were somewhat confused by my project. Food? Why food? It seemed a trivial area to pursue, not worthy of serious academic attention. Today, however, there is a wealth of new research, archives are more accessible and devote attention to this category, and the notion of writing about food seems, if anything, mundane. Print publications and Internet sources are engaged in a process of collecting and organizing historical material about food, reclaiming advertisements and packaging, and surveying restaurants. The culinary scene in Israel has changed as well, blossoming to support a wealth of local growers and manufacturers, creative local chefs, an abundance of foreign cuisine restaurants and ingredients, cooking schools, and television shows that cater to an educated and sophisticated audience. Even the service in restaurants has changed, becoming more professional and solicitous. A visit to Tel Aviv affords the same access to current culinary trends as does a visit to New York or London. I am proud that this project is part of this culinary revolution.

When we think of a national cuisine, our instinctive response seems to be to create a list: schnitzel, chopped vegetable salad, hummus . . . Perhaps that list corresponds to the way we think of nations more broadly: flag, national anthem, geographical borders, currency . . . But lists are limited and limiting. Understanding cuisine as a process, as a changing, adaptable construct, and with it the nation that engendered it is what I hope to contribute in this study. Food is changeable and adaptable, it travels and morphs, it plays a role in all aspects of society, in the private and the public spheres. Food products and practices are concrete and grounded in reality, their travels and changes clear and measurable. It is easy for us to accept that the potato originated in the New World, but today the potato is an indispensable part of Irish cuisine. Because food is disarming, it does not read as a product of high culture, and as such it is more readily acceptable, reflecting other, more nuanced changes.

As I have shown throughout this book, food is particularly intimately linked to the evolution of Jewish nationalism in the state of Israel. From agriculture to religion, economic changes to education, it reflects socio-economic, political, and ideological changes, and it is affected by them. It therefore offers a concrete and inclusive window to the study of a variety of aspects relating to national identity and identification.

In Israel everything seems to be accelerated: processes that should take generations happen in a decade. Due to Israel's size and circumstances, every change (an immigration wave, a war, an advertising campaign) has profound effects on the entire population and is seen and felt everywhere. Beyond these more objective parameters, Israel is still in the process of becoming. It is still trying to define the idea of Jewish nationalism (a secular concept), its definition as the "Jewish state" constantly tested—in recent years more acutely than ever, with immigration waves from Ethiopia and the FSU and with the influx of foreign workers and refugees. Israel is a perfect laboratory for thinking through questions of national identity and immigration.

Food is one of the vehicles we use to perform national, communal, ethnic, or family affiliations. It is a tangible way for us to demonstrate the most elusive constructs in our lives, like love, care, and loyalty. Foodways allow us to perform (to show and to practice) care and love for our family, ideological or moral commitment (to the environment, to a religion), affiliation with a community or an identity. The changeable and ephemeral nature of foodways allows us to constantly reexamine and negotiate these constructs and identities in our daily lives. Thus the study of food as a performance medium offers us a tangible object of study (or, rather, a tangible process) that may offer greater understanding of some of these intangible, constantly changing constructs.

# APPENDIX

## *Historical Context*

JEWISH COMMUNITY IN THE LAND OF ISRAEL BEFORE ZIONISM

Prior to the beginning of the First Aliya (immigration wave) in 1882, the Yishuv (which refers to the entire Jewish community in Palestine before 1948) numbered some twenty-six thousand people residing mainly in the urban centers. The Jewish population in Palestine at that time was known as ha-Yishuv ha-Yashan (the Old Settlement) and consisted of immigrants from both Islamic countries and European countries. These immigrants came to the land of Israel because of their religious convictions in small but consistent numbers starting in the eighteenth century. They subsisted largely on support from Jewish communities abroad (known as the *haluka*, or "handout"), most lived in an environment segregated from the Arab population, and they had no immediate political-national aspirations. Two unique ventures, Petach-Tikva, a *moshava* (capitalist settlement) established in 1878, and Mikve Israel, an agricultural school established in 1870, were early attempts at agricultural work by Jewish people in the land of Israel prior to the First Aliya.[1] They mark the seeds of the attempt to bring Jewish people out from behind the city walls and into a new, more independent existence.

*The First Zionist Congress in Basel, Switzerland (1897)*

THE FIRST ALIYA (1884–1903)

The main difference between ha-Yishuv ha-Yashan and ha-Yishuv ha-Hadash (the New Settlement), which begins roughly with the First Aliya, is that the immigrants of the First Aliya had a national awareness.[2] They saw themselves as pioneers, building the foundation for a multitude of Jewish immigrants who would follow them.[3] They established the center for the new Yishuv in Jaffa and from 1884 to 1904 founded twenty-five new agricultural settlements (*moshavot,* plural of moshava). These agricultural settlements should be distinguished from the *moshavim* (plural of *moshav*), established in the early 1920s, because the early moshavot were not structured as communes or cooperatives but as more traditional villages with private plots and hired help.

Each immigration wave can be understood in terms of the background against which the subsequent immigration wave positioned itself. One of the central differences between the Second Aliya and all prior Jewish immigration to Palestine (including the First Aliya) is the immigrants' attitude toward the Jewish religion. The new ways of negotiating Jewish nationality and Jewish religion and culture led to a new distinction between Jewish and Erez-Israeli (of the land of Israel) identification. The other important difference lies in the dominant social structure during the two periods: the immigrants of the Second Aliya tried to create a social revolution in addition to a national one, while many of the settlers of the First Aliya arrived with their families and with some capital and did not wish to disrupt the traditional family structure. These differences were reflected in the immigrants' attitude toward food and kitchen work. Since they were not attempting a social revolution, they did not need to use food as an ideologically charged tool.

The members of the First Aliya perceived agriculture as a means for achieving a new Jewish existence, but this attitude was not accompanied by the wish to create a new Jewish society, a wish that would characterize later immigrants. On the domestic front, food helped maintain the traditional family and community structure, create a sense of comfort, extend hospitality, and sometimes establish ties with the new land and neighbors.

The emphasis on self-labor ("Hebrew" labor), particularly agricultural labor, was one of the main innovations of the First Aliya.[4] Another important contribution of the First Aliya was the revival of Hebrew as the national tongue and the creation of a national educational system that advocated

Hebrew as a national language. Hebrew was to set the Jewish people apart from their neighbors and would serve to unite them with each other. Hebrew schools were created in the moshavot, and secular studies (such as mathematics) were initiated in Hebrew. Courses were offered in agriculture and in knowledge of the land and its nature, all of which aimed to establish roots in the land of Israel. Courses in physical education promoted the ideology of the new Jewish person: healthy, strong, and physically active. Finally, there was the study of the history of the land of Israel and the new Erez-Israeli literature. These changes mark a break with former immigration waves in their conscious effort to promote a national Jewish culture in the land of Israel.[5] The term *Hebrew culture* was created to distinguish it from Jewish culture in the Diaspora.

The study of secular subjects in Hebrew came as an addition to religious studies. The immigrants of the First Aliya were observant Jews, and the settlements they established had a distinctly religious character. But the members of the old Yishuv criticized the laxity of religious practice of the immigrants of the First Aliya, particularly in the moshavot, outside the more established urban centers, and controversies kept erupting between the religious governing bodies of the old Yishuv and the new settlers. The First Aliya also included the group known as the Billuyim, whose ideals were modern secular-national. They wished to create a national and social revolution based on an ideal of communal living and mutual aid and became a symbol of the entire First Aliya because they anticipated the ideology of later immigration waves. However, even the Billuyim adhered to a certain religious code and at one point, due to criticism from the old Yishuv, allowed a religious supervisor to monitor their lifestyle.[6] Even though they were a very small minority and only established one moshava (Gdera), they have come to occupy an important place in the national imagery.

The new Jewish settlers lived in close proximity to their Arab and Bedouin neighbors. The Jewish settlers learned about and adopted many of their neighbors' food products and customs out of necessity. "The Arabs bring different things for sale: milk, eggs, chickens, wood, grapes, and several kinds of fruit. Everything is sold cheap," wrote Mrs. Kalman Shlomo

Kantor to her sister-in-law.[7] Upon visiting the moshava Yesod ha-Maala, Gershon Horowitz, another member of the First Aliya, was impressed by the method of exchange that provided the settlement with a catch of fish: a Bedouin brought over the fish, and the settlers bought them for some olive oil and tobacco. Horowitz experienced his first taste of pita bread with olive oil in Yesod ha-Maala as well. He confesses that despite the enthusiasm of his hosts he had a difficult time eating it.[8] As the settlers of the First Aliya became more successful and established, they could afford to hire workers and generally preferred the more experienced and less expensive Arab workers to the new Jewish immigrants, whose lifestyle, in terms of religious observance, was questionable in the settlers' eyes. In return, the members of the Second and Third Aliyot would criticize the employment of Arab workers in the moshavot and question the First Aliya's definition of self-labor.

The adoption of Arab ways was often the result of difficult conditions in the early days of the settlements and the unavailability of more familiar products. Beyla Likerman was among the early settlers of the moshava Yesod ha-Maala. The most difficult experience for Likerman was having to watch her children go hungry or fight over a piece of bread.[9] She described the difficulty of getting flour and how, in order to economize, they had to bake pita bread as the Bedouins did instead of European-style bread. Likerman reported that one of the settlers learned the method of baking pita bread, along with other practices, from the Bedouins and taught the rest of them. They baked the bread on a *saj* (a rounded tin pan) placed directly over the fire. The flattened dough, placed on the saj, was ready in a few minutes. (The baking of the bread was considered an honored task among the Bedouin and was done by the men.)[10] Likerman's account does more than describe the local Arab and Bedouin influence on the new settlers; it highlights her position as a wife and mother and the way these roles influenced the way she negotiated the new reality in Palestine. Unlike the young, single members of the next immigration wave, many of the members of the First Aliya arrived in Palestine with their children and families.

The First Aliya ended in 1903. During its nineteen years the Jewish population in Palestine rose to fifty-five thousand, five thousand of them in twenty-five new agricultural settlements.[11] The Second Aliya, which began a year later, was highly critical of the members of this earlier wave for its "betrayal" of the ideal of self-labor.

Despite the many differences between the dominant ideology and social structure of the First and the Second Aliya, some of the seeds of the phenomenon that would be central to the character of the Yishuv in later periods were planted at this time. The immigrants of the First Aliya established the foundation for Jewish agricultural settlements and an economy centered on agricultural products. The ideal of self-labor, particularly agricultural labor, also has its roots in this period, though the precise meaning of "self-labor" would change by the next immigration wave. The concept of Hebrew culture and the revival and use of the Hebrew language as the national language is one of the central contributions of the First Aliya to Jewish culture in Palestine. Finally, even though they did not create governing bodies or push for political solutions, the immigrants of the First Aliya did have a national consciousness and a sense of laying the groundwork of life in the land of Israel for future immigrants and generations.

THE SECOND ALIYA (1904–1914) AND THE THIRD ALIYA (1919–1922)

The immigration wave known as the Second Aliya (1904–14) spawned some of the central myths and icons of Israeli society that would endure for generations. The Second Aliya created the basic structure of local government in Palestine, which was to become the basis for the later state of Israel, and produced some of the most influential leaders of the Yishuv and the state, as well as some important writers. In a sense, the members of the Second Aliya got to write history and, as a result, the historiography of the Zionist movement.

The members of this immigration wave broke with previous Jewish immigration to Palestine in their dominant socialist ideology and their new perception of the relationship between religion and nation in Jewish identity. Their ideals were developed and enhanced in the subsequent period of the Third Aliya (1919–22). Literary accounts describing the time of the Second Aliya do their part in promoting an idealized picture of this influential historical period.

The dominant ideology among the new immigrants from Eastern Europe was nationalist-socialist. They dreamed of creating a society that would be radically different in its social makeup from the Jewish existence in the Diaspora. These immigrants were named *halutzim* (pioneers), a term presenting them as the vanguard, leading the way for future immigrants to forge a new Jewish nation in the land of Israel. The *halutz* was the ideal new Jewish figure: strong, independent, and rooted in the land. Ideally presented as an agricultural worker, the halutz embodied a physical connection to the land and a new foundation for Jewish society in manual agricultural labor. The nationalist-socialist ideology implied putting the nation and the community before any one individual. It dictated a way of life that is intentionally ascetic, diminishing the importance of individual needs and comforts, among them food. Not only was the individual relegated to a subservient position in this "new order," but so was the nuclear family, which was presented as an extension of the individual—a bourgeois luxury. During the first two decades of the twentieth century, the Zionist national movement used food to subjugate the individual and the nuclear family to the greater community and the nation.

Food was reduced to the bare essentials during this period for both practical and ideological reasons. The reality the new immigrants encountered in Palestine was harsh. Food products were very limited, particularly in the more isolated new settlements. The new immigrants were unfamiliar with many of the products available to them in the new land, which, combined with the inexperience of the cooks and the inadequacy of the cooking facilities, often resulted in inedible meals. These practical conditions were easier to bear given the ideology of frugality and asceticism that characterized the Second Aliya. The Second Aliya's antibourgeois philosophy advocated setting aside individual luxuries and comforts. The pleasures of the individual, such as food and sex, were marginal compared with the greater good of society. The same applied to the nuclear family—its interests, its very existence, had to be secondary to that of the community. Food, beyond basic sustenance, was deemed a frivolity and a waste. Resources would be better spent on creating or enhancing the means of production that would contribute to the future of the nation.

*The End of the Ottoman Empire and the Beginning*
*of the British Mandate in Palestine (1918)*

THE FOURTH ALIYA (1924–1926)

By the late 1920s the Yishuv had begun to see food as a useful tool of Zionist propaganda. Nationalizing foodstuffs was one way to strengthen and legitimize Jewish national claims and to set the Jewish population apart from the local inhabitants. This transformation was largely due to the immigration wave known as the Fourth Aliya, which was comprised chiefly of immigrants from Central Europe. These immigrants were different from their predecessors in their social makeup and their ideology. The immigrants of the earlier immigration waves wished to create a drastic break with Jewish life in the Diaspora. They upheld socialist ideals and were willing to sacrifice individual needs and comforts for the sake of the future of the nation. The majority of the members of the Fourth Aliya, however, were bourgeois. The percentage of women and families was greater in this Aliya than in previous immigration waves, and the men were mostly merchants and craftsmen. The majority of these immigrants gravitated toward the urban centers and away from agricultural work. They held the view that the national home should be built "naturally," with private capital, making the "family man," small businessman, and merchant, rather than the agricultural laborer, the backbone of the new Jewish society. Merchants, farmers, and craftsmen, this model advocated, should all enjoy the prestige of the halutz. The members of the Fourth Aliya precipitated an ideological dispute in Palestine between socialist and bourgeois worldviews.[12]

The more established socialist immigrants of the Second and Third Aliyot, who constituted the dominant force in the political institutions of the Yishuv, criticized the new capitalist attitude. Moshe Lissak cites David Ijmojik, a public figure, speaking in 1926: "[There is] a proliferation of restaurants, coffeehouses, and carnal parties and dancing on the roofs. . . . [T]hey lived like this in Tel Aviv for two years, the streets busy, the restaurants full, in the coffeehouses singing, music, and dancing until two a.m."[13] In 1933 Chaim Arlozerov made a comment describing the Fourth Aliya: "[that which] raised its new flags in the commercial centers, put up signs for realty agencies, hung its store windows with colorful bills of money."[14] Despite the Yishuv's criticism, the Fourth Aliya made an impact on the ideological climate of the Yishuv, which can be seen in the way that the national movement began its active "recruitment" of the kitchen to further its political agenda. The family and individual needs became more important to Jewish society in Palestine, as did women, food, and kitchen work. Embracing food and kitchen work was a way of enlisting women to the Zionist cause.

### THE LATE 1930S AND WORLD WAR II

The Arab Revolt in 1936–38 gave local Jewish products and Jewish labor a boost, since competing local Arab products and Arab labor were not available for an extended period of time. The outbreak of World War II shortly thereafter, with its effect on transportation and food availability in Europe, forced the Yishuv to rely more on local products. Cookbook author Lillian Cornfeld writes, "The import has decreased significantly, because totzeret ha-aretz . . . has taken its place. From that aspect the war has helped totzeret ha-aretz more than . . . many years of . . . national propaganda."[15] Since local industries and products were still limited at this time, the British government established a rationing program in Palestine throughout the war years. Food became, once again, instrumental in recruiting the public's help to further a political agenda. Wartime rationing, though, was different in some significant respects from the totzeret ha-aretz campaign: it was driven by economic need and enforced by a colonial government. Several Yishuv institutions and Zionist agencies assisted the British government in "educating" the public, encouraging cooperation with the rationing program, and shunning the black market. These agencies, however, often had their own agenda, which they promoted alongside the British government's. The Zionist movement continued its attempts to create a homogeneous and united nation out of an increasingly diverse population, using food habits as an agent of transformation.

Wartime and the few postwar years leading up to Israel's independence in 1948 were times of relative prosperity for the Yishuv. Despite the difficult economic situation brought about by the war, economic conditions in

Palestine actually improved compared to earlier in the century. During the war, Palestine served as an important base for the British in their campaign in the Middle East, creating jobs for the local population and boosting local industries that produced food and supplies for the British army. This development, combined with the rising numbers of nonsocialist immigrants, helped enhance the realm of consumer goods and the attention given to food. Most of the new immigrants who arrived in Palestine during and following World War II were not dedicated halutzim and halutzot, but refugees from Central Europe, the Middle East, and North Africa. Many of them settled in the urban centers rather than in the kibbutzim and moshavim. Due to these demographic and economic changes, food matters no longer needed a cloak of scientific or national benefits to receive growing attention.

INDEPENDENCE AND MASS IMMIGRATION (1948–EARLY 1950S)

David Ben-Gurion, Israel's first prime minister, advocated the "melting pot" ideology as a necessary tool for the merging of multitudes of new immigrants who arrived in Israel during its early years with their varied languages and cultures into one culture and one nation. Ben-Gurion believed that the special circumstances of the state of Israel required adopting the melting pot consciously, as government policy.[16] The Hebrew term for this policy is *mizug-galuyot* (literally, "melding Diasporas").

Between May 1948 and the end of 1951 some seven hundred thousand new immigrants arrived in the recently independent Israel. This immigration wave was called ha-Aliya ha-Hamonit (the Mass Immigration), and it changed the demographics of Israel significantly. To understand the effect this immigration had on the local population, it is helpful to compare it with the number of immigrants who arrived in Palestine during the thirty years of British rule over Palestine—483,000 in total. During the three and a half years following independence, Israel became the primary immigration destination for the world's Jews, and its population more than doubled.[17] This immigration wave was different from those that preceded it not only in size but also in character. About half of the new immigrants came from Asia and Africa, and a major segment arrived as part of an entire community that was transferred to Israel with the assistance of the Jewish Agency and the Joint Distribution Committee (the remains of communities from the displaced persons camps in Europe, as well as the Yemenite community in 1949–50 and the Iraqi Jews in 1950–51).[18] This immigration wave included a high percentage of children and elderly people, often arriving in family groups, and a fairly low number of working-age immigrants. The formal education level of these immigrants was on the whole lower than that of the earlier immigrants, and many had lower-status professions that were often redundant in Israel. These qualities, combined with their poor knowledge of modern Hebrew, forced many of these immigrants (about 80 percent) to change their former professions and positioned them in the lower economic and social strata of Israeli society.[19] The new Israeli government was concerned about social and economic chasms opening up between the new arrivals and the existing population, particularly between immigrants from Europe and those arriving from Asia and Africa.

During the 1950s the government concentrated its efforts on supplying shelter and employment to the new arrivals.[20] The government allocated large amounts of money to projects geared toward absorbing the massive immigration productively. Needing to house and feed these immigrants, the government encouraged primarily construction and agriculture as fields that could supply both jobs and living necessities. By choosing this solution, the government was following earlier Zionist priorities designed to encourage taking literal possession of the country while creating a more diversified Jewish society that is also spiritually connected to the land.[21]

Consistent with Prime Minister David Ben-Gurion's belief that settling as much of the country as possible is an important security measure, new immigrants were housed in abandoned Arab houses, in temporary camps (*mahanot olim* and, later, *ma'abarot*), and in development towns (*ayarot pituah*). The government's primary wish was to encourage agricultural settlements for the new immigrants, but urban solutions such as the planned development towns were established in order to further certain social goals, including maximum distribution of the population, quick absorption of the immigrants, and development of industry.[22]

The government's economic policy encouraged rapid growth over cautious development. According to Yitzhak Greenberg, the government of the Labor

Party (ha-Avoda) continued its earlier policy of "economic nationalism," that is, not "rational" economic behavior designed to maximize profits. This policy manifested itself in several ways, among them an "emphasis on industrialization . . . [and] efforts to attain a higher level of self supply."[23] The government's "expansionist" policy was partly designed to help in the absorption of the massive immigration in Israel's early years, in addition to developing Israel's economy and expanding its economic basis. These objectives combined with security problems, the great financial drain of the War of Independence, and socialist ideology to produce a government with unusually deep involvement in the economy.[24]

The trend of an improving economic situation and rising standard of living in Palestine was interrupted with the Declaration of Independence in 1948. The mass immigration and the War of Independence took their toll, and the new Israeli government had to take certain steps to cope with the economic crisis. The main government initiative was implementing a rationing program (Zena).

*The 1950s and Early 1960s*

Toward the end of this decade the melting pot ideology was slowly replaced by a more pluralistic approach. The 1950s began with a big public debate around the question of whether to accept monetary compensation from Germany as some form of atonement for the Holocaust (1952). The decade ended with an even greater and more violent breach of national "harmony" with the Wadi Saleeb Riots (1959), an outbreak of violence by frustrated Moroccan youths in one of Haifa's neighborhoods. They complained of social injustice and limited opportunities due to their ethnic background. These riots were the culmination of growing unrest among the new immigrants, especially in the ma'abarot, and led for the first time to public awareness in Israel of the link between ethnic divisions and socioeconomic situation and opportunities (or lack thereof). This period also marks the beginning of the break between the non-Ashkenazi groups and the Labor Party (the governing party at the time and throughout Israel's early decades).

During the late 1950s and early 1960s the feeling of imminent danger and threat to Israel's existence abated somewhat. The initial chaos of the mass immigration during the state's first years gave way to a slower, more manageable pace of immigration. For the first time in its short history, Israel was free of the rationing program. The developing economy led to a rise in national wealth and in the standard of living, which was accompanied by a burgeoning middle class and greater inequality in the distribution of wealth and a less idealized view of manual labor and farming as white-collar jobs gained in prestige.[25] Israel became a consumerist culture prepared to indulge individual comforts and pleasures and "nonproductive" interests, such as fashion and entertainment. However, a greater correspondence between class and ethnic division appeared in this period. The growing unrest and self-awareness among new immigrants from Middle Eastern and North African countries and their complaints of inequality forced Israeli society to reexamine the prevailing ideology of obliterating difference in favor of a unified (Ashkenazi, i.e., European) culture. That unrest and self-awareness also created the cracks in the idealization of the government.

The 1960s brought not only tolerance for the individual but also open critique of the government. One of the landmarks of the deterioration of the absolute authority of the government and the growing power of the Israeli media as a voice of criticism and condemnation was the Lavon scandal (*parashat* Lavon), which was exposed in 1954 but was kept secret (under censorship) until 1960. This was a political scandal involving the discovery of an espionage plot to deploy bombs in some American sites in Egypt and to blame the National Egyptian movement for them in order to sabotage American-Egyptian relations. A widescale investigation in Israel had a difficult time finding the person responsible for the order and resulted in firing Pinhas Lavon, the minister of security. This scandal marked the beginning of leaks from government meetings to the press, the rising power of the newspapers and radio, and the faltering of the power of the political parties, which until then had been able to infiltrate all aspects of everyday life.[26]

Despite these far-reaching changes, official ideology largely prevailed, although there was a shift in priorities. The government and related organizations began to focus their efforts on presenting a "united front" and forging symbols that would project an Israeli identity, rather than creating actual unity within the country, as they had in the previous decade. This "outward" orientation is apparent in the realm of food both in the development of the tourist industry and in the related infrastructure (such as hotels, restaurants, and El Al Airline). These institutions looked abroad for models of behavior (to France and Italy for the upscale dining experience and to the United States for modern supermarkets and convenience foods).

Cookbooks, newspaper columns, and advertisements from this period display an increased awareness of the world outside Israel. Modern inventions and conveniences, sophisticated table manners and presentation, and greater tolerance of difference all derive from the new outward orientation of these publications. The rise of professional cookery indicates a similar trend. Fine hotels and restaurants, catering mostly to tourists, hired professional chefs from Europe. They considered sophisticated and kosher food two necessary requirements. The development of "culinary icons," products or phenomena that were created and shaped in order to convey a unified portrait of Israel, are further examples of how food began to function as a symbol of national culture rather than as a tool in its crafting.

## THE LATE 1960S AND 1970S

The effects of the 1967 Six-Day War on Israeli society were numerous and varied, but it appears that for many Israelis this war was somehow life affirming. The first two decades following independence were a time of economic hardship and social dilemmas, security was a prime concern, and the nation's future was in constant peril. Now, for the first time, there was a sense that immediate danger had been alleviated and that more time and resources could be directed at making life better, rather than preserving one's existence. With the improvement in the economic situation and the rise in the standard of living, Israelis began to venture outside their country as tourists. With their country's survival apparently assured they could allow themselves to look outward and to embrace some influences from Europe and the United States that in earlier times had been shunned in the struggle to fashion an independent and new Jewish state. It was a time for the individual: the trends that budded in the 1960s were now blossoming.

Anita Shapira marks the 1970s as the period when Israel "retreat[ed] from the idea of negating exile."[27] The boost in national confidence and security was accompanied by a growing number of native-born Israelis, for whom Israel was an actual *moledet* (homeland, literally "birthplace") and who had no knowledge or nostalgia for any Diaspora. The world outside Israel could now be explored and imported safely. This attitude was enforced by the incentive of the close economic ties with the United States that were formed following the 1967 war.

Shlomo Swirski makes a case for 1967 as a major turning point for Israeli economic policy for several reasons. Swirski argues that Israel's geopolitical position changed following the Six-Day War. This change manifests in three arenas. First, Israel became a preferred partner of the United States and its strategic anchor in the Middle East. This partnership led to generous financial and military support for Israel that allowed it to greatly increase its security budget. Second, the Israeli government elected to retain control of the territories that were seized during the fighting (the West Bank, East Jerusalem, the Gaza Strip, and the Golan Heights) and establish its control through Jewish settlements within them. Finally, Israel, reinventing itself as a military power, decided to develop military industries significantly.[28] The generous financial support from the United States allowed Israel to increase its military budget significantly while maintaining and even increasing the standard of living of its citizens. Military products quickly became Israel's most important export industry and overtook agricultural products as Israel's major export. During the 1970s products of the military industry reached 25 percent of Israel's export, causing a comparable rise in the number of employees in the military sector.[29]

The development of industries for the mass production of utilitarian objects (such as textiles and food), which were the focus of Israeli industry during the 1950s and 1960s, served to create jobs for the multitude of new immigrants and required a low degree of skill, with comparably low pay and status. The new focus on military industries and their derivatives was an opportunity for Israel to break into new world markets, yet these products benefited only a small segment of Israeli society: mostly highly skilled labor, including engineers, scientists, technicians, computer operators, and graduates of certain military units. The military associations and high degree of specialized expertise required caused women, Israeli Arabs, and older factory workers from the more traditional industries to remain, for the most part, outside the nascent elite group that benefited from the new developing industry and related services and, later, from the blossoming high-tech industry, which was a kind of by-product of the military work.[30] The increased buying power, ability to travel, and exposure to the outside world that characterize this period were mostly limited to a small segment of the Israeli population, although they trickled down into and affected the broad Israeli population in different ways. One of the results of these new industries is indeed a widening social and economic gap within Israeli society.

During the 1970s more public funds were directed toward cultural projects: the Ha-Bima Theater building was renovated in 1970, the Jerusalem Theater building was inaugurated in 1971, and the Tel Aviv Museum of Art opened that same year. At the same time, more funds were being directed toward establishing settlements in the new territories instead of the not-yet-quite-established development towns and new immigrant settlements and their infrastructure. The 1970s also saw an explosion of Israeli cookbooks, some of them seminal works that have left their mark and are used in almost every Israeli kitchen to this day.

The abating of the immediate threat to survival had another major effect: the emergence of critique and cynicism. Up until this time criticism or condemnation of the government's actions or of Zionist ideology in general was very rare and mostly took the form of constructive criticism. The 1970s saw the beginning of serious, unabashed satire and social protest. Hanoch Levin's play *Malkat Ambatya* (Queen of the bathtub), a satirical review comprised of short sketches that criticized and ridiculed Israeli society and government following the 1967 war, was produced and performed to general outrage in 1970; the Black Panthers' fight for the rights of non-Ashkenazi groups in Israeli society managed to influence the start of legislation on social matters such as unemployment, housing, and education in an attempt to mend some of the damage done during the period of mass immigration.

In 1973 the Yom Kippur War disrupted the sense of security. The mounting criticism of the government's actions eventually caused the most significant political change in Israel: the rise of the Likud Party into power in

1977 with Menachem Begin as prime minister. Some scholars cite the Yom Kippur War as the marker for growing doubts and criticism of Zionism in general.[31] The political change from the dominant Labor Party and its socialist ideology to the capitalist approach of the Likud Party had many economic repercussions (such as canceling the supervision over foreign currency and radically reducing subsidies for basic food products). This shift corresponded to the rise in power and influence of the non-Ashkenazi groups within Israeli society (the main supporters of the Likud Party) and the rise in the standard of living and increased buying power of Israeli citizens. This change is evident in many facets of social and cultural life in Israel. The political change also brought about the Camp David talks and the signing of the peace treaty with Egypt in 1979. Despite criticism of government actions and political repercussions, the 1970s were still a time of general consensus in Israel of the unfortunate necessity of war, of the sense that Israel's fight was for its survival and that it was a just fight, a view that would change in the following decade.

THE 1980S AND 1990S

This period, termed "post-Zionism" by several scholars, can be said to start following the War in Lebanon in 1982 and to increase in significance more recently, with the large wave of immigration from the Former Soviet Union (FSU). The roots of this ideological shift could be traced to the Yom Kippur War and the rise of the Likud Party to power, described above. The signing of the peace accord with Egypt in 1979 was followed closely by the war in Lebanon in 1982. This war spawned a wave of protests within Israeli society and a political rift that would grow over the following decades.[32]

Beginning with the late 1970s, Israel has become increasingly a Western, consumerist culture, with the United States as its most significant influence. American-style supermarkets became the preferred venue for food shopping (over small grocery stores), American fast-food chains opened branches in Israel (the first McDonald's branch was opened in 1993; today there are 180 branches throughout the country, including 50 kosher ones), and television's range and influence have increased dramatically (with the introduction of satellite and cable channels).[33]

The late 1980s and 1990s introduced new immigration waves into Israeli society. Like previous waves, these too made their mark on Israeli culture. Immigrants from both Ethiopia and the FSU forced the question of difference to the front of national thinking because the way they looked and the way they engaged with Judaism were obviously different from previous immigration waves. These immigrants' relationship with their country of origin was also unique compared to former immigration waves: they maintained close ties to their country of origin and a clear identity as separate communities within Israel. These new relationships to the nation correspond to the rise of consumer culture and capitalism and mirror the focus on diversity and individual choice that became more prevalent in Israeli culture in general.

Ethiopian immigration to Israel began in 1985. In Mivtza (Operation) Moshe, seven thousand Ethiopian Jews were flown to Israel; and in 1991 (in Mivtza Shlomo), fifteen thousand more. These Jewish Ethiopians are known as Falashas (in Ethiopia mostly) and, more recently, as Beta-Israel. This relatively small number of immigrants was overshadowed by the mass immigration from the FSU shortly thereafter. Their marginal position within Israeli society was due to prejudice regarding their skin color and to doubts about their Jewish status. Unlike the FSU population, which includes many who do not identify as Jewish, the Ethiopians see themselves as Jewish, but their status as such is suspect in the eyes of the religious Orthodox bodies in Israel.[34] The Ethiopians were the first group of immigrants to force Israeli society to reexamine ideas about the unified nature of Jewish nationalism: by looking different, Ethiopians forced Israeli society to create room for difference within the definition of the nation.[35] Whether by choice or due to the treatment they received in Israeli society, the Ethiopian immigrants tend to sustain separate social ties and an identity as a coherent community within the broader society. Even in terms of food, no Ethiopian dish has achieved broad appeal or become part of the Israeli diet yet. Though a few Ethiopian restaurants and ingredients can be found in Israel, they mostly cater to Ethiopians. A significant number of Ethiopian immigrants maintain business relationships with their country of origin (import-export businesses of food products, music, and clothes). This too separates them from previous immigration waves and contributes to the sense of a community with dual cultural affiliations.[36]

The 1990s witnessed a major immigration wave to Israel from the Former Soviet Union. Between 1990 and 1997 more than seven hundred thousand immigrants from the FSU arrived in Israel, and in the early twenty-first century they constituted 20 percent of the Israeli population. About 80 percent of these immigrants came from the European republics (Russia and the Ukraine) and 20 percent from the Asian republics, mainly Uzbekistan. Unlike previous immigration from this area to Israel, this immigration wave hailed, to a large degree, from the urban centers (Moscow, St. Petersburg, and Kiev). These immigrants see themselves as the intelligentsia of this group and include many writers, poets, journalists, artists, and scientists, as well as architects and engineers, doctors, dentists, nurses, and teachers. This immigration wave included a large percentage of women, many of them single parents (either divorced or widowed), and a relatively low percentage of children. Many had higher education degrees and were employed in white-collar professions.[37] Their connection to Judaism was often tenuous. Most spoke no Hebrew, and many were nonreligious. Most of them defined themselves as Jewish mostly due to being defined that way by the society in their place of origin. Due to the restrictions and prohibitions on religious practice during Soviet rule, most of these immigrants did not practice any element of Jewish life in public; and due to processes of modernization, among other influences, practices in the home diminished as well. Both Larrisa Remennick and Baruch Kimmerling comment on the problematic nature of their Jewish identity: according to the Israeli Law of Return, a person may be considered Jewish for the purpose of receiving Israeli citizenship if that person's father or one of that person's grandparents was Jewish, whereas according to Jewish Halacha, only children of Jewish mothers may be considered Jewish.[38] This complicated the life of many FSU immigrants in a country that has no separation of state and religion in many areas of life (e.g., marriage and burials). This group of immigrants is different from most others in that it was spurred almost exclusively by the wish to leave the Soviet Union rather than by a wish to come to Israel. In other words, Zionism played no part in the decision to immigrate to Israel. This immigration wave resembles immigration in other parts of the world, such as in the United States, because it was a result of economic considerations, frustration, and pessimism regarding life in the country of origin rather than an ideological commitment and devotion to the new country.[39]

Another element that sets this immigration apart from previous immigration waves to Israel and links it with the immigration from Ethiopia is that it maintained close ties to the country of origin. One reason for this change is the lack of ideological motivation for migration, resulting in no particular incentive to become immersed in the new culture and society.[40] Another reason has more to do with global changes: as a result of cable and satellite television, the Internet, and the greater ease and accessibility of transportation, many immigrants maintain business ties and/or residences in their countries of origin, as well as business and family ties to other countries such as the United States and Germany. Not only did these immigrants retain physical and economic ties to their country of origin, they also maintained significant cultural elements that enforced their connection to it, such as the Russian language, separate schools, music and literature, and food practices. All these elements have resulted in a community of immigrants that, rather than working to become part of Israeli society, tries to maintain distinct social and cultural characteristics and networks.[41]

The case of Zionism is unique in this respect compared to voluntary immigration to other parts of the world in that it was very much motivated by ideological considerations, an expressed wish to become part of the Jewish nation and state. This may not have been true to the same degree for all immigrant groups, nor was it necessarily the only reason for immigration, but the wish for assimilation does characterize immigration to Israel throughout its history to a large degree. One of the prominent demonstrations of this wish is the success of Hebrew as the dominant language across all ethnic groups. Other languages, including Yiddish, French, and Arabic, were shunned and replaced by Hebrew. Today, it is no longer obvious that the goal of immigrants is to merge into the new culture and society as soon as possible. The staying power of the language from their countries of origin in both the Ethiopian and the Russian cases is a prime example of this change. It is perhaps no coincidence that the rise of these new communities coincides with greater skepticism regarding Zionist ideology within Israeli society and a change in attitude toward immigration of Israelis to other countries (earlier referred to as Yordim, literally "descending," a rare term these days).[42]

The FSU immigration had a strong impact on Israeli food practices. Their encounter with local products and habits obviously affected their own cooking and eating habits, but I wish to focus here on the reverse process and the impact on the host society. Every immigrant community always brings with it some products and ingredients from its country of origin. Some of them play a more central role in daily diet, some are important for special occasions, and some are nostalgic reminders of a different time and place. These products and dishes remain secluded, restricted to a particular ethnic group, or they cross over and gain popularity, sometimes erasing their origins in the process, to be embraced by the entire population. Perhaps the most obvious change instigated by the FSU immigrants is the greater demand for nonkosher food products in Israel. In this particular case, these food products carry a complex meaning. Since Jewish nationalism is so intertwined with religion, and since food and dietary restrictions and rituals play an important part in Jewish religion, any obvious, particularly public, breach of these restrictions and practices within the Jewish state has implications regarding the presentation of national identity. Keeping a kosher kitchen, or even the appearance of *kashrut*, was one of the hallmarks of representations of Israel to the world. It is therefore a particularly rich issue for questioning and rethinking Jewish nationalism and affiliation.

## 2000 TO THE PRESENT

The migration of asylum seekers from Eritrea and Sudan to Israel began in 2005. This latest wave of new residents enhanced the earlier influx of foreign labor migrants who arrived in Israel on temporary work visas or tourist visas, mostly from West Africa and Asia during the 1990s, and stayed past their visa's limitation in order to work and establish families in Israel. Many of these immigrants left Israel around 2000 due to policy changes. In 2005, however, the migration of refugees filled the void, and these immigrants were granted legal status and protection in Israel under international law. By 2012 there were more than forty thousand African immigrants in Israel, the largest group residing in the southern neighborhoods of Tel Aviv.[43] This group of non-Jewish immigrants has changed the ethnic and religious makeup of Israeli society and, in fact, the very landscape of Tel Aviv. They brought with them new ingredients and opened new restaurants that cater almost exclusively to other immigrants. They are the latest wave of immigration to Israel, and they present an even greater departure from the early Zionist immigrants than the Ethiopian and FSU immigrants. Their liminal status as refugees in particular raises many new questions regarding the definition of the nation. Most of their influence on the Israeli street and on the perception and image of the Israeli nation is still unclear, but looking at their negotiation of new Israeli food products and habits and those brought from their home countries may offer a window into their inroads into Israeli society. As their presence becomes more permanent and visible, the issues they raise regarding the nature of the Jewish state and the lack of separation between religious and state institutions might force far-reaching changes.

# NOTES

The author is responsible for all translations from Hebrew to English throughout the manuscript unless otherwise specified.

### INTRODUCTION

1. Bhabha, *The Location of Culture*.
2. Kalcik, "Ethnic Foodways," cited in Bell and Valentine, *Consuming Geographies*, 116.
3. Hobsbawm, *Nations and Nationalism*, 11.
4. See, for example, Bell and Valentine, *Consuming Geographies*; Ohnuki-Tierney, *Rice as Self*; Pilcher, *Que Vivan Los Tamales!*; and Trubek, *Haute Cuisine*.
5. See Diner, *Hungering for America*; and Ray, *The Migrant's Table*.
6. Diner, *Hungering for America*, 10.
7. Wheaton, *Savoring the Past*, xix.
8. Appadurai, "How to Make a National Cuisine."
9. Pilcher, *Que Vivan los Tamales!*
10. Kirshenblatt-Gimblett, "Playing to the Senses."
11. Conquergood, "Performance Studies."
12. Shavit, "Bein Uma Yotzeret Tarbut le-Tarbut Yotzeret Uma," 149.
13. Zubaida, "National, Communal, and Global Dimensions," 39–41.
14. Berkowitz, *Zionist Culture*.
15. Ben-Yehuda, *The Masada Myth*; Zerubavel, *Recovered Roots*.
16. Zerubavel, *Recovered Roots*, 8.
17. Zerubavel, *Recovered Roots*, 8–19.
18. Ben-Yehuda, *The Masada Myth*.
19. Anderson, *Imagined Communities*, 6, 11; Hobsbawm, *Nations and Nationalism*.
20. Gellner, *Nations and Nationalism*.
21. Falafel's "history" is described by several cookbook authors, including Nathan, *The Foods of Israel Today*, 70–71; and Roden, *The Book of Middle Eastern Food*, 47–48.

22. Roden, *The Book of Middle Eastern Food*.

23. Barbara Kirshenblatt-Gimblett, talk at Feast and Famine Colloquium, New York University, 21 September 2001.

24. "Bishvil Akeret ha-Bayit" (For the housewife), *Ha-Aretz*, 27 May 1940, 3.

25. *Beyond Milk and Honey*, 4.

26. Yehuda Litani, quoted in Yaniv Zach, "Nuevo-Falafel," *Ha-Aretz*, 2 November 2000.

27. Zuckerman, "Falafel." I would like to thank Eve Jochnowitz for finding and bringing this song to my attention.

28. WIZO, Department of Education, *Kakh Nevashel*, 215.

29. Cornfeld, *Ha-Mitbah ha-Meshubah*, 181.

30. Uri Guttman, interview, 10 January 1999.

31. For an example of the rumor about engine oil, see Tami Ninyo, "Ve-Lanu Yesh" (And we have), *Ma'ariv*, 30 January 1998.

32. Zach, "Nuevo-Falafel."

33. Ella Shein, quoted in Zach, "Nuevo-Falafel."

34. Levin, "Ishel and Romanechka," 187.

35. Lehman-Wilzig and Blum, *The Melting Pot*.

36. Isis Egypt, *A Taste of Egypt: Quick and Easy Egyptian Recipes*. (There are no publication details on the book itself, bought in Lebanon, but it was traced by Dalia Carmel to Palphot Ltd. in Israel.) I wish to thank Dalia Carmel for sharing these books with me and for all her help in my research for this chapter.

37. From a conversation with Daniel Bar-Tal.

38. Jodi Kantor, "A History of the Mideast in the Humble Chickpea," *New York Times*, 10 July 2002.

39. Aziz Shihab, quoted in Kantor, "A History."

40. Shihab, *A Taste of Palestine*, 103.

41. Helou, *Mediterranean Street Food*, 152.

42. Nasser, *Classic Palestinian Cookery*, 61.

43. Uvezian, *Recipes and Remembrances*, 113.

44. Ridgwell, *Middle Eastern Cooking*, 26.

### 1. PUTTING DOWN ROOTS

1. Agnon, *Temol Shilshom*, 50.

2. Agnon, *Temol Shilshom*, 79.

3. Tammuz, *Ha-Zikit veha-Zamir*.

4. Tammuz, *Ha-Zikit veha-Zamir*.

5. See Bardenstein, "Threads of Memory."

6. Mordechai Eliav, "Yichuda Shel ha-Aliya ha-Rishona—Mavo" (The uniqueness of the First Aliya—introduction), in Eliav, *Sefer ha-Aliya ha-Rishona*, 1:xi–xii.

7. Bar-Tal, "Al ha-Rishoniyut," 15–24.

8. Bar-Tal, "Al ha-Rishoniyut," xiii.
9. Etinger and Bartal, "Shorshei ha-Yishuv ha-Hadash be-Eretz Israel," 2.
10. Etinger and Bartal, "Shorshei ha-Yishuv ha-Hadash be-Eretz Israel," 17.
11. Bardenstein, "Threads of Memory."
12. Bardenstein, "Threads of Memory."
13. Some examples include the work of Ran Morin (see fig. 4), Avner Bar-Hama, Naama Orbach, Sliman Mansour, and Ednan Zbeidi.
14. Steve Stiffler's work on chicken processing in the United States, Carey McWilliams's work on migrant labor in California, and Krishnendu Ray's work on immigrant labor in the restaurant industry are a few recent examples.
15. Zerubavel, *Recovered Roots*.
16. Erel Margalit, a successful Israeli entrepreneur, is quoted in Senor and Singer, *Start-Up Nation*: "You feel like a *fallah* ('farmer' in Arabic), a farmer of high tech. . . . The new pioneering, Zionist narrative is about creating things." The quote appears in the final chapter, titled "Farmers of High Tech," 228.
17. Kimmerling, *Invention and Decline*.
18. Kimmerling, *Invention and Decline*.
19. Manya Shohat, "Bishvil ha-Dor ha-Ba" (For the next generation), a collection of letters, 29 November 1946, in *Al ha-Giva'a*, 2 October 1950.
20. Deborah Dayan, quoted in Shazar, *The Ploughwomen*, in Safir, "An Historical Perspective," 111.
21. Dayan, quoted in Shazar, *The Ploughwomen*, in Safir, "A Historical Perspective," 112.
22. Yosef Baraz, "Kalkalat ha-Oved ha-Hakla'i," *Davar*, 1 September 1925, 2.
23. Givalder, "Ba-Mitbach ha-Kibutzi."
24. Ida Friber, quoted in Erez, *Sefer ha-Aliya ha-Shlishit*, 738.
25. Tzipora Shtozin, quoted in Erez, *Sefer ha-Aliya ha-Shlishit*, 731.
26. Shoshana Bluwstein, 1940, quoted in Shilo, "The Women's Farm," 133.
27. Lapid, *Havat ha-Alamot*, 124.
28. Lea, quoted in Ofaz, *Sefer ha-Kvutsa*, 127.
29. This brochure is from 1960, but most of the songs in it date much earlier, from the 1930s and 1940s, even though the exact date is often unavailable.
30. Haim Nahman Byalik, "Ba-Gina" (In the garden), in Biribis et al., *Zemer Hen*, 53.
31. Refael Sporta, "Ginati" (My garden), in Biribis et al., *Zemer Hen*, 40.
32. A. L. Yaron, "Batzal" (Onion), in Biribis et al., *Zemer Hen*, 39.
33. Y. Karni, "Agbaniya" (Tomato), in Gorali and Samburski, *Sefer Shirim u-Manginot*, 62.
34. Sarah Levi, "Harish va-Zera" (Plowing and planting), in Goralis and Samburski, *Sefer Shirim u-Manginot*, 17.
35. Anon., "Yad le-Yad" (Hand to hand), in Goralis and Samburski, *Sefer Shirim u-Manginot*, 96.
36. Almog, *Preida mi-Srulik*, 633–40.

## 2. PATRIOTIC DISTRIBUTION

1. Lissak, "Aliya, Klita u-Binyan," 175–77, 181.
2. Bell and Valentine, *Consuming Geographies*; Ashley et al., *Food and Cultural Studies*.
3. Antebi-Yemini, "Being an Oleh."
4. The presence of foreign workers is another, more recent influence on Israel's culinary scene and marketplace. That influence is present in specialty shops and restaurants, as well as in the variety of available ingredients. This group of non-Jewish workers is also part of the growing clientele for nonkosher products.
5. Sulamith Schwartz, "Zionism in the Kitchen," *Hadassah Newsletter*, April 1940. Thank you to Eve Jochnowitz for bringing this source to my attention.
6. *Davar*, 2 June 1925, 4.
7. Igud le-Ma'an Totzeret ha-Aretz (Union for Totzeret ha-Aretz), Agricultural Department, Flyer No. 2, Coffeehouses and Eating Establishments Branch, 12 January 1936, Printed Matter Collection 12.9, Central Zionist Archives, Jerusalem (hereafter cited as CZA).
8. Igud le-Ma'an Totzeret ha-Aretz (Union for Totzeret ha-Aretz), Agricultural Department, Coffeehouses and Eating Establishments Branch, 13 November 1939, Printed Matter Collection 12.9, CZA.
9. "Survey of the Actions of the Agricultural Department of the Union for Totzeret ha-Aretz in the Second Part of 1938," Printed Matter Collection 12.9, CZA.
10. Max Yakobson, "Tafkidei Tnuva be-Shivuk ha-Yerakot" (Tnuva's duties in the distribution of vegetables), *Ha-Aretz*, 16 September 1937, 4.
11. Roland Barthes, "Steak and Chips," in Barthes, *Mythologies*; Ohnuki-Tierney, *Rice as Self*.
12. Igud le-Ma'an Totzeret ha-Aretz (Union for Totzeret ha-Aretz), "An Exhibit of Food, Agriculture, and Groceries," 1939, Printed Matter Collection 12.9, CZA.
13. Miryam Baraz, "La-Haverot ba-Ir!" (To the comrades in the city!), *Devar ha-Poelet*, nos. 4–5, 12 July 1936, 75.
14. Cover of *Devar ha-Poelet*, nos. 11–12, 1 March 1936.
15. Ytschak Ziv-Av, "Boycott Nationalism," in *Ha-Boker*, 31 October 1935.
16. Ziv-Av, "Boycott Nationalism."
17. Schwartz, "Zionism in the Kitchen."
18. *Ha-Tzofe*, 8 April 1945, 3.
19. *Ha-Tzofe*, 19 April 1945, 5.
20. See Bentley, *Eating for Victory*.
21. Lakerda (dried bonito fish) was a popular, cheap protein substitute that appeared often in recipes created during wartime and later, as well as in the time of Zena rationing following Israel's independence.
22. *Tafritim u-Mirshamim Lefi Shitat ha-Nekudot* (Menus and recipes according to the point system), November 1942, F49-1340, CZA.

23. WIZO, *Tzunatenu li-Sha'at Herum le-Hodshei ha-Kayitz* (Our nutrition in a time of emergency in the summer months), June 1940, F49-1340, CZA.

24. Bentley, *Eating for Victory*, 66.

25. Bentley, *Eating for Victory*, 66.

26. "Agira" (Hoarding), *Olam ha-Isha*, no. 128, 19 April 1948, 10.

27. "Agira," 10.

28. *Ha-Aretz*, 27 April 1949, 1.

29. *Ha-Aretz*, 27 April 1949, 1.

30. See Bentley, *Eating for Victory*, 16–17.

31. Cornfeld, *Ma Avashel*, 8.

32. Cornfeld, *Ma Avashel*, 8.

33. Ziona Katinski-Rabao, "Tzunat 'Bimkom'" ("Instead-of" nutrition), *Devar ha-Poelet*, no. 12, year 15, 30 December 1949, 370.

34. Lillian Cornfeld, "Mediniyut ha-Tzuna ve-ha-Isha ha-Tzarkhanit" (Nutritional policy and the woman consumer), *Ha-Aretz*, 2 May 1950, 3.

35. Cornfeld, "Mediniyut ha-Tzuna," 3.

36. Anon., "La-Isha ve-la-Bayit" (For the woman and home), *Ha-Aretz,* 6 June 1950, 3.

37. Anon., "Tafritim la-Hag" (Menus for the holiday), *Ha-Boker*, 30 March 1950, 3.

38. Daniella, "Yom Hag Beli Manot Hag" (A holiday without holiday rations), *Ha-Boker*, 30 April 1950, 3.

39. Dov Yosef, introduction to Cornfeld, *Ma Avashel*.

40. Cornfeld, *Ma Avashel*.

41. Cornfeld, *Ma Avashel*, 15.

42. Ya'akov Lishanski, interview with the author, Haifa, December 1998.

43. Lillian Cornfeld, "Tafritim u Matkonim" (Menus and recipes), *Ha-Aretz*, 14 February 1950.

44. Aliza Holdheim, "Ta'arukhot Shel Mazon" (Food shows), *Ha-Aretz*, 30 May 1950, 3.

45. Holdheim, "Ta'arukhot Shel Mazon," 3.

46. Summary of Report by WIZO, Department of Education, 1948–49, F49-2940, CZA.

47. Tikva, "Reshamim mi-Ta'arukhat ha-Mazon" (Impressions from the food show), *Ha-Boker*, 23 February 1950, 3.

48. Tikva, "Reshamim," 3.

49. Tikva, "Reshamim," 3.

50. Tikva, "Reshamim," 3.

51. Halter, *Shopping for Identity*.

52. Ashley et al., *Food and Cultural Studies*.

53. Bell and Valentine, *Consuming Geographies*.

54. Super-Sal advertisement, early 1960s, Binyamina Gallery, Tel Aviv.

55. See www.shufersal.co.il, accessed 16 May 2007.

56. Rivka Grinker, "'Supermarket' ba-Aretz?" ("Supermarket" in Israel?), *Devar ha-Poelet*, no. 12, 23 December 1957.

57. Bat-Oren, *365 Shulhanot Arukhim*.

58. Luntz and Livingston, *Mass Consumption*, cited in Ashley et al., *Food and Cultural Studies*, 109.

59. Yael Gross, "Supermarket and Makolet," *Ma'ariv*, 30 January 1998.

60. According to several websites (e.g., Mapa.co.il and 2Eat), the number of kosher restaurants in Israel in 2010 was around 2,000 (the numbers vary from 1,800 to 2,300), no more than 25 percent of the total number of restaurants in Israel. This figure, however, does not include hotel restaurants. I was not able to obtain official government data to support this information. This is not the place to elaborate on the variety and degrees of kosher-keeping schools. Kosher, in this context, will broadly refer to *not* consuming pork and seafood products (other than fish with scales) and *not* mixing dairy and meat products in the same meal.

61. Moshe Gerti, interview with the author, Kibbutz Mizra, 5 January 2007.

62. Chicken schnitzel is considered by many to be the Israeli food par excellence: a breaded and fried chicken cutlet is the local, budget version of the Viennese veal schnitzel. Since the Arab population does not eat pork either, the company has developed special products for that market, such as a type of mortadella without pork fat and other products that do not include pork.

63. Ze'ev Ben-Gal (Zibon), interview with the author, Rosh ha-Nikra, Israel, 5 January 2007.

64. See www.tivtaam.co.il, accessed 2 May 2007.

65. Unlike earlier examples, such as Amos Keinan's cookbook from the late 1960s, discussed further in chapter 4.

66. Remennick, *Russian Jews*.

67. Bell and Valentine, *Consuming Geographies*, 77.

68. Bernstein and Carmeli, "Food for Thought."

### 3. KITCHEN LESSONS

1. Izraeli, "The Zionist Women's Movement," 93.

2. Izraeli, "The Women's Workers' Movement," 185.

3. Aliza Shidlovelski, quoted in Habas, *Sefer ha-Aliya ha-Shniya*, 557.

4. Izraeli, "The Zionist Women's Movement," 95; see also notes 3–6.

5. M. Baraz, Y. Zenter, and R. Machnimit, quoted in Blum, "Ha-Isha be-Tenuat," 39–40.

6. Givalder, "Ba-Mitbah ha-Kibutzi."

7. R. Bonik, "Al Mitbahei ha-Poalim," *Davar*, 22 August 1925, 4.

8. Bonik, "Al Mitbahei ha-Poalim."

9. B.B., quoted in Shazar, *The Ploughwomen*, in Safir, "An Historical Perspective," 6:113–14.

10. N. Gerdi, quoted in Erez, *Sefer ha-Aliya ha-Shlishit*, 534.

11. Feldman, *No Room of Their Own*, 30.

12. See Bernstein, *Pioneers and Homemakers*; Izraeli, "The Zionist Women's Movement"; Blum, "Ha-Isha be-Tenuat ha-Avoda"; and Rosen, "Tmurut be-Ma'amadan."

13. Near, *The Kibbutz Movement*, 53–54.

14. Near, *The Kibbutz Movement*, 51.

15. Ziona Katinski, "Instruction in the Kibbutz Kitchen," in *Ten Years of Guidance*, WIZO (in English) (Tel Aviv: WIZO, 1938).

16. Katinski, "Instruction."

17. "Din ve-Heshbon al ha-Matzav ha-Kalkali ve-ha-Senitary Shel ha-Poalim ha-Ivriy'im ba-Moshavot" (A report on the economic and sanitary state of the Hebrew workers in the moshavot), June 1926, DD2.12, CZA.

18. "Din ve-Heshbon al ha-Matzav."

19. Givalder, "Ba-Mitbah ha-Kibbutzi."

20. Alfa, *Anu Mevashlim*.

21. Alfa, *Anu Mevashlim*, 79.

22. Alfa, *Anu Mevashlim*, 11.

23. Haifa Experiment Group, "Torat ha-Hazana" (The science of nutrition), *Davar*, 25 August 1925.

24. WIZO, "Report," n.d., F49-2184, WIZO, Advertising Department: Articles 1929–31, CZA.

25. A. Yaffe, "Excerpts from a Talk at the 10th Anniversary Reunion," in *Eser Shnot Hadrakha* (Ten years of instruction) (Tel Aviv: WIZO, 1936), F41-134, CZA.

26. Hadassah, Children's Welfare Program, 1939, File RG 171, Hadassah Archive, New York (hereafter cited as HA).

27. A. Chahanski, "Yahasenu El Avodat ha-Bayit" (Our attitude toward housework), *Ha-Isha*, no. 8 (1927): 26–28, F49-3161, CZA.

28. Chahanski, "Yahasenu El Avodat ha-Bayit," 26–28.

29. Tila Poper, "Keitsad Linhog be-Bishul Yerakot" (How to cook vegetables), *Ha-Isha*, no. 3 (1929): 25, F49-3161, CZA.

30. WIZO, Department of Education, F49-1344, CZA.

31. Esther Rozov-Uzieli, "Li-She'elat Hadrakhat ha-Isha be-Meshek ha-Bayit" (On the question of instructing women in home economics), *Ha-Isha*, no. 8 (1927): 25, F49-3161, CZA.

32. WIZO, Department of Education, "Report 1954–1955," F49-2184, CZA.

33. Shochat, "Sepharadim in Israel," 24.

34. Lissak, "Ha-Mahapekha ha-Demographit-Hevratit," 24–32.

35. Lissak, "Ha-Mahapekha ha-Demographit-Hevratit."

36. Shochat, "Sepharadim in Israel," 22.

37. Levenstein, *Revolution at the Table*, quoted in Pilcher, *Que Vivan los Tamales!*, 93–94.

38. WIZO, Department of Education, "A Report on the Activities of the Department for Nutrition and Home Economics Instruction, 1950–1951," F49-1340, CZA.

39. Mina Meyir, "Hadrakha Bein Olim" (Teaching among olim), lecture given at a conference for WIZO's Institute for Nutritional Guidance, 28 June 1950, F49-2941, CZA.

40. Meyir, "Hadrakha Bein Olim."

41. Simha, "From the Notebook of an Instructress," WIZO Publicity Department, no. 462, April 1954, F49-2941, CZA.

42. Simha, "From the Notebook."

43. Almog, "It's Not Just a Game."

44. Mrs. Granouvsky, "Report on Child Welfare, February 1946" (in English), File RG 23, HA.

45. Granouvsky, "Report."

46. M. Simconith, "Eating a Hadassah Lunch" (in English), 1920s, reprinted from *Devar ha-Poelet*, File RG 171, HA.

47. Simconith, "Eating a Hadassah Lunch."

48. "Cooking Exam—Eighth Grade," Haifa, 1939, RG 5, box 2, HA.

49. Minutes of the National Board Meeting, 26 December 1945, File RG 23, HA.

50. Cornfeld, *Israeli Cookery*, 12.

51. Yehudit Hitron, interview with the author, Tel Aviv, 20 August 2000.

52. E. Rigger, introduction to Bromberg, *Tzunatenu*, v.

53. Hitron, interview.

54. Rigger, introduction, viii.

55. Rigger, introduction, viii.

56. Bromberg, *Tzunatenu*, 117–18.

57. Bromberg, *Tzunatenu*, 118.

58. Shimon Reshef, "National Aims and Educational Policy," *Jerusalem Quarterly* 20 (Summer 1981): 99.

59. Reshef, "National Aims."

60. Ministry of Education and Culture, School Curriculum, Seventh Grade, Jerusalem 1963, 8.123/14, 73–74, Archive for Jewish Education in Israel and the Diaspora, Tel Aviv University.

61. Ministry of Education and Culture, School Curriculum, Seventh Grade.

62. Ministry of Education and Culture, School Curriculum, Eighth Grade, Jerusalem 1963, 8.123/14, 86, Archive for Jewish Education in Israel and the Diaspora, Tel Aviv University.

63. Ministry of Education and Culture, School Curriculum, Eighth Grade.

64. Hitron, interview.

65. Hitron, interview.

66. Peled, "Education," 391.
67. Ministry of Education and Culture, Supervision of Home Economics, *Matkonim le-Ugiyot ve-le-Manot Shonot* (Recipes for cookies and different dishes), a brochure for school cafeterias, 1967.
68. Hobsbawm, *Nations and Nationalism*, 141–42.
69. Hobsbawm, *Nations and Nationalism*, 141–42.
70. Bavly, *Minhagei ha-Akhila*, 5–7.
71. Bavly, *Minhagei ha-Akhila*, 9.
72. Bavly, *Minhagei ha-Akhila*, 10.
73. Bavly, *Minhagei ha-Akhila*, 18–20.
74. Bavly, *Tzrikhat Mazon*.
75. Bavly, *Minhagei ha-Akhila*, 25.
76. Almog, *Mat'amei Israel*, 6.
77. Almog, *Mat'amei Israel*, 7–8.
78. Almog, *Mat'amei Israel*, 7–8.
79. Almog, *Mat'amei Israel*, 9.
80. Almog, *Mat'amei Israel*, 9.
81. Almog, *Mat'amei Israel*, 10.
82. Almog, *Mat'amei Israel*, 25.

### 4. THE VIRTUAL KITCHEN

1. Meyer, *Eikh le-Vashel*. This is one of the earliest published cookbooks from Palestine. Only small, single-subject brochures and some recipes published in the daily press predate it. It is one of only a handful of cookbooks from the decades prior to Israeli independence and immediately following it.
2. Meyer, *Eikh le-Vashel*, xiii.
3. Meyer, *Eikh le-Vashel*, 71.
4. Meyer, *Eikh le-Vashel*, 80.
5. Cornfeld, *Keitzad Mevashlim*.
6. J. Walsh, "Opening Remarks," in Cornfeld, *Keitzad Mevashlim*.
7. Walsh, "Opening Remarks."
8. Cornfeld, *Keitzad Mevashlim*, 4.
9. Cornfeld, *Keitzad Mevashlim*.
10. *Recipes of the Season*, issued by the food controller with the aid of Hadassah and WIZO, June 1945, HA.
11. *Recipes of the Season*.
12. WIZO, Department of Education, *Sefer ha-Bishul* (The cookbook) (Tel-Aviv: Masada, 1948), 3.
13. WIZO, Department of Education, *Sefer ha-Bishul*, 3.
14. WIZO, Department of Education, *Sefer ha-Bishul*, 3.
15. WIZO, Department of Education, *Sefer ha-Bishul*, 3.

16. WIZO, Department of Education, *Kakh Nevashel*, 3.

17. WIZO, Department of Education, *Kakh Nevashel*, 216.

18. Cornfeld, *Israeli Cookery*, 92.

19. Cornfeld, *Ha-Mitbah ha-Meshubah*, 5.

20. Cornfeld, *Ha-Mitbah ha-Meshubah*, 5.

21. Bat-Oren, *365 Shulhanot Arukhim*.

22. Cornfeld, *Ha-Mitbah ha-Meshubah*, 52.

23. Hanna Heiman, Mitbah (Kitchen) column, *La-Isha*, no. 637, 22 June 1959.

24. Cornfeld, *Ha-Mitbah ha-Meshubah*, 29–31.

25. Anon., Ba-Mitbah (In the kitchen) column, *La-Isha*, no. 622, 10 March 1959, and no. 625, 31 March 1959.

26. Keinan, *Sefer ha-Ta'anugot*, 35.

27. *Burda Sefer ha-Bishul*, 33.

28. It is important to note, however, that the book was published by a different (much smaller) publishing house (Adam) than Aharoni's other, kosher cookbooks (published by Modan Publishing).

29. Sirkis, *Me-Hamitbah be-Hana'a*, 6–7.

30. Sirkis, *Me-Hamitbah be-Hana'a*, 6.

31. Sirkis, *Me-Hamitbah be-Hana'a*, 6.

32. Kleinberg, "Siha im–Ruth Sirkis," 143.

33. At the time Sirkis's book was published, there were already a handful of other recent cookbooks available to the Israeli public. One of them was Aviva Goldman's *Sefer ha-Bishul—Kasher* (The cookbook—kosher), which was published in 1970. In her introduction, Goldman stresses her amateur status: "I am not a professional cook. . . . I have never learned how to cook." She shares her own experience with other housewives, teaching them recipes in a cookbook version of traditional culinary learning: through being in the kitchen and watching another woman cook. Among other recipes, she offers a wide variety of avocado and eggplant dishes. These two ingredients have become very common in the Israeli kitchen, demonstrating the effects of diligent propaganda. Nira Russo was another cookbook author whose work had a significant impact on Israeli cooking practices. Her cookbook, also published in the early 1980s, is titled *Sodot me-Hamitbah* (Secrets from the kitchen), and her introduction speaks to the same issues raised by Sirkis, namely, the "busy cook of the 1980s" and the new technology and new ingredients available to Israeli home cooks. She, too, utilizes recipes from a variety of international influences. Russo's readership, like Sirkis's, seemed to comprise mostly working women who were looking for quick, easy-to-make, yet new and interesting meals for their family.

34. Ashley et al., *Food and Cultural Studies*, 112.

35. Almog, *Preida mi-Srulik*, 92.

36. Sarah Bavly, "Report on the Nutrition Department of the Nathan and Lina Straus Health Center of Hadassah, Jerusalem," January–December 1944, PCH / B1 / School Lunch Correspondence, HA.

37. "List of Topics Treated on the P.B.C.," PCH / B1 / School Lunch Correspondence, HA.

38. *Nutrition Cycles*, sponsored by the food controller, produced by Asher Hirshberg, in conjunction with the Nutrition Department of Hadassah, Jerusalem, 24 October 1944, HA.

39. *Nutrition Cycles*, 21 November 1944.

40. "The Sephardim," *Nutrition Cycles*, 16 October 1944.

41. "The Sephardim."

42. "The Sephardim."

43. "The Sephardim."

44. "The Arab Food," *Nutrition Cycles*, 5 December 1944.

45. Tchiya Bat-Oren, interview with the author, Herzliya, 23 April 1998.

46. The show was hosted by Gloria Stewart, produced by Ester Sofer, and edited by Rivka Friedman.

47. Tova Aran, phone interview with the author, 15 March 2004.

48. Aran, phone interview.

49. Aran, phone interview.

50. Eugene Wolf, phone interview with the author, 14 January 2004.

51. Wolf, phone interview.

52. Gil Hovav, phone interview with the author, 26 January 2004.

53. Eylon Goyten, interview with the author, New York, 26 February 2004.

54. Goyten, interview.

55. Goyten, interview.

56. Goyten, interview.

57. Goyten, interview.

58. Shiri Katz, "Keren Pensiya" (Pension fund), *Ha'ir*, 30 January 2003, 24–25.

59. Katz, "Keren Pensiya."

60. Katz, "Keren Pensiya."

61. McLuhan, *Understanding Media*, 317–18.

### 5. THE PROFESSIONAL KITCHEN

1. Cornfeld, *Israeli Cookery*, 87.

2. Long, "Culinary Tourism," 21.

3. Both of these recipes are in Cornfeld, *Israeli Cookery*, 266, 277.

4. Cornfeld, *Israeli Cookery*, 269, 278.

5. Semberg, *The Story of the King David Hotel*.

6. Semberg, *The Story of the King David Hotel*.

7. Avraham Weiner, interview with the author, New York, 22 January 2002.

8. The quote is from Semberg, *The Story of the King David Hotel*.

9. Anon., a notebook of menus and recipes, 1965, King David Archives.

10. Weiner, interview.

11. Weiner, interview.

12. Recipes for these dishes are included in Cornfeld, *Israeli Cookery*, 298–312.

13. Haim Ohel in *Ha-Mitbah ha-Kar* (The cold kitchen), vol. 1 of Nikolai and Efraim, *Madrich le-Omanut ha-Bishul*.

14. Hirsch, *An American Housewife*.

15. Recipes are included in Cornfeld, *Israeli Cookery*, 319–20.

16. A 2010 online survey showed the number of kosher restaurants in Israel (excluding hotel restaurants) at somewhere between 1,800 and 2,300, depending on the source, around 22–23 percent of the total number of restaurants in Israel. Based on www.mapa.co.il and www.2eat.co.il (accessed April 2014).

17. Uri Guttman, interview with the author, Ramat-Gan, 10 January 1999.

18. See www.danhotels.com/Luxury-Hotel-Jerusalem-Restaurants, accessed February 2009 and January 2014.

19. Herzog, "Women's Status," 332.

20. David Ben-Gurion, *Military and Defense*, 257, quoted in Moshe Lissak, "The Civilian Components of Israel's Security Doctrine," in Troen and Lucas, *Israel*, 580.

21. Eliezer Don-Yehiya, "Political Religion in the New State: Ben-Gurion's Mamlakhtiyut," in Troen and Lucas, *Israel*, 181.

22. Micha Popper, "The Israel Defense Forces as a Socializing Agent," in Bar-Tal, Jacobson, and Klieman, *Security Concerns*, 169.

23. "Stan be-Livuy Sir Bishul" (*Stan* accompanied by a cooking pot), *Davar*, 2 August 1948.

24. Kline, "Heil Tahazuka," 148.

25. Kline, "Heil Tahazuka," 148.

26. Kline, "Heil Tahazuka," 148.

27. Ostfeld, *Tzava Nolad*, 480.

28. Ostfeld, *Tzava Nolad*, 494.

29. B. Zinner and Y. Sharvit to David Ben-Gurion, 11 December 1952, 1955/540, file 50, p. 24, IDF Archive, Tel Aviv.

30. List of products for 16 June 1948, 1950/2289, file 6, IDF Archive.

31. Supply forms, 1952/249, no. 293, IDF Archive.

32. Nir Cohen, "Al Marak Limonim Kevar Shama'atem?" (Have you heard of lemon soup?), *Ba-Mahane*, no. 39, 31 May 1995, 81.

33. Cohen, "Al Marak Limonim Kevar Shama'atem?," 81.

34. Nir Cohen and Uri Nisim, "Ve-Hu Bikhlal Ahav Naknik Me'ushan" (And he actually liked smoked sausage), *Ba-Mahane*, no. 39, 31 May 1995, 30–31.

35. Tami Zilber, "Rav ha-Luf" (General Luf [sounds like *rav-aluf*, meaning "general" in the IDF]), *Ba-Mahane*, no. 39, 31 May 1995, 28.

36. Raviv and Shaham, *Bishul la-Gever ha-Meshuhrar*, 85.
37. Raviv and Shaham, *Bishul la-Gever ha-Meshuhrar*, 86.
38. *Ba-Mahane*, no. 39, 31 May 1995.
39. Command Center of the Chief Supply Officer, *Bishul u-Tzuna be-Tzahal* (Cooking and nutrition in the IDF), 1962.
40. Command Center of the Chief Supply Officer, *Bishul u-Tzuna be-Tzahal*.
41. Command Center of the Chief Supply Officer, *Bishul u-Tzuna be-Tzahal*.
42. Letter from the head of the Afsana'ut Branch to the Chief of Staff regarding IDF nutrition, December 1952, 1955/540, file 50, p. 42, IDF Archive.
43. Letter from Z. Rakovehik, head of the Nutrition Division, 1952, 1955/540, file 50, p. 43, IDF Archive.
44. Avraham Meron, "Ha-Im Ata Ra'ev?" (Are you hungry?), *Ba-Mahane*, no. 36, 28 May 1958.
45. Eli Sahaf, "Ha-Okhel she-Hu Okhel" (The food he is eating), Ma Matrid et ha-Hayal, Helek 1 (What is ailing the soldier, part 1), *Ba-Mahane*, no. 19, 24 January 1961.
46. Chief Maintenance Officer, *Ha-Bishul be-Tzahal* (Cooking in the IDF), 1976.
47. Ali Mohar, "14 Manot, bi-Fkuda" (14 dishes, on command), *Ba-Mahane*, no. 9, 17 November 1976.
48. The IDF cookery manual for the 1990s goes a step further, boasting color photographs, a glossy cover, and consultation with Israel Aharoni, a famous Israeli chef who owns both a Chinese and an upscale French restaurant and has published several popular cookbooks. Is a trend evident?
49. Yehudit Klienman, "Avirat Bayit be-Hazit" (A feeling of home at the front), *Devar ha-Poelet*, no. 5, year 24, May 1948, 103.
50. Klienman, "Avirat Bayit be-Hazit," 103.
51. Molly Bar-David, "Hadassah Nutrition Officers in the Jerusalem Battle Area," July 1948, RG 5, box 1, HA.
52. See Herzog, "Women's Status," for more on this issue.
53. Meron, "Ha'im Ata Ra'ev?"
54. Kline, "Heil Tahazuka," 158.
55. For example, Avi Eliyahu, "Ha-Mtkonim ha-Zvaiim shel Kol ha-Zmanim" (Army recipes of all times), PZM, July 2012 (accessed 8 February 2013).
56. FXP, November 2010, and Israelbody.org, April 2007 (accessed 8 February 2013).
57. Yael Bnaya and Mikey Galss, "Hayalim Mamlizim al Pizeriyot ha-Bayit" (Soldiers recommend their home pizzerias), *Ba-Mahane*, February 2013, http://www.mako.co.il/pzm-soldiers (accessed 8 February 2013).

## 6. NO TABLE REQUIRED

1. Kirshenblatt-Gimblett, "Making Sense of Food," 72.
2. *Al ha-Giva'a*, 2 October 1950.

3. B. Z. Kolman, quoted in Erez, *Sefer ha-Aliya ha-Shlishit*, 595.

4. Tzvi Vardi, "Divrei Preida me-Hadar ha-Okhel ha-Yashan" (Words of farewell from the old dining room), *Devar ha-Poelet*, nos. 10–11, year 11, 12 December 1945.

5. Anonymous, *Al ha-Givaʾa*, 18 August 1939.

6. Near, *The Kibbutz Movement*, 295.

7. Bina Peleg, *Devarim Tovim be-Geva* (Good things in Geva), brochure for the seventieth anniversary celebration of Kibbutz Geva.

8. Ganiel, *"Borre Minei Mezonot."*

9. Keikh, *Efshar le-Hitpakeʾa!*

10. Shani, Groner, and Ivri, *Matkonim ba-Shaʾar.*

11. Shani, Groner, and Ivri, *Matkonim ba-Shaʾar.*

12. Shani, Groner, and Ivri, *Matkonim ba-Shaʾar.*

13. Katriel, *Milot Maftehach*, 12.

14. Almog, *Ha-Tzabar*, 369.

15. Almog, *Ha-Tzabar*, 368.

16. Hefer and Wilenski, "Shir ha-Finjan," 4; Gil Dor and Achinoam Nini, "Ha-Stav Biladav," 2001.

17. Almog, *Ha-Tzabar*, 307.

18. Katriel, *Milot Maftehach*, 118–20.

19. Bachelard, *The Psychoanalysis of Fire*, 10.

20. Almog, *Ha-Tzabar*, 369.

21. Lag ba-Omer is a shorthand way of saying the thirty-third day of counting the Omer (the days between the Exodus from Egypt and the Giving of the Torah). There are several explanations of its origins: commemorating the Bar Kochva revolt during the Roman occupation, as well as the death of Rabbi Simon Bar Yochai, writer of the Kabbalistic text, the Zohar. It is customary to celebrate the holiday by lighting bonfires and going out into nature.

22. Raviv and Saham, *Bishul la-Gever ha-Meshuhrar*, 79.

23. Amnon Shapira, "Leshonenu la-Am" (1994), in Asaf, "Al ha-Esh," 14.

24. Yair Nitzani, "Shir ha-Mangal" (The mangal song) (1986), a very loose adaptation of the original love song "Brother Louie" by Dieter Bohlen Lyrics, Warner/Chappell Music, Inc.

25. This is more obvious in the original Hebrew text than in the translation, since the adjectives in Hebrew are gendered. For example, the "wash" in "wash the dishes" is in the female form.

26. Lamdani, "Misdar Abirey ha-Mangal," 50–51.

27. Kalka, "Mangal or BBQ," 61.

28. Gilboʾa, *Melah ha-Aretz.*

29. Gilboʾa, *Melah ha-Aretz.*

30. Gilbo'a, *Melah ha-Aretz*, 173.

31. Levy, "To Morocco and Back."

32. Gidon Alon, "Picnic u-Shmo Mimouna" (A picnic called Mimouna), *Ha-Aretz*, 22 April 1973, 12.

33. Roden, *The Book of Jewish Food*, 554.

34. Goldberg, "Hagigot ha-Mimouna be-Marocco," 108.

35. Web page *Mimouna, a Jewish-Moroccan Festival in Israel*, http://www.jafi.org.il /education/festivls/pesach/m3.html, accessed 29 March 2005.

36. Goldberg, "Hagigot ha-Mimouna be-Marocco"; Hirschberg, "Ha-Mimouna ve-Hagigot"; Einhorn, "Origins and Nature."

37. Ben-Gurion interviewed in *Le Monde*, 1962, cited in Sammy Smouha, "Ashkenazy Hegemony," *New Outlook Middle East Monthly*, July–August 1981, 20.b.

38. Ben-Gurion in an interview with Moskin, in Smouha, "Ashkenazy Hegemony."

39. Zeev Jabotinski, "The Orient," *Ha-Derech* 7 (1972): 18, in Smouha, "Ashkenazy Hegemony."

40. Shochat, "Sepharadim in Israel," 13.

41. Shochat, "Sepharadim in Israel," 24.

42. Shochat, "Sepharadim in Israel," 25.

43. Gidon, "Picnic u-Shmo Mimouna," 12.

44. *Mimouna, a Jewish-Moroccan Festival in Israel.*

45. *Mimouna, a Jewish-Moroccan Festival in Israel.*

46. Daniel Ben Simon, "Either Mimouna or Likud Has Lost Magic," *Ha-Aretz*, 8 April 1999.

47. Alon, "Picnic u-Shmo Mimouna," 12.

48. Alon, "Picnic u-Shmo Mimouna," 12.

49. Baruch Ha-Meiri, "Hagigot ha-Mimouna Mashhu Olim mi-Kol Rahvei Tevel" (The Mimouna celebration attracted immigrants from all corners of the globe), *Maariv*, 8 April 1980, 11.

50. Ha-Meiri, "Hagigot ha-Mimouna."

51. Dov Goldshtein, "Ha-Mimouna shel Avoteinu be-Marocco, veha-Mimouna Shelanu be-Yerushalayim" (Our ancestors' Mimouna in Morocco, and our Mimouna in Jerusalem), an interview with Sam Ben-Shitrit, *Maariv*, 6 April 1980, 20.

52. Goldshtein, "Ha-Mimouna shel Avoteinu be-Marocco."

53. Amelia Uzeri, interview with the author, Even-Menachem, 5 January 2007, and phone interview with the author, 8 February 2007.

54. Ray, "Ethnic Succession," 97–114.

55. See, among others, Wu, "Global Encounter," 75–103; and Collingham, *Curry*.

56. Hamis Aboulafia, "A Moroccan Peace Overture," *Maariv International*, 19 April 2005.

1. Eliav, "Yichuda Shel," 1:xi–xii.
2. In recent years, there has been much debate and resentment around the title "First" given to this immigration wave, referring to both earlier settlements and other organized groups of immigrants from various geographical points, but the "First Aliya" remains unique in its place in the Zionist narrative and in the prominence it placed on "modern," Western concepts in contrast to Jewish religion and traditions valorized by its predecessor.
3. Eliav, "Yichuda Shel," 1:xiii.
4. Eliav, "Yichuda Shel," 1:xiii.
5. Etinger and Bartal, "Shorshei ha-Yishuv ha-Hadash," 1:23.
6. Eliav, "Yichuda Shel," 1:xiv.
7. Mrs. Kalman Shlomo Kantor, 1889, quoted in Eliav, *Sefer ha-Aliya ha-Rishona*, 2:180.
8. Gershon Leib Horowitz, 1887, quoted in Berlowitz and Ze'evi, *E'ebra-na ba-Aretz*, 65–69.
9. Beyla Likerman, 1886, quoted in Eliav, *Sefer ha-Aliya ha-Rishona*, 2:105–6.
10. Moshe Smilanski, 1894, quoted in Berlowitz and Ze'evi, *E'ebra-na ba-Aretz*, 180.
11. Eliav, *Sefer ha-Aliya ha-Rishona*, 2:ix.
12. Lissak, "Aliya, Klita u-Binyan Hevra," 175–77, 181.
13. David Ijmojik, 1926, quoted in Lissak, "Aliya, Klita u-Binyan Hevra," 293.
14. Chaim Arlozerov, 1933, quoted in Lissak, "Aliya, Klita u-Binyan Hevra," 293.
15. Lillian Cornfeld, "Tzunatenu be-Kayitz Ze" (Our nutrition this summer), *Olam ha-Isha*, no. 28, 11 June 1941, 12.
16. Gutwein, "From Melting Pot to Multiculturalism," 247.
17. Sikron, "Ha-Aliya ha-Hamonit," 31–32.
18. Sikron, "Ha-Aliya ha-Hamonit," 32.
19. Sikron, "Ha-Aliya ha-Hamonit," 34–45.
20. Ben-Porat, "Ha-Meshek ha-Israeli," 119.
21. Gross, "The Economic Regime," 234–35.
22. Lissak, "Ha-Mahapekha ha-Demografit-Hevratit."
23. Greenberg, "The Contribution of the Labor Economy," 280–81.
24. Greenberg, "The Contribution of the Labor Economy," 285.
25. Lissak, "Patterns of Change," 141–46.
26. Almog, *Preida mi-Srulik*, 84–91.
27. Shapira, "Whatever Became of 'Negating Exile'?," 69–108.
28. Swirski, "1967," 91–116.
29. Swirski, "1967."
30. Swirski, "1967."
31. Liebman and Yadgar, "Israeli Identity"; Ram, "Post-Zionist Studies"; Silberstein, *Postzionism Debates*; Gutwein, "Left and Right Post-Zionism."

32. In the aftermath of the war, Prime Minister Begin resigned, and a "unity government" with Shimon Peres as prime minister was instituted (a government comprised of representatives from both Likud and Labor Parties). In 1987 the first Palestinian *Intifada* began. These political and ideological changes were only aggravated with the aftermath of the Oslo Peace Accord (1993) and the assassination of Prime Minister Yithak Rabin, which led to disappointment and growing pessimism regarding the possibility for peace on both sides of the conflict.
33. See www.mcdonalds.co.il, accessed April 2014.
34. Kimmerling, *Invention and Decline.*
35. Kimmerling, *Invention and Decline.*
36. Antebi-Yemini, "Being an Oleh."
37. Leshem and Lisak, "Hitgabshuta ha-Hevratit"; and Friedgut, "Immigrants from the Former Soviet Union."
38. Kimmerling, *Invention and Decline*; and Remennick, *Russian Jews.*
39. See Bernstein and Carmeli, "Food for Thought"; Friedgut, "Immigrants from the Former Soviet Union."
40. Kimmerling, *Invention and Decline.*
41. Antebi-Yemini, "Being an Oleh"; and Remennick, *Russian Jews.*
42. See Shapira, "Whatever Became of 'Negating Exile'?"
43. For a rare and thoughtful study of this group's foodways, see Sabar and Posner, "Remembering the Past," 197–222.

# BIBLIOGRAPHY

Agnon, S. Y. *Temol Shilshom* (Only yesterday). Tel Aviv: Shoken Publishing House Ltd., 1975.

Aharoni, Israel, and Dan Daor. *Ha-Bishul ha-Sini shel Haharoni* (Aharoni's Chinese cooking). Tel Aviv: Modan, 1986.

Aharoni, Israel, and Shaul Evron. *Ha-Bishul ha-Italki* (Italian cooking). Tel Aviv: Adam Motzi'im Laor, 1989.

Alfa, Peninna, ed. *Anu Mevashlim: Nose Limudi u-Mikra'a li-Shnat ha-Limudim 2–3* (We are cooking: A study subject and reader for grades 2–3). Merhavia, Israel: Ha-Kibbutz ha-Artzi, Sifriyat ha-Poalim, 1952.

Almog, Bella, ed. *Mat'amei Israel: Mivhar ha-Mat'amim she-Hugshu le-Taharut "Malkat ha-Mitbah ha-Israeli" 1964* (Delicacies of Israel: A selection of the dishes that were submitted to the contest "The Israeli Queen of the Kitchen" 1964). Jerusalem: Mitzad Mat'amei Israel, 1964.

Almog, Oz. *Ha-Tzabar—Deyokan* (The sabra—a profile). Tel Aviv: Am Oved, 1997.

———. "It's Not Just a Game." In *A Trip across the Country: Games from Mr. Barlevy's Store*. Tel Aviv: Eretz-Israel Museum, 1999.

———. *Preida mi-Srulik: Shinuy Arahim ba-Elita ha-Israelit* (Farewell to Srulik: Changing values among the Israeli elite). Haifa: Haifa University Press and Zmora-Bitan, 2004.

Almog, Shmuel. *Zionism and History: The Rise of a New Jewish Consciousness.* New York: St. Martin's Press, 1987.

Amir, Bela. *Ta'am Shel Pa'am* (A taste of long ago). Tel Aviv: Modan, 1986.

Anderson, Benedict. *Imagined Communities.* London: Verso, 1983.

Antebi-Yemini, Lisa. "Being an Oleh in a Global World: From Local Ethnic Community to Transnational Community." In *Israelis in Conflict*, edited by A. Kemp, D. Newman, U. Ram, and O. Yiftachel. Brighton: Sussex Academic Press, 2004.

Appadurai, Arjun. "How to Make a National Cuisine: Cookbooks in Contemporary India." *Comparative Studies in Society and History* 30, no. 1 (1988): 3–24.

———. *Modernity at Large: Cultural Dimensions of Globalization.* Minneapolis: University of Minnesota Press, 1996.

Asaf, David. "Al ha-Esh." In *Mangal.* Tel Aviv: Ha-Galerya le-Itzuv Shel Askola, 1996.

Ashley, Bob, Joanne Hollows, Steve Jones, and Ben Taylor. *Food and Cultural Studies.* London: Routledge, 2004.

Avineri, Shlomo. *The Making of Modern Zionism: The Intellectual Origins of the Jewish State.* London: Weidenfeld and Nicolson, 1981.

Bachelard, Gaston. *The Psychoanalysis of Fire.* Translated by Alan C. M. Ross. 1938; Boston: Beacon Press, 1964.

Bar-David, Molly. *The Israeli Cook Book.* New York: Crown Publishers, 1964.

Bardenstein, Carol. "Threads of Memory and Discourses of Rootedness: Of Trees, Oranges, and the Prickly-Pear Cactus in Israel/Palestine." *Edebiyat* 8 (1998): 1–36.

———. "Trees, Forests, and the Shaping of Palestinian and Israeli Collective Memory." In *Acts of Memory: Cultural Recall in the Present*, edited by M. Bal, J. Crewe, and L. Spitzer. Hanover: Dartmouth College, University Press of New England, 1999.

Bar-Itzhak, Haya. "'The Unknown Variable Hidden Underground' and the Zionist Idea: Rhetoric of Place in an Israeli Kibbutz and Cultural Interpretation." *Journal of American Folklore* 112, no. 446 (1999): 497–513.

Bar-Tal, Daniel, Dan Jacobson, and Aharon Klieman, eds. *Security Concerns: Insights from the Israeli Experience.* Stamford CT: JAI Press, 1998.

Bar-Tal, Israel. "Al ha-Rishoniyut: Zman u-Makom ba-Aliya ha-Rishona" (Of primacy: Time and place in the First Aliya). In *Lesoheah Tarbut im ha-Aliya ha-Rishona* (Talking culture: The First Aliya), edited by Yafa Berlovitch and Yosaf Lang. Tel Aviv: Ha-Kibbutz ha-Meuchad, 2010.

———, ed. *Ha-Aliya ha-Shniya: Mehkarim* (The Second Aliya: Studies). Jerusalem: Yad Ben-Zevi, 1997.

Barthes, Roland. *Mythologies.* Translated by A. Lavers. New York: Hill and Wang, 1972.

———. "Toward a Psychology of Contemporary Food Consumption." In *Food and Culture,* edited by Carol Counihan and Penny Van Esterik. New York: Routledge, 1997.

Bat-Aliya, Rivka. *Ma Nokhal?* (What should we eat?). Tel Aviv: Moria, 1930.

Bat-Oren, Tchiya. *365 Shulhanot Arukhim* (365 set tables). Jerusalem: Hagal, 1961.

Bavly, Hanah, and Ugenya Simchoni. *Eich Ochlim At Ze?* (How to eat this?). Tel Aviv: Shoken, 1970.

Bavly, Sarah. *Food Habits and Their Changes in Israel*. Jerusalem: Ministry of Education and Culture and the College of Nutrition and Home Economics, 1964.

———. *Minhagei Ha-Akhila ve-ha-Shinuyim ha-Halim ba-Hem be-Israel* (Eating habits and the changes in them in Israel). Jerusalem: Ministry of Education and Culture and the College of Nutrition and Home Economics, 1964.

———. *Tzrikhat Mazon ve-Ramat Tzuna Shel Mishpahot Skhirim Ironiyot be-Israel 1956–57* (Food consumption and nutritional level of urban employee families in Israel 1956–57). Jerusalem: Central Statistics Bureau, 1960.

Belasco, Warren, and Philip Scranton, eds. *Food Nations: Selling Taste in Consumer Societies*. New York: Routledge, 2002.

Bell, David, and Gill Valentine. *Consuming Geographies: We Are Where We Eat*. London: Routledge, 1997.

Ben-Porat, Yoram. "Ha-Meshek ha-Israeli: Hevlei Tzmiha" (The Israeli economy: Growing pains). In *Azma'ut: 50 ha-Shana ha-Rishonot* (Independence: The first fifty years), edited by Anita Shapira. Jerusalem: Zalman Shazar Center, 1998.

Ben-Rafael, Eliezer. *The Emergence of Ethnicity: Cultural Groups and Social Conflict in Israel*. Westport CT: Greenwood Press, 1982.

Bentley, Amy. *Eating for Victory: Food Rationing and the Politics of Domesticity*. Urbana: University of Illinois Press, 1998.

Ben-Yehuda, Nachman. *The Masada Myth: Collective Memory and Mythmaking in Israel*. Madison: University of Wisconsin Press, 1982.

Berkowitz, Michael. *Zionist Culture and West European Jewry before the First World War*. Chapel Hill: University of North Carolina Press, 1996.

Berlowitz, Yafa, and Rechavam Ze'evi, eds. *E'ebra-na ba-Aretz: Mas'ot be-Eretz Israel Shel Anshei ha-Aliya ha-Rishona* (Wandering in the land). Tel Aviv: Ministry of Defense, 1992.

Bernstein, Deborah S., ed. *Pioneers and Homemakers: Jewish Women in Pre-state Israel*. Albany: State University of New York Press, 1992.

Bernstein, Julia, and Yoram Carmeli. "Food for Thought: The Dining Table and Identity Construction among Jewish Immigrants from the Former Soviet Union in Israel." In *Consumption and Market Society in Israel*, edited by Y. Carmeli and K. Applebaum. Oxford: Berg, 2004.

*Beyond Milk and Honey: Traditional Recipes from an Israeli Kitchen*. Washington DC: Embassy of Israel, Office of Public Affairs, 1994.

Bhabha, Homi K. *The Location of Culture*. London: Routledge, 1994.

————, ed. *Nation and Narration*. London: Routledge, 1990.

Biribis, H., M. Dafna, E. Amiran, and A. Omer. *Zemer Hen: Shiron le-Ganei ha-Yeladim ve-Lekitot ha-Yesod* (Lovely song: Songbook for preschools and the elementary grades first and second). Tel Aviv: Union of Composers in Israel, 1960.

*Bishul u-Tezuna be-Tzahal* (Cooking and nutrition in the IDF). Office of Senior Supply Officer, 1962.

Blum, Shlomit. "Ha-Isha be-Tnu'at ha-Avoda be-Tkufat ha-Aliya ha-Shniya" (The women in the Labor movement in the period of the Second Aliya). Master's thesis, Tel Aviv University, 1980.

Brent, Moshe, Yosef Aggasi, and Yehudit Buber-Aggasi. *Toda'a Le'umit Israelit* (Israeli national awareness). Tel Aviv: Tel Aviv University, Sapir Institution of Development, 1988.

Bromberg, Sarah (Sarah Bavly). *Tzunatenu* (Our nutrition). Jerusalem: Ever, 1939.

Brow, James. "Notes on Community, Hegemony, and the Uses of the Past." *Anthropological Quarterly* 63, no. 1 (1990): 1–6.

*Burda Sefer ha-Bishul* (Burda, the cookbook). Translated from *Burda-Kochbuch*, Verlag Aenne Burda, Offenburg. Tel Aviv: Ahiasaf-Brinfman Publishing, 1974.

Chambers, Ian. *Migrancy, Culture, Identity*. London: Routledge, 1994.

Chang, Kwang-chih, ed. *Food in Chinese Culture: Anthropological and Historical Perspectives*. New Haven CT: Yale University Press, 1977.

Charles, Simon R. *Wedding Cakes and Cultural History*. London: Routledge, 1992.

Cohen, E. "Israel as a Post-Zionist Society." *Israel Affairs* 1, no. 3 (1995): 203–214.

————. "The Representation of Arabs and Jews on Postcards in Israel." *History of Photography* 19, no. 3 (1995): 210–220.

Collingham, Lizzie. *Curry: A Tale of Cooks & Conquerors*. Oxford: Oxford University Press, 2006.

Connerton, Paul. *How Societies Remember*. Cambridge: Cambridge University Press, 1989.

Conquergood, Dwight. "Performance Studies: Interventions and Radical Research." *TDR* 46, no. 2 (2002): 145–156.

Cornfeld, Lillian. *Ha-Mitbah ha-Meshubah* (The superb kitchen). Tel Aviv: Published by the author, 1960.

————. *Israeli Cookery*. Westport CT: Avi Publishing Company, 1962.

————. *Keitzad Mevashlim Biyemei Milhama?* (How to cook in a time of war?). Tel Aviv: Olam ha-Isha, 1942.

————. *Ma Avashel mi-Manot ha-Zena?* (What will I cook from the Zena rations?). Tel Aviv: Published by the author, 1949.

Cotter, Colleen. "Claiming a Piece of the Pie: How the Language of Recipes Defines a Community." In *Recipes for Reading: Community Cookbooks, Stories, Histories,* edited by Anne L. Bower. Amherst: University of Massachusetts Press, 1997.

Crang, P. "Displacement, Consumption, and Identity." *Environment and Planning A* 28, no. 1 (1996): 47–67.

Csikszentmihalyi, Mihaly, and Eugene Rochberg-Halton. *The Meaning of Things: Domestic Symbols and the Self.* Cambridge: Cambridge University Press, 1981.

Dabdoub, Christiane N. *Classic Palestinian Cookery.* London: Saqi Books, 2001.

Diner, Hasia R. *Hungering for America: Italian, Irish, and Jewish Foodways in the Age of Migration.* Cambridge MA: Harvard University Press, 2001.

Dominguez, Virginia R. *People as Subject, People as Object: Selfhood and Peoplehood in Contemporary Israel.* Madison: University of Wisconsin Press, 1989.

———. "The Politics of Heritage in Contemporary Israel." In *Nationalist Ideologies and the Production of National Culture,* edited by Richard G. Fox, 130–147. Washington DC: American Ethnological Society, 1990.

Douglas, Mary. "Deciphering a Meal." In *Food and Culture,* edited by Carole Counihan and Penny Van Esterik. New York: Routledge, 1997.

———, ed. *Food in the Social Order: Studies of Food and Festivities in Three American Communities.* New York: Russell Sage Foundation, 1984.

Einhorn, Itzhak. "The Origins and Nature of the Mimouna." *Tarbiz* 2 (1972): 211–219.

Eisenstadt, Shmuel N. *Israeli Society: Background, Development, and Problems.* London: Weidenfeld and Nicolson, 1967.

Eisenstadt, Shmuel N., Rivkah Bar-Yosef, and Chaim Adler, eds. *Integration and Development in Israel.* New York: Praeger, 1970.

Eliav, Mordechai, ed. *Sefer ha-Aliya ha-Rishona* (The book of the First Aliya). Jerusalem: Yad Ben-Tzvi and Ministry of Defense, 1981.

Erez, Yehuda, ed. *Sefer ha-Aliya ha-Shlishit* (The book of the Third Aliya). Tel Aviv: Am-Oved, 1964.

Etinger, Shmuel, and Israel Bartal. "Shorshei ha-Yishuv ha-Hadash be-Eretz Israel" (The roots of the new settlement in the land of Israel). In *Sefer ha-Aliya ha-Rishona,* edited by Mordechai Eliav, vol. 1. Jerusalem: Yad Ben-Tzvi, Ministry of Defense Publishing, 1981.

Even-Zohar, Itamar. "The Emergence of a Native Hebrew Culture in Palestine: 1882–1948." *Studies in Zionism* 4 (1981): 167–184.

Evron, Boas. *Jewish State or Israeli Nation?* Bloomington: Indiana University Press, 1995.

Farb, Peter, and George Armelagos. *Consuming Passions: The Anthropology of Eating.* Boston: Houghton Mifflin Company, 1980.

Feeley-Harnik, Gillian. *The Lord's Table: The Meaning of Food in Early Judaism and Christianity*. Washington DC: Smithsonian Institution Press, 1881.

Feldman, Yael. *No Room of Their Own: Gender and Nation in Israeli Women's Fiction*. New York: Columbia University Press, 1999.

Fenton, Alexander, and Eszter Kisban, eds. *Food in Change: Eating Habits from the Middle Ages to the Present Day*. Edinburgh: John Donald Publishers, 1986.

Fine, Elizabeth C., and Jean Haskell Speer. *Performance, Culture, and Identity*. New York: Praeger, 1992.

Fischler, Claude. "Food, Self, and Identity." *Social Science Information* 27, no. 2 (1988): 275–292.

Friedgut, Theodore H. "Immigrants from the Former Soviet Union: Their Influence and Identity." In *Israeli Identity in Transition*, edited by Anita Shapira. Westport CT: Praeger, 2004.

Ganiel, Sheli, ed. *"Borre Minei Mezonot" Uga, Uga: Matconei Ugot u-Mat'amim Kalim* ("Creator of many foods" cake, cake: Cake recipes and easy delicacies). Kibbutz Tirat Tzvi: Tirat Tzvi, 1988.

Gellner, Ernest. *Nations and Nationalism*. Ithaca NY: Cornell University Press, 1983.

Gilbo'a, Rami. *Melah ha-Aretz: Bishul ba-Shetah im Meitav ha-Shefim ba-Israel* (Salt of the earth: Outdoor cooking with the best Israeli chefs). Tel Aviv: Moto Media, 2004.

Gillis, John, ed. *Commemorations: The Politics of National Identity*. Princeton NJ: Princeton University Press, 1994.

Givalder, Rivka. "Ba-Mitbah ha-Kibbutzi" (In the kibbutz kitchen). *Devar ha-Poelet*, nos. 8–9, year 11, 16 October 1945, 128–130.

Goldberg, Harvey. "Hagigot ha-Mimouna be-Marocco." In *Yehudey ha-Mizrah*, edited by S. Deshen and M. Shaked. Tel Aviv: Shoken, 1981.

Goldscheider, Calvin. *Israel's Changing Society: Population, Ethnicity, and Development*. Boulder CO: Westview Press, 1996.

Gorali, M., and D. Samburski, eds. *Sefer Shirim u-Manginot* (A book of songs and melodies). Jerusalem: Kiryat ha-Sefer, 1950.

Greenberg, Yitzhak. "The Contribution of the Labor Economy to Immigrant Absorption." In *Israel: The First Decade of Independence*, edited by Ilan S. Troen and Noah Lucas. Albany: State University of New York Press, 1995.

Grosglik, Rafi. "Organic Hummus in Israel: Global and Local Ingredients and Images." *Sociological Research Online* 16, no. 2 (2011): 3.

Gross, Nachum. "The Economic Regime during Israel's First Decade." In *Israel: The First Decade of Independence*, edited by Ilan S. Troen and Noah Lucas. Albany: State University of New York Press, 1995.

Grossman, Ronit. "Tourism and Change in the Galilee Kibbutz: An Ethnography." In *Consumption and Market Society in Israel*, edited by Yoram Carmeli and Kalman Applbaum. New York: Berg, 2004.

Gutierrez, Paige C. *Cajun Foodways*. Jackson: University Press of Mississippi, 1992.

Gutwein, Daniel. "From Melting Pot to Multiculturalism; or The Privatization of Israeli Identity." In *Israeli Identity in Transition*, edited by Anita Shapira. Westport CT: Praeger, 2004.

———. "Left and Right Post-Zionism and the Privatization of Israeli Collective Memory." In *Israeli Historical Revisionism: From Left to Right*, edited by D. J. Penslar and A. Shapira. New York: Routledge, 2013.

Habas, Bracha, ed., with E. Shochat. *Sefer ha-Aliya ha-Shniya* (The book of the Second Aliya). Tel Aviv: Am Oved, 1947.

*Ha-Bishul be-Tzahal* (Cooking in the IDF). Office of the Senior Maintenance Officer, 1976.

Halter, Marylin. *Shopping for Identity: The Marketing of Ethnicity*. New York: Schocken Books, 2000.

Handler, Richard. *Nationalism and the Politics of Culture in Quebec*. Madison: University of Wisconsin Press, 1988.

Hefer, Haim, and Moshe Wilenski. "Shir ha-Finjan." In *Haim Hafer: Tavim "le-Tachmoshet Kalla"* (Haim Hefer: Musical notes for "light ammunition"). Tel Aviv: Sifriyat Poalim, 1949.

Helou, Anissa. *Mediterranean Street Food*. New York: HarperCollins, 2002.

Herzog, Hanna. "Women's Status in the Shadow of Security." In *Security Concerns: Insights from the Israeli Experience*, edited by Daniel Bar-Tal, Dov Jacobson, and Aharon Klieman. Stamford CT: JAI Press, 1998.

Hirsch, Shula. *An American Housewife in Israel*. New York: Citadel Press, 1962.

Hirschberg, Haim Ze'ev. "Ha-Mimouna ve-Hagigot Isru-Hag Shel Pesach" (The Mimouna and the celebrations of the day following Passover). In *Zchor Le-Avram* (Remembrance for Avraham), edited by H. Z. Hirshberg. Bar-Ilan University, 1972.

Hobsbawm, Eric J. "Introduction: Inventing Traditions." In *The Invention of Tradition*, edited by E. J. Hobsbawm and Terence Ranger. Cambridge: Cambridge University Press, 1983.

———. *Nations and Nationalism since 1780: Programme, Myth, Reality*. Cambridge: Cambridge University Press, 1990.

Horowitz, Dan, and Moshe Lissak. *Mi-Yishuv le-Medina* (The origins of Israeli polity). Tel Aviv: Am Oved, 1977.

Izraeli, Dafna N. "The Women's Workers' Movement: First Wave Feminism in Pre-state Israel." In *Pioneers and Homemakers: Jewish Women in Pre-state*

*Israel*, edited by Deborah S. Bernstein. Albany: State University of New York Press, 1992.

———. "The Zionist Women's Movement in Palestine, 1911–1927: A Sociological Analysis." *Signs* 7, no. 1 (1981): 87–114.

Izraeli, Dafna N., and Bernstein Dvora. "Ha-Poelet ba-Aliya ha-Shniya" (The female worker in the Second Aliya). In *Ha-Aliya ha-Shniya: Mehkarim* (The Second Aliya: Studies), edited by Israel Bartal. Jerusalem: Yad Yzchak Ben-Zevi, 1997.

Kalcik, S. "Ethnic Foodways in America: Symbols and the Performance of Identity." In *Ethnic and Regional Foodways in the United States*, edited by L. K. Brown and K. Mussell. Knoxville: University of Tennessee Press, 1984.

Kalka, Iris. "Changing Nutrition Values and Self-Image in Israel." *ICAF Occasional Report* 7 (1990): 7–10.

———. "Coffee in Israeli Suburbs." *Leisure Studies* 10 (1991): 119–131.

———. "Mangal or BBQ." In *Mangal*. Tel Aviv: Ha-Galerya le-Itzuv Shel Askola, 1996.

Kamon, Azriel. "Ha-Shiva la-Mizrah, ha-Markiv ha-Romanti ve-Hamotiv ha-Autokhtoni ba-Yisuv bi-Tkufat ha-Aliya ha-Shniya" (Return to the east, the romantic component, and the autochtonic motive in the Yishuv during the time of the Second Aliya). MA thesis, Tel Aviv University, 1989.

Katriel, Tamar. *Communal Webs: Communication, Culture, and Acculturation in Contemporary Israel*. Albany: State University Of New York Press, 1991.

———. *Milot Maftehach: Dfusei Tarbut ve-Tikshoret be-Israel* (Key words: Patterns of culture and communication in Israel). Tel Aviv: Haifa University and Zmora-Bitan, 1999.

———. *Performing the Past: A Study of Israeli Settlement Museums*. Mahwah NJ: Lawrence Erlbaum, 1997.

Keikh, Gidi. *Efshar le-Hitpake'a! Karikaturot me-Hayey ha-Kibbutz* (You could burst! Caricatures of kibbutz life). Tel Aviv: Mifalei Tarbut ve-Hinukh Ltd., 1966.

Keinan, Amos. *Sefer ha-Ta'anugot* (The book of pleasures). Tel Aviv: Levin-Epshtein, 1970.

Keinan, Gadi. *Ha-Bishul be-Tzahal* (The cookery in the IDF). Tel Aviv: Ministry of Defense Publishing House, 1991.

Keller Brown, Linda, and Kay Mussell, eds. *Ethnic and Regional Foodways in the United States: The Performance of Group Identity*. Knoxville: University of Tennessee Press, 1984.

Kellerman, Aharon. *Society and Settlement: Jewish Land of Israel in the Twentieth Century*. Albany: State University of New York Press, 1993.

Kimmerling, B. "Academic History Caught in the Cross-Fire: The Case of Israeli-Jewish Historiography." *History & Memory* 7, no. 1 (1995): 41–65.

——. *The Invention and Decline of Israeliness*. Berkeley: University of California Press, 2001.

——. *Zionism and Territory: The Socio-territorial Dimension of Zionist Politics*. Berkeley: University of California Press, 1983.

Kirshenblatt-Gimblett, Barbara. "Edible Icon: A Social History of the Bagel in the United States." Lecture at Feast and Famine, Humanities Colloquium, New York University, 2001.

——. "Making Sense of Food in Performance: The Table and the Stage." In *The Sense in Performance*, edited by Sally Banes and Andre Lepecki. New York: Routledge, 2007.

——. "Playing to the Senses: Food as a Performance Medium." *Performance Research* 4, no. 1 (1999): 1–30.

Kleinberg, Aviad. "Siha im–Ruth Sirkis" (A conversation with Ruth Sirkis). In *Beten Mele'a: Mabat Aher al Ohel ve-Hevra* (A full belly: A different look at food and society), edited by Aviad Kleinberg. Jerusalem: Keter Publishing, 2005.

Kline, Ze'ev. "Heil Tahazuka" (Maintenance Corps). In *Tzahal be-Heilo: Intziklopedi'a le-Tzava u-le-Bitahon* (IDF: Encyclopedia for army and security), edited by Y. Erez and Y. Shif. Israel: Revivim, 1983.

Krausz, Ernest, ed. *Studies of Israeli Society: Migration, Ethnicity, and Community*. New Brunswick NJ: Transaction Books, 1981.

Lamdani, Dalia. "Misdar Abirey ha-Mangal" (Order of the mangal knights). In *Mangal*. Tel Aviv: Ha-Galerya le-Itzuv Shel Askola, 1996.

Lapid, Shulamit. *Havat ha-Alamot* (The damsels' farm). Jerusalem: Keter Books, 2006.

Laqueur, Walter. *A History of Zionism*. New York: Schocken Books, 1976.

Lehman-Wilzig, Tami, and Miriam Blum. *The Melting Pot: A Quick and Easy Blend of Israeli Cuisine*. Hertzelia, Israel: Palphot Ltd., n.d.

Leshem, Elazar, and Moshe Lisak. "Hitgabshuta ha-Hevratit ve-Hatarbutit shel ha-Kehila ha-Rusit be-Israel" (Social and cultural consolidation of the Russian community in Israel). In *Me-Russia le-Israel* (From Russia to Israel), edited by M. Lissak and E. Leshem. Tel Aviv: He-Kibbutz ha-Meuhad, 2004.

Levenstein, Harvey. *Paradox of Plenty: A Social History of Eating in Modern America*. New York: Oxford University Press, 1993.

——. *Revolution at the Table: The Transformation of the American Diet*. New York: Oxford University Press, 1988.

Levin, Hanokh. "Ishel and Romanechka." In *Taʿam ha-Haʾim* (A taste of life), edited by Yaron Avitov and Ran Yagil. Jerusalem: Carmel, 2002.

Levy, Andre. "To Morocco and Back: Tourism and Pilgrimage among Moroccan-Born Israelis." In *Grasping Land Space and Place in Contemporary Israeli Discourse and Experience*, edited by Y. Bilu and E. Ben-Ari, 25–46. New York: SUNY Press, 1997.

Libman, Ishayahu C. "Ha-Musag 'Medinat Israel' u-Tfisotav ba-Hevra ha-Israelit" (The concept "state of Israel" and its understandings in Israeli society). *Medina, Mimshal ve-Yahasim Bein-Leumiyim* (State, government, and international relations) 30 (1989): 51–60.

Liebman, Charles S., and Eliezer Don-Yehiya. *Civil Religion in Israel: Traditional Judaism and Political Culture in the Jewish State*. Berkeley: University of California Press, 1983.

Liebman, Charles S., and Yaakov Yadgar. "Israeli Identity: The Jewish Component." In *Israeli Identity in Transition,* edited by A. Shapira. Santa Barbara: Praeger, 2004.

Lissak, Moshe. "Aliya, Klita u-Binyan Hevra be-Eretz Israel bi-Shnot ha-Esrim (1918–1930)" (Immigration, absorption, and building the land of Israel in the 1920s). In *The History of the Jewish Community in Eretz-Israel since 1882, the Period of the British Mandate*, edited by Anita Shapira, Gabriel Cohen, and Moshe Lissak. Jerusalem: Bialik Institute, 1994.

———. "Ha-Mahapekha ha-Demografit-Hevratit bi-Shnot ha-Hamishim: Klitat ha-Aliya ha-Gedola" (The social-demographic revolution in the fifties: The great immigration wave). In *Azmaʾut: 50 ha-Shana ha-Rishonot* (Independence: The first fifty years), edited by Anita Shapira. Jerusalem: Zalman Shazar Center, 1998.

———. "Patterns of Change in Ideology and Class Structure in Israel." In *Integration and Development in Israel*, edited by Shmuel N. Eisenstadt, Rivka Bar-Yosef, and Chaim Adler. New York: Praeger, 1970.

Long, Lucy M. "Culinary Tourism: A Folklorist Perspective on Eating and Otherness." In *Culinary Tourism*, edited by Lucy M. Long. Lexington: University Press of Kentucky, 2004.

Luntz, Peter, and Sonia Livingston. *Mass Consumption and Personal Identity*. Buckingham: Open University Press, 1992.

Lupton, Deborah. "Food, Memory, and Meaning: The Symbolic and Social Nature of Food Events." *Sociological Review* 42, no. 4 (1994): 665–685.

Luz, Ehud. *Makbilim Nifgashim: Dat-Leumiyut ba-Tnuʾa ha-Tziyonit be-Reshita (1882–1904)* (Parallels meet: Religion and nationalism in the early Zionist movement, 1882–1904). Tel Aviv: Am Oved Publishers Ltd., 1985.

McLuhan, Marshall. *Understanding Media: The Extensions of Man*. 1964; Cambridge MA: MIT Press, 1994.

Mennell, Stephen. *All Manners of Food: Eating and Taste in England and France from the Middle Ages to the Present*. Chicago: University of Chicago Press, 1996.

Metzer, Jacob. "Economic Structures and National Goals: The Jewish National Home in Interwar Palestine." In *Essential Papers on Zionism*, edited by Anita Shapira and Yehuda Reinhartz. New York: New York University Press, 1996.

Meyer, Erna. *Aikh Levashel be-Erez-Israel?* (How to cook in the land of Israel?). Tel Aviv: WIZO, 1935.

Mintz, Sidney. *Tasting Food, Tasting Freedom: Excursions into Eating, Culture and the Past*. Boston: Beacon Press, 1996.

Mosse, George L. *Confronting the Nation: Jewish and Western Nationalism*. Hanover NH: Brandeis University Press, 1993.

Naor, Mordechai, ed. *Olim u-Ma'abarot, 1948–1952*. Jerusalem: Yad Ben Tzvi, 1986.

Nasser, Christiane Dabdoub. *Classic Palestinian Cookery*. London: Saqi Books, 2001.

Nathan, Joan. *The Foods of Israel Today*. New York: Alfred A. Knopf, 2001.

Near, Henry. *Ha-Kibbutz ve-ha-Hevra (1923–1933)* (Kibbutz and society). Jerusalem: Yad Ben-Zvi, 1984.

——. *The Kibbutz Movement: A History, Vol. I, Origins and Growth 1909–1939*. Oxford: Oxford University Press, 1992.

Nikolai, Yizhak, and Hanan Efraim. *Madrich le-Omanut ha-Bishul* (A guide to the art of cooking). Tel Aviv: Published by the authors, n.d.

Ofaz, Aviva, ed. *Sefer ha-Kvutza, Kvutzat ha-Sharon 1922–1936*. Jerusalem: Yad Ben-Tzvi, 1996.

Ofer, Daliya, ed. *Bein Olim le-Vatikim: Israel ba-Aliya ha-Gedola (1948–1953)* (Israel in the great wave of immigration [1948–1953]). Jerusalem: Yad Ben-Zvi, 1996.

Ohnuki-Tierney, Emiko. *Rice as Self: Japanese Identities through Time*. Princeton NJ: Princeton University Press, 1993.

Orbach, Naama. *Eich Ossa Yalda* (What a girl does). Tel Aviv: Shoken Books, 2004.

Ostfeld, Zehava. *Tzava Nolad* (An army is born). Tel Aviv: Ministry of Defense Publishing House, 1994.

Owen, Sri. "Introducing Children to Food and Table Manners in Java." In *Food, Culture, and History*, edited by Gerald Mars and Valerie Mars, 61–73. London: London Food Seminar, 1993.

Pearce, Susan M., ed. *Interpreting Objects and Collections*. London: Routledge, 1994.

Peled, Elad. "Education: The Social Challenge." In *Israel: Social Structure and Change*, edited by Michael Curtis and Mordechai S. Chertoff. New Brunswick NJ: Transaction Books, 1973.

Pilcher, Jeffrey M. *Que Vivan los Tamales! Food and the Making of Mexican Identity*. Albuquerque: University of New Mexico Press, 1998.

———. "Recipes for Patria: Cuisine, Gender and Nation in Nineteenth-Century Mexico." In *Recipes for Reading: Community Cookbooks, Stories, Histories*, edited by Anne L. Bower. Amherst: University of Massachusetts Press, 1997.

Ram, U. "Zionist Historiography and the Invention of Modern Jewish Nationhood: The Case of Ben-Zion Dinur." *History & Memory* 7, no. 1 (1995): 91–124.

———. "Glocommodification: How the Global Consumes the Local-McDonald's in Israel." *Current Sociology* 52, no. 1 (2004): 11–31.

———. "Post-Zionist Studies of Israel—the First Decade." *Israel Studies Forum* 20, no. 2 (Winter 2005): 22–45.

Raviv, Amiram, and Asher Shaham. *Bishul la-Gever ha-Meshuhrar* (Cooking for the liberated man). Tel Aviv: Masada, 1979.

Ray, Krishnendu. "Ethnic Succession and the New American Restaurant Cuisine." In *The Restaurant Book: Ethnographies of Where We Eat*, edited by D. Berriss and D. Sutton. Oxford: Berg, 2007.

———. "Meals, Migration and Modernity: Food and the Performance of Bengali-American Ethnicity." PhD diss., State University of New York, 2000.

———. *The Migrant's Table*. Philadelphia: Temple University Press, 2004.

Regev, Menahem. "Ha-Zehut ha-Le'umit be-Sifrut ha-Yeladim ha-Israelit" (The national identity in Israeli children's literature). *Shdemot* 126, no. 2 (1994): 49–52.

Reinhartz, Yehuda, and Anita Shapira, eds. *Essential Papers on Zionism*. New York: New York University Press, 1996.

Reinhartz, Yehuda, Gidon Shimoni, and Yosef Salmon, eds. *Le'umiyut u-Politica Yehudit: Perspectivot Hadashot* (Jewish nationalism and politics: New perspectives). Jerusalem: Zalman Shazar Center for Jewish History and Tauber Institute at Brandeis University, 1996.

Remennick, Larrisa. *Russian Jews on Three Continents*. New Brunswick NJ: Transaction Publishers, 2007.

Renan, Ernest. "What Is a Nation?" In *Nation and Narration*, edited by Homi K. Bhabha. London: Routledge, 1990.

Ridgwell, Jenny. *Middle Eastern Cooking*. London: Ward Lock, 1986.

Roach, Joseph. *Cities of the Dead: Circum-Atlantic Performance*. New York: Columbia University Press, 1996.

Roden, Claudia. *The Book of Jewish Food*. New York: Alfred A. Knopf, 1996.

———. *The Book of Middle Eastern Food*. New York: Random House, Vintage Books, 1972.

Rosen, Ora. "Tmurut be-Ma'amadan Shel ha-Nashim ba-Hityashvut ha-Ovedet, ha-Ra'ayon ve-Hama'ase" (Changes in the conditions and status of women in the worker's settlement, the idea and its realization). Master's thesis, Tel Aviv University, 1984.

Sabar, Galia, and Rachel Posner. "Remembering the Past and Constructing the Future over a Communal Plate: Restaurants Established by African Asylum Seekers in Tel Aviv." *Food, Culture and Society* 16, no. 2 (2013): 197–222.

Sabar, Naomi, and Shimon Sabar. *Ma'akhalim Teimanyim u-Mizrahyim* (Yemenite and Oriental dishes). Tel Aviv: Sadan, 1962.

Safir, Marilyn P. "An Historical Perspective: The Kibbutz as an Experiment in Social and Sexual Equality." In *Sexual Equality: The Israeli Kibbutz Tests the Theories*, edited by Micha Palgi, Joseph Raphael Blasi, Menachem Rosner, and Marilyn P. Safir. Kibbutz Studies Book Series, vol. 6. Norwood PA: Norwood Editions, 1983.

Sanjur, Diva. *Social and Cultural Perspectives in Nutrition*. Englewood Cliffs NJ: Prentice-Hall, 1982.

Schechner, Richard. *Between Theater and Anthropology*. Philadelphia: University of Pennsylvania Press, 1985.

Segev, Tom. *1949—the First Israelis*. New York: Free Press, 1986.

Semberg, Fiona, ed. *The Story of the King David Hotel*. Jerusalem, 1993.

Senor, Dan, and Saul Singer. *Start-Up Nation: The Story of Israel's Economic Miracle*. New York: Hachette Books, 2009.

Shalev, Meir. *Esau*. Tel Aviv: Am-Oved, 1991.

Shapira, Anita. "Ha-Motivim ha-Datiyim Shel Tenu'at ha-Avoda" (The religious motifs of the Labor movement). In *Tziyonut ve-Dat (Zionism and religion)*, edited by Yehuda Reinhartz, Anita Shapira, and Shmuel Almog. Jerusalem: Zalman Shazar Center for Jewish History, 1994.

———. "Whatever Became of 'Negating Exile'?" In *Israeli Identity in Transition*, edited by Anita Shapira. Westport CT: Praeger, 2004.

Shapiro, Laura. *Perfection Salad*. New York: Henry Holt and Company, 1986.

Shani, D., A. Groner, and S. Ivri, eds. *Matkonim ba-Sha'ar: Matkonim mi-Mitbaham ha-Prati Shel Haverot ve-Haverei Kibbutz Sha'ar ha-Golan* (Recipes at the gate: Recipes from the private kitchens of the members of kibbutz Sha'ar ha-Golan). Sha'ar ha-Golan: Kibbutz Sha'ar ha-Golan, 2000.

Shavit, Ya'akov. "Bein Uma Yotzeret Tarbut le-Tarbut Yotzeret Uma" (The Yishuv between national regeneration of culture and cultural generation of the nation). In *Le'umiyut u-Politica Yehudit: Perspectivot Hadashot* (Jewish nationalism and politics: New perspectives), edited by Yehuda Reinhartz, Gidon Shimoni, and Yosef Salmon. Jerusalem: Zalman Shazar Center for Jewish History and Tauber Institute at Brandeis University, 1996.

Shazar, R. K. *The Ploughwomen*. New York: Herzl Press, 1932.

Sheran, Shlomo. "Al ha-Mashber ba-Zehut ha-Yehudit be-Israel" (Regarding the crisis of Jewish identity in Israel). *Nativ* 5 (1988): 21–28.

Shihab, Aziz. *A Taste of Palestine*. San Antonio TX: Corona Publishing Company, 1993.

Shilo, Margalit. "The Women's Farm at Kinneret, 1911–1917." In *Pioneers and Homemakers: Jewish Women in Pre-state Israel*, edited by Deborah S. Bernstein. Albany: State University of New York Press, 1992.

Shochat, Ella. "Sepharadim in Israel: Zionism from the Standpoint of Its Jewish Victims." *Social Text* 9, no. 20 (1988): 9–35.

Shwartz, Dora. *Sefer ha-Bishul* (The cookbook). Zikhron Ya'akov: Published by the author, 1956.

Siegel, Dina. *The Great Immigration: Russian Jews in Israel*. New York: Berghahn Books, 1998.

Sikron, Moshe. "Ha-Aliya ha-Hamonit: Memade'a, Me'afyene'a, ve-Hashpa'ote'a" (The mass immigration: Its dimensions, characteristics, and influences). In *Olim u-Ma'abarot, 1948–1952*, edited by M. Naor. Jerusalem: Yad Ben-Tzvi, 1968.

Silberman, Neil Asher. *Between Past and Present: Archeology, Ideology, and Nationalism in the Modern Middle East*. New York: Doubleday, 1989.

Silberstein, Laurence J., ed. *New Perspectives on Israeli History*. New York: New York University Press, 1991.

———. *The Postzionism Debates: Knowledge and Power in Israeli Culture*. New York: Routledge, 2013.

Sirkis, Ruth. *Me-Hamitbah be-Hana'a* (From the kitchen with pleasure). Tel Aviv: Bait va-Gan Publishing, 1982.

Soler, Jean. "The Semiotics of Food in the Bible." In *Food and Culture*, edited by Carole Counihan and Penny Van Esterik. New York: Routledge, 1997.

Someck, Ronny. *Gan Eden le-Orez* (Rice paradise). Tel Aviv: Zmora-Bitan, 1996.

———. *Mahteret ha-Halav* (The milk underground). Tel Aviv: Kineret, Zmora-Bitan, Dvir, 2005.

Stewart, Susan. *On Longing: Narratives of the Miniature, the Gigantic, the Souvenir, the Collection*. Durham NC: Duke University Press, 1993.

Stoler-Lees, Sahlav. "'Kach Agadel Tinok Tzioni': Nituah Antropology Shel Sifrei Hadrakha le-Horim" ("This is how I shall raise a Zionist baby": Anthropological analysis of parental guidebooks). Master's thesis, Tel Aviv University, 1998.

Swirski, Shlomo. "1967: Tafnit Calcalit-Medinit be-Israel" (1967: A political-economic turning point in Israel). In *Hevra ve-Calcala be-Israel: Mabat History ve-Achshavi* (Society and economy in Israel: Historic and contemporary perspectives), edited by A. Bareli, D. Gutwein, and T. Friling. Jerusalem: Yad Ytzhak Ben-Tzvi and Machon Ben-Gurion le-Haker Israel, 2005.

Tamuz, Benyamin. *Ha-Zikit veha-Zami r* (The chameleon and the nightingale). Tel Aviv: Keter, 1989.

Taylor, Diana. *Disappearing Acts: Spectacles of Gender and Nationalism in Argentina's "Dirty War."* Durham NC: Duke University Press, 1997.

Toomre, Joyce. "Food and National Identity in Soviet Armenia." In *Food in Russian History and Culture*, edited by Musya Glants and Joyce Toomre. Bloomington: Indiana University Press, 1997.

Tremayne, Soraya. "We Chinese Eat a lot: Food as a Symbol of Ethnic Identity in Kuala Lumpur." In *Food, Culture and History*, edited by Gerald Mars and Valerie Mars, 74–92. London: London Food Seminar, 1993.

Troen, Ilan S., and Noah Lucas, eds. *Israel: The First Decade of Independence.* Albany: State University of New York Press, 1995.

Trubek, Amy. *Haute Cuisine: How the French Invented the Culinary Profession.* Philadelphia: University of Pennsylvania Press, 2000.

Turner, Victor. *The Anthropology of Performance.* New York: PAJ Publications, 1987.

Uvezian, Sonia. *Recipes and Remembrances from an Eastern Mediterranean Kitchen.* Austin: University of Texas Press, 1999.

Weingrod, Alex. *Israel: Group Relations in a New Society.* London: Pall Mall, 1965.

Weintraub, Dov, M. Lissak, and Y. Azmon. *Moshava, Kibbutz and Moshav: Patterns of Jewish Rural Settlement and Development in Palestine.* Ithaca NY: Cornell University Press, 1969.

Wheaton, Barbara. *Savoring the Past: The French Kitchen and Table from 1300 to 1789.* Philadelphia: University of Pennsylvania Press, 1983.

WIZO, Department of Education. *Kakh Nevashel—Sefer ha-Bishul* (Like so we shall cook—the cookbook). Tel Aviv: Ner Publishing, 1937.

———. *Sefer ha-Bishul* (The cookbook). Tel Aviv: Masada, 1948.

Wu, David Y. H. "Global Encounter of Diasporic Chinese Restaurant Food." In *Chinese Food and Foodways in Southeast Asia and Beyond*, edited by Tan Chee-Beng. Singapore: Nus Press, 2011.

Yerushalmi, Yoseph H. *Zakhor: Jewish History and Jewish Memory*. Seattle: University of Washington Press, 1982.

Yoshino, Kosaku. "Rethinking Theories of Nationalism: Japan Nationalism in a Marketplace Perspective." In *Consuming Ethnicity and Nationalism: Asian Experiences*, edited by Kosaku Yoshino. Honolulu: University of Hawaii Press, 1999.

Zerubavel, Yael. "Documenting Israeli Folk Culture." In *Documenting Israel: Proceedings of a Conference Held at Harvard University on May 10–12, 1993*, edited by Charles Berlin. Cambridge MA: Harvard University Press, 1995.

———. *Recovered Roots: Collective Memory and the Making of Israeli National Tradition*. Chicago: University of Chicago Press, 1995.

Zubaida, Sami. "National, Communal and Global Dimensions in Middle Eastern Food Cultures." In *Culinary Cultures of the Middle East*, edited by Sami Zubaida and Richard Tapper. London: I. B. Tauris, 1994.

Zubaida, Sami, and Richard Tapper, eds. *Culinary Cultures of the Middle East*. London: I. B. Tauris, 1994.

Zuckerman, Leora. *Ha-Bishul u-Meshek ha-Bayit* (Cooking and the household). Tel Aviv: Amihai Ltd., 1963.

Zuckerman, Y. "Falafel." Tel Aviv: Ha-Zemer, 1949.

# INDEX

*Page numbers in italic indicate illustrations.*

Aboulafia, Hamis, 207–8

Adoni, Meir, 155, 166

African immigrants, 232–33

afternoon tea ritual, 187–88

"Agira" (poem), 63–64

Agnon, S. Y., 29–30

agricultural labor: in the First Aliya, 34–36, 215–16, 217; gender divisions in, 42–46, 87–89; "Hebrew" labor, 34, 37–41, 215, 217; importance to Zionist ideology, 37–39, 42; shifting focus away from, 50–51; used in propaganda, 39–40, 47–49

agriculture: connections to the land through, 6, 28–29, 222; during the First Aliya, 28–29, 34–37, 214–16; prior to the First Aliya, 34, 213; role in identity formation, 4, 10–11; role in Israeli culture, 46–47; training in, 96–97; used in propaganda, 10–11, 39–40, 47–49

Aharoni, Israel, 134, 138–39, 244n28, 247n48

*Al ha-Giva'a* (newsletter), 184

ha-Aliya ha-Hamonit (Mass Immigration), 221–23

Almagor, Dan, 20

Almog, Oz, 106, 191

Alpert, Hila, 147

Alterman, Nathan, 192, 195

Anderson, Benedict, 13

Antebi-Yemini, Lisa, 51

Appadurai, Arjun, 7

Arab cuisine: influence of, 16, 70–71, 110, 124–25, 126–27, 143, 167; kumzits, 192, 193–94; Mimouna celebration, 200–208

Arab-Israeli conflict, 16, 103, 129, 131, 203–4, 220, 225–26

Arab Revolt (1936–38), 220

Aran, Tova, 145–47

*Ha-Aretz* (newspaper), 17–18, 55, 64, 67–68, 72

Arlozerov, Chaim, 220

army. *See* Israeli Defense Forces (IDF)

"Around the Fire" (Alterman), 192, 195

art: falafel presented in, 22–23; food's relation to, 26; in the Mimouna, 205; oranges presented in, 37, 38. *See also* Zionist propaganda

asceticism, 6, 17, 41–42, 218–19

Ashley, Bob, 51, 74–75, 138

Askola (design school), 197–98

assimilation: food in process of, 6–7, 29, 48, 84–85, 101–6; maintaining ties to origin country, 84–85, 229, 231; role of culinary education in, 87; through school systems, 106–7, 110–11, 113. *See also* immigration

Bachelard, Gaston, 194
baking, 188–89. *See also* kitchen work (cooking)
*Ba-Mahane* (magazine), 171, 173, *174*
Baraz, Miryam, 58, 89
Baraz, Yosef, 44
Bar-David, Molly, 128, 177–78
Bardenstein, Carol, 36
Bar-Tal, Daniel, 24
Bar-Tal, Israel, 34
Barthes, Roland, 1
Bat-Oren, Thiya, 76, 77, 127, 128, 129, 144–45
Bavly, Sarah, 108–10, 114–15, 139, 144
Bedouins, 192, 193–94, 215–16
Begin, Menachem, 228, 251n32
Beit-Brener cooperative kitchen, 158
Bell, David, 51, 75, 84
Ben-Gal, Ze'ev (Zibon), 80–81
Ben-Gurion, David, 64, 168, 203, 221
Ben-Shitrit, Sam, 205
Bentley, Amy, 63, 65
Ben-Yehuda, Nachman, 11
Bernstein, Julia, 84
Bhabha, Homi, 3
Billuyim, 215
*Ha-Bishul ha-Sini shel Aharoni* (Aharoni), 138–39
*Bishul la-Gever ha-Meshuhrar* (Raviv and Shaham), 172–73, 196
*Ha-Bishul ve-Meshek ha-Bayit* (Tzukerman), 127

black market, 74
Black Panthers, 227
blogs (culinary), 153–55
Bluwstein, Shoshana, 45
boar hunting, 80–81
*Ha-Boker* (newspaper), 68, 73
Bonik, R., 90
*The Book of Jewish Food* (Roden), 201
Bookshtater, Zachi, 147
bourgeois ideology, 50–51, 119–20, 219–20
breakfast, 159
British food controller, 60, 73, 123–25, 139–40
British Mandate, 53–54; cookbooks during, 123–25; improvement projects, 161; rationing program of, 60–64, 220; role in economic prosperity, 221
*Burda Sefer ha-Bishul* (cookbook), 133–34
Byalik, Haim Nahman, 47

Carmeli, Yoram, 84
Ha-Casba (restaurant), 165
Central European cuisine, 160, 163, 164
Central European immigrants, 50–51, 96–97, 219–20
Chahanski, A., 99
Chanit (blog writer), 153–54
chefs, 157, 161, 163–65
chicken schnitzel, 80, 240n62
childcare, 92
children: communal care for, 92; nutritional education of, 106–13; school lunch programs for, 97–98; training in communal cooking, 94–95
Chinese cuisine, 138–39
citrus fruits, 18, 35–37, 58–59

coffee ritual, 192, 193–94
Cohen, Haim, 150
Cohen, Nir, 171
collectivism, 41, 43–45, 49, 218–19
colonialism. *See* British Mandate
communal childcare, 92
communal dining: changes in service
  in, 185–86; changes to private dining,
  186–91; sociocultural role of, 184–85.
  *See also* kibbutzim
communal working groups (*kvutzot*),
  88–92
Conquergood, Dwight, 9
consumerism, 74–78, 224, 228–29
cookbooks: by chef Nikolai, 163–65;
  didactic approach in, 120–23, 125–26,
  136–37, 244n33; ethnic diversity in,
  138–39, 244n33; falafel recipes in,
  20, 24, 25; as historical artifacts,
  7–8; of the IDF, 173–77, 247n48; of
  kibbutzim, 188–90; leisure activity approach in, 116–18, 129–32,
  134; nonkosher recipes in, 132–34;
  for outdoor cooking, 199; prior to
  independence, 243n1; during rationing programs, 66–71, 123–25; shifting
  approaches to, 126–32, 134–38. *See
  also* culinary education
cooking. *See* kitchen work (cooking)
*Cooking and Nutrition in the IDF*
  (Lamdani), 173–76
"cooking corner" TV program, 145–46
cooking equipment, 187–88, 196, 199
*Cooking in the IDF* (manual), 176–77
cooking shows, 71–73, 120. *See also*
  culinary education
co-op stores, 75–76
Cornfeld, Lillian, 20, 66, 67, 68–71,
  123–25, 127, 128, 158, 160, 220

culinary apps, 155–56
culinary blogs, 153–55
culinary education, 66–73, 86–87, 90,
  94–95, 119–20
culinary tourism, 159–60
culinary vocabulary, 73–74, 136, 190–91
culinary websites, 152–53, 154–55
cultural Zionism, 10

dairy products, 46, 62–63, 112–13, 142
Daor, Dan, 139
Daughters of Zion. *See* Hadassah
  (women's organization)
*Davar* (newspaper), 44, 53, 90, 96, 169
Dayan, Deborah, 42–43
*Devar ha-Poelet* (magazine), 58
Diaspora, 2, 9–12, 39, 215
Diner, Hasia, 6
dining rooms. *See* communal dining

Eastern European cuisine, 95, 160, 163
Eastern European immigrants, 29, 160
eating practices. *See* food consumption
economic inequality, 224, 226–28
economic nationalism, 223
economy: First Aliya's contribution
  to, 35; government's role in, 223;
  impact of the Mass Immigration on,
  222; impact of tourism on, 160–
  61; impact on kibbutz life, 186–87;
  increased stability of, 128, 156, 198;
  postwar improvement in, 221; and
  shifts in political ideology, 39, 83, 138;
  Six-Day War's impact on, 225–27;
  and the *totzeret ha-aretz* campaign,
  52–59, 69
education: culinary education, 66–73,
  86–87, 90, 119–20; in the First Aliya,
  215; focused on immigrants, 62, 103–
  6; home economics, 96–100, 109–10,

education (*continued*)
111; nutritional studies for children,
94–95, 106–13; school lunch programs, 97–98
Efraim, Hanan, 164
Egypt, 16, 24, 224, 228
*Eich Ossa Yalda* (Orbach), 182
El Al Airline, 36, 78
"electric kettle syndrome," 187
equality, 44–46, 87–94, 178, 196
*Esau* (Shalev), 50
Ethiopian immigration, 51, 229–30
European cuisine, 95, 160, 163, 164, 167, 175
Evron, Shaul, 134
export industries, 35–37, 226–27

"Falafel" (song), 19–20
falafel: as national symbol, 15–16, 22–26; origins of, 16; stages to national symbol status, 16–21; tensions surrounding, 24–26
*Falafelman* (Maya-Gur), 22, 23
family structure: early attempts to restructure, 41, 92, 218–19; in the First Aliya, 214; ideological changes toward, 100, 106, 138, 186, 188, 191
Federman family, 163
Feldman, Yael, 91–92
"The Finjan Song," 192–93
*finjan* tradition, 192, 193–94
fire, 194
First Aliya (immigration), 28–29, 34–37, 213–17, 250n2
folk songs, 19–20, 47–49, 95, 192–93
food: attempts to create unity through, 30–37, 96, 168–69, 220; ephemeral nature of, 7; and identity formation, 2–5; and nationalism, 5–8, 26–27, 113;

as national symbol, 25–26, 29–37, 55–57, 225; performative nature of, 8, 211; role in assimilation, 102–6; role in the First Aliya, 214; role in the Second Aliya, 218–19; shifts in approach to, 4, 143–44, 198–99, 210; stages of cultural assimilation of, 16–21; street foods, 182–83; used in propaganda, 10, 28, *31, 33,* 47–49, 219
food consumption: 1964 survey on, 113–15; and economic stability, 198; and identity formation, 74–78, 84–85; in the kibbutz, 184–91; outdoor dining, 191–200; and the school system, 106–9, 112–13; shifts in approaches to, 50–51; of street foods, 182–83; and tourism, 159–60
food distribution: black market, 74; and identity formation, 74–78; impact of foreign workers on, 238n4; increased importance of, 51–52; kosher food in, 78–79; and local products, 52–59; nonkosher products in, 81–82. *See also* rationing programs
food preparation. *See* kitchen work (cooking)
food production. *See* agriculture
food rationing. *See* rationing programs
food shortages, 19, 69, 70, 89–90, 184, 218. *See also* rationing programs
food shows, 71–73, 120. *See also* culinary education
food substitutes, 19, 63, 66–67, 70, 238n21
foreign workers, 40–41, 238n4
Former Soviet Union (FSU) immigrants, 51–52, 79–80, 84–85, 229, 230–32

Fourth Aliya, 50–51, 97–98, 219–20

French cuisine, 131, 160, 163, 164–65, 207

Friber, Ida, 44

*From the Kitchen with Love* (Sirkis), 134–38

fruits, 18, 30, 32–35, 58–59

Ganiel, Sheli, 188

Gellner, Ernest, 13

gender equality, 87–94, 178, 196

Gerdi, N., 90

Gerti, Moshe, 79–80

Geva (kibbutz), 187–88, 190

Gilbo'a, Rami, 199

Givalder, Rivka, 44, 89–90, 94

globalization, 51, 209–10, 231

Goldberg, Esther, *108*

Goldman, Aviva, 244n33

Goyten, Eylon, 148–49

grapes, 32–35

Great Britain. *See* British Mandate

Greenberg, Yitzhak, 223

grocery stores, 75–78. *See also* food distribution

Guttman, Uri, 21, 166–67

Hadassah (women's organization), 97–99, 107–8, 139–43, 177–78

Halter, Marilyn, 74

*haluka* (distribution), 35, 141, 190, 213

*halutzim* (pioneers), 218; of the Second Aliya, 41–42, 50, 88–92, 192, 193–94, 217–19; of the Third Aliya, 42, 50, 92–93, 218

*Ha-Mitbah ha-Meshubah* (Cornfeld), *130*

Ha-Shomer organization, 193–94

*Havat ha-Alamot* (Lapid), 45–46

Hebrew language: culinary vocabulary, 73–74, 136; increase in speakers of, 128; limitations in, 132; as the national language, 215, 231

"Hebrew" labor, 34, 37–41, 215, 217

Hebrew Workers Union, 54

Helou, Anissa, 25

Herbert Samuel Restaurant, 166

high-tech industry, 39, 227, 237n16

Hilton Hotel (Tel Aviv), 159

Hirsch, Shula, 165

Hitron, Yehudit, 109, 112–13

Hobsbawm, Eric J., 5, 13, 113

Holdheim, Aliza, 71–72

Hollows, Joanne, 51

home economics, 99–100, 109–10, 111

homeland (*moledet*), 2

Horowitz, Gershon, 216

hotel restaurants: King David Hotel, 161–64; kosher food in, 78, 165–67; role in Israeli cuisine, 157–58, 159–61

Hovav, Gil, 148–49, 150

*How to Cook in a Time of War?* (Cornfeld), 69–71

*How to Cook in the Land of Israel?* (Meyer), 120–23, 243n1

"How to Eat in Palestine" (radio program), 140–43

hummus, 24, 25, 169, 176

hunting, 80–81

identity. *See* national identity

IDF (Israeli Defense Forces). *See* Israeli Defense Forces (IDF)

Ijmojik, David, 219–20

Ilan (chef), 153

immigration: challenges of, 3, 29–30, 86–87, 203–4; economic impact of, 221–23; First Aliya, 28–29, 34–37,

immigration (*continued*)
213–17, 250n2; Fourth Aliya, 50–51,
97–98, 219–20; globalization's impact
on, 51, 209–10, 231; impact on eating
habits, 79–80, 84–85; impact on
Israeli culture, 207–8; Mass Immigration wave (1948–51), 221–23;
pluralistic approach to, 223–24;
post-independence wave, 101–6; during the post-Zionism period, 228–32;
role of ideology in, 231–32; role of
religion in, 214, 215; Second Aliya,
41–42, 50, 88–92, 192, 193–94, 217–19;
Third Aliya, 42, 50, 92–93, 218; and
the Zena program, 64–65. *See also*
assimilation
imported products, 83, 84–85
individualism, 41, 43–45, 49, 218–19
Internet, 120, 151–55
"In the Garden" (Byalik), 47
*Ha-Isha* (journal), 99, 100
*La-Isha* (magazine), 129
Israel: demographic changes, 221–
22; demographic changes in, 196;
economic inequality in, 223–24,
226–28; ethnic diversity within,
69–70, 126–27; foreign workers in,
40–41, 238n4; globalization's impact
on, 51–52, 209–10; impact of change
on, 211; impact of the Six-Day War
on, 225–27; increased criticism of
government, 224, 227–28; as Jewish
homeland, 2; postwar economic
policy of, 222–23; relationship to
Diaspora, 12–13; television in, 145
*The Israeli Cookbook* (Bar-David), 128
*Israeli Cookery* (Cornfeld), 127, 128, 158
Israeli cuisine: Arab food's impact on,
16, 70–71; attempts to unify, 167–69;
ethnic diversity in, 151, 154–56,
166–67; and national identity, 15–16,
116–18, 120, 151; professional chefs'
influence on, 164–65; role of hotel
dining, 157–58, 160–61; role of street
foods, 182–83
Israeli Defense Forces (IDF): cookbooks of, 173–77, 247n48; cooks in,
177–81; ethnic diversity of food, 181;
food supply concerns in, 169–73;
influence on Israeli cuisine, 168–69;
kosher food in, 78, 171; Luf used by,
171–73
Israeli national identity. *See* national
identity
Izraeli, Dafna, 88

Jabotinski, Zeev, 203
Jaffa oranges, 36–37
Jewish Halacha, 230
Jewish National Fund, 79
Jewish national identity. *See* national
identity
Jewish religion: changes in observance,
69–70, 214, 215; food as connection
to, 32–34; of FSU immigrants, 230;
relationship to nationalism, 11–12,
158, 232; role in the Second Aliya,
217–18
Jones, Steve, 51

Kalcik, S., 3
Kalka, Iris, 198
Kantor, Kalman Shlomo, 216
*kashrut* (dietary laws), 12, 117, 158, 163,
165–66, 232. *See also* kosher food
Katinski-Rabao, Ziona, 66–67, 93–94
Katriel, Tamar, 190, 194
"Kav ha-Oni" (Someck), 100–101

Keich, Gidon, 185–86, 189
Keinan, Amos, 119, 129–33
*Keitzad Mevashlim bi-Yemei Milhama?*
   (Cornfeld), 123–25
Keren (restaurant), 150
Keren Kayemet (Jewish National
   Fund), 79
Kfar Giladi (kibbutz), 41–42, 184
kibbutzim: dining rooms of, 184–91;
   greater diversity in, 189; ideology
   of, 92–93, 95; impact of economic
   prosperity on, 186–87; kitchen work
   in, 93–95; kosher foods in, 79; typical
   diet of, 95
Kimmerling, Baruch, 41, 230
Kinetic Art (company), 155–56
King David Hotel (Jerusalem), 161–64,
   167
Kinneret Women's Farm, 45–46
Kirshenblatt-Gimblett, Barbara, 8, 16,
   183
The Kitchen column (*La-Isha*), 129
kitchen work (cooking): in the army,
   178; in communal kitchens, 43–46,
   88–95; in the domestic kitchen,
   86–87; growing professionalism
   of, 131, 138, 160–61; in institutional
   kitchens, 158–59; shifts in approaches
   to, 98–100, 119–20, 150–51. *See also*
   cookbooks; culinary education
Kleinberg, Aviad, 137
Klienman, Yehudit, 177
Kline, Ze'ev, 169, 179
Kolman, B. Z., 184
Kol Yerushalayim (radio station), 139
Kol Yisrael (radio station), 139
kosher food: in the army, 158, 171; in
   cookbooks, 133–34, 165; in cooking
   shows, 149; defined, 240n60; and

early religious Zionists, 91; in hotel
   restaurants, 160, 163, 166–67; and
   identity, 232; in the marketplace, 78–
   79; in the public sphere, 78–79, 158,
   166–67; in restaurants, 78, 165–66,
   240n60, 246n16; in the school system, 112–13. *See also kashrut* (dietary
   laws)
kosher restaurants, 78, 165–66, 240n60,
   246n16
*kumzits*, 183, 191–95
*kvutzot* (communal working groups),
   88–92

labor. *See* agricultural labor
Labor Party, 138, 223, 228
Lag ba-Omer celebration, 195, 248n21
lakerda (dried bonito fish), 61–62,
   238n21
Lamdani, Dalia, 173, 198
Landau, Eli, 152
Lapid, Shulamit, 45–46
Latovitch, Ayelet, 148–49
Lavon, Pinhas, 224
Lavon scandal, 224
Law of Return, 230
Levenstein, Harvey, 102
Levi, Richard, 171
Levin, Hanokh, 22, 227
Likerman, Beyla, 216
Likud Party, 138, 205, 228
Lilien, E. M., 40
Lishankski, Ya'akov, 71
Lissak, Moshe, 102, 219–20
literature, 49
Livingston, Sonia, 78
local products. See *totzeret ha-aretz*
   (local products)
Long, Lucy, 159

Look & Cook (app), 155–56
Luf (canned meat), 171–73
Lumina (restaurant), 166
Luntz, Peter, 78

ma'abarot (temporary camp), 103, 112, 222, 223
Ma'adaney Mizra (manufacturer), 79–80, 240n62
*Madrich le-Omanut ha-Bishul* (Nikolai and Efraim), 164–65
*Malkat ha-Ambatya* (Levin), 227
Malkat ha-Mitbah competition, 115–18
Malkot ha-Falafel (restaurant), 21
*mangal* (BBQ), 195–98
Margalit, Erel, 237n16
marketplace, 51–52, 74–79, 81–82, 238n4. *See also* food distribution
Mass Immigration wave (1948–51), 221–23
*Matkonim ba-Sha'ar* (brochure), 189
Maya-Gur, Dorit, 22
meat consumption, 63, 198
media: impact of, 120; Internet, 120, 151–55; radio programs, 139–45; television programs, 145–52
*Me-ha-Mitbah be-Hana'a* (Sirkis), 135
Meisel, Hanna, 45
"melting pot" ideology, 102, 116, 221, 223
*Menus and Recipes According to the Point System* (WIZO), 61–62
Merchavia (kibbutz), 184
Meron, Avraham, 176
*Mevashlim* (website), 154
Meyer, Erna, 120–23
Meyir, Mina, 104
Middle Eastern cuisine: in army cooking, 169, 175; in cookbooks, 124–25, 126–27; falafel in, 25; in hotel dining, 160, 164, 167; in outdoor cooking, 196–98; in radio programs, 143; in television programs, 148
Middle Eastern immigrants, 101–6, 103, 107, 110
Mikve Israel (agricultural school), 34, 213
military. *See* Israeli Defense Forces (IDF)
military industry, 226–27
Mimouna celebration, 183, 200–208
Ministry of Education and Culture, 108–9, 111–12, 113–15
"Misaviv la-Medura" (Alterman), 192, 195
*Ha-Mitbah ha-Meshubah* (Cornfeld), 127, 129
Mizra (kibbutz), 79–80
Mohar, Ali, 176–77
*moledet* (homeland), 2
Morin, Ran, 37, 38
Moroccan Jewish community, 200–208
*moshavim*, 34, 59, 214
*moshavot*, 34–35, 59, 94, 214
*mufleta*, 201
"My Garden" (Sporta), 47–48
*My Mom's Recipes and More* (blog), 153–54

Na'arei Raful program, 179
Nagar, Lilith, 145
Nasser, Christiane Dabdoub, 25
nation: concept of, 26–27, 210; immigration's impact on, 3; performative aspects of, 8
National Committee (Va'ad Leumi), 53, 108
national identity: and consumption patterns, 74–75; First Aliya's impact

on, 217; food as symbols of, 15–16, 29, 225; globalization's impact on, 51–52, 209–10, 229; impact of non-Jewish immigration, 233; kumzits tradition and, 199–200; and multiple identities, 83–85; and professional cooking, 157–58; role of army in shaping, 168–69; role of culture in, 10; role of food in forming, 2–4, 120–21, 151, 211, 219; role of kosher food in, 166; role of religion in, 230; Second Aliya's impact on, 217–18

nationalism: challenges to unified ideal of, 41, 229; ethnic influences on, 208, 232; and food, 5–8, 26–27, 113; and religion, 11–12, 158, 232

Near, Henry, 92

Nikolai, Yizhak, 163–65

Nitzani, Yair, 197

nonkosher food: in cookbooks, 132–34; impact of foreign workers on, 238n4; impact of immigration on, 52, 232; shifts in approaches to, 82–83; sources of, 79–82

North African cuisine, 126–27, 148. *See also* Mimouna celebration

North African immigrants, 101–6, 107

nuclear family structure. *See* family structure

"Nutritional Policy and the Woman Consumer" (Cornfeld), 67

Nutrition Department (Ministry of Education), 108–9

*Olam ha-Isha* (magazine), 63–64, 68–69, 124

*olim / olot* (immigrants), 101. *See also* immigration

olives, 30–32

"Onion" (Yaron), 48

*Oranger Suspendu* (Morin), 37, *38*

oranges, 18, 35–37

Orbach, Naama, 182

Osem, 152

*Our Nutrition at a Time of Emergency* (wizo), 62–63

outdoor eating: and changing approach to food, 198–200; *kumzits*, 183, 191–95; the *mangal*, 195–98; Mimouna celebration, 202, 203–5; picnic, 195–98, 202, 203, 207

Palestinian Broadcasting Company, 139–43

Palestinians, 16–18, 24–26, 32, 39–40, 143, 145–46, 167, 213, 215–16

Palmach (paramilitary), 192, 194–95

Palphot Ltd. (publisher), 24, 236n36

Pan-Lerner, Dalia, 149

Parade of Israeli Delicacies, 115

Peleg, Bina, 187–88

Peres, Shimon, 251n32

Peretz, Dan, 155

performance: agriculture as, 28–29; aspects of, 8; and diversity, 156; food as medium of, 2–4, 54-55, 59, 209–12

performance studies, 9

Petach-Tikva (moshava), 34, 90, 213

picnics, 195–98

Pilcher, Jeffrey, 7

Poel ha-Mizrachi movement, 91

poetry, 49

political Zionism, 10, 91

Popper, Micha, 168

pork products, 79–81, 82, 132–33

post-independence immigration wave, 101–6

post-Zionism period, 228–32

processed foods, 182–83

Queen of the Kitchen competition, 115–18

Rabin, Itzhak, 193
Rabinowitz, Joseph, 160
radio programs, 139–45
Rashut ha-Shidur (national broadcasting system), 148–49
rationing programs: during British Mandate, 60–64; food substitutes during, 238n21; opposition to, 74; wartime, 140–44, 220; Zena, 19, 64–74, 101, 175, 223, 238n21
Raviv, Amiram, 196
Ray, Krishnendu, 207
recipe booklets, 99–100. *See also* cookbooks
*Recipes of the Season* (brochure), 125
refugees, 232–33
religion. *See* Jewish religion
Remennick, Larissa, 83–84, 230
Reshef, Shimon, 110–11
restaurants, 74, 78, 118, 157, 165–66, 240n60, 246n16. *See also* hotel restaurants
Ribua Kahol (supermarket), 75–76
Richter, Ruth, 117
Ridgwell, Jenny, 25
Rigger, E., 109–10
Roden, Claudia, 201
Roshfeld, Yonathan, 166
Rosh ha-Nikra (kibbutz), 80–81
Rothschild, Edmond James de, 34–35
Rozov-Uzieli, Esther, 100
Russo, Nira, 138, 244n33

*sabra* (native Israeli plant/nickname for native Israeli person), 127. See also *tzabar*

Sahaf, Eli, 176
*Salt of the Earth* (Gilbo'a), 199
Savir, Ami, 208
school lunch programs, 97–98, 107–9, 114
school system: influence of, 106–7, 113; lunch program, 107–9; nutrition and home economics studies, 109–13
Schwartz, Sulamith, 52–53, 55, 59
"The Science of Nutrition" (article), 96
scientific approach to nutrition, 96–97, 98, 109–10, 111
seafood products, 79, 132, 240n60
Second Aliya, 41–42, 50, 88–92, 192, 193–94, 217–19
*seer peleh* (wonder pot), 188
*Sefer ha-Bishul* (WIZO), 125–26
*Sefer ha-Bishul—Kasher* (Goldman), 244n33
*Sefer ha-Kvutza* (Ofaz), 46
*Sefer ha-Ta'anugot* (Keinan), 119, 129–33
self-labor ("Hebrew" labor), 34, 37–41, 215, 217
Sephardic Jewish community, 141–43, 148, 197–208
"The Sephardim" (radio program), 141–43
service (communal dining), 185–86
Sha'ar ha-Golan (kibbutz), 189, 190–91
Shaham, Asher, 196
Shalev, Meir, 50
Shamuti oranges, 36
Shapira, Anita, 226
Shavit, Ya'akov, 10
Shein, Ella, 21
Shenkar, Irit, 150
Shidlovelski, Aliza, 88–89
Shihab, Aziz, 25
Shilo, Margalit, 45

"Shir ha-Mangal" (song), 197–98
"Shir Patrioti" (song), 86
Shohat, Ella, 203
Shohat, Manya, 42
Ha-Shomer organization, 192
shopping. *See* food distribution
Shtozin, Tzipora, 44–45
*Shum, Pilpel, ve-Shemen-Zayit* (TV program), 148–51
Sirkis, Ruth, 134–38
Six-Day War, 129, 131, 225–26
snack foods, 182–83
socialist ideology, 44–45, 87–92, 138, 217–19
*Sodot me-Hamitbah* (Russo), 244n33
Someck, Ronny, 86, 101
songs, 19–20, 47–49, 95, 192–93
Sporta, Refael, 47–48
"Ha-Stav Biladav" (Yonathan), 193
Steiner (chef), 160
Stewart, Susan, 209
street foods, 182–83
substitutions (food), 19, 63, 66–67, 70, 238n21
supermarkets, 74–79, 81–82
Super-Sal (supermarket), 75–77
Supply Service (IDF), 170
Swirski, Shlomo, 226
Szold, Henrietta, 107

Tadmor (hotel management school), 115–18, 160, 164
Talmus Torah Temini (school), 98
Tamuz, Benyamin, 30
*A Taste of Palestine* (Shihab), 25
Taylor, Ben, 51
*Te'amim* (TV show), 147–48
technology, 39, 156, 227, 237n16
television cooking programs, 145–52

Telma food products, 161, *162*
*Temol Shilshom* (Agnon), 29–30
textbooks (nutrition studies), 109–10
Third Aliya, 42, 50, 92–93, 218
*365 Set Tables* (Bat-oren), 76, *77*, 127, 128
*tish* (table), 183
Tiv Ta'am (supermarket), 79, 81–82
Tnuva (company), 55, 146
*totzeret ha-aretz* (local products): campaign for, 18, 52–59, 63; changes in demand for, 83; emphasized in cookbooks, 116–17, 121–23, 126; emphasized on radio shows, 140–43; emphasized on TV shows, 148–49; and national identity, 18; wartime reliance on, 220
tourism industry, 116, 118, 156, 157–58, 159–61, 166
*tzabar* (Israel-born Jew), 192
*Ha-Tzofe* (newspaper), 60
Tzukerman, Ilana, 127
*Tzunatenu* (Bavly), 109–10

Union for Totzeret ha-Aretz, 53–57
Union for Working Mothers, 177
United States: ethnic identities in, 74, 102–3; food rationing programs in, 61, 63; immigrant cuisine in, 207; partnership with Israel, 226
Uvezian, Sonia, 25
Uzeri, Amelia, 206–7

Va'ad Leumi (National Committee), 53, 108
Valentine, Gil, 51, 75, 84
Vardi, Tzvi, 184
vegetables, 46, 48–49, 141–42

Wadi Saleeb Riots (1959), 223

wage inequality, 44–45

Wallish, Otte, 56

Walsh, J., 123–24

"We Are All Cooks Here" (song), 95

*We Are Cooking,* 94–95

websites (culinary), 152–53, 154–55

Weiner, Avraham, 163, 164

*What Shall I Cook This Week?* (food show), 73

*What Will I Cook from the Zena Rations?* (Cornfeld), 66, 68–71

Wheaton, Barbara, 7

wild plants, 194, 195

WIZO (Women's International Zionist Organization): and the army, 169, 178; cookbooks, 20, 121–23, 125–26; food shows, *72,* 72–73; home economics work, 95–97; main goal of, 96–97; during rationing programs, 61–63; recipe booklets, 99–100; work in the kibbutzim, 93; work with immigrants, 103–6

Wolf, Eugene, 147–48

women: as army cooks, 177–78; culinary education for, 71–73; during the Fourth Aliya, 220; and home economics, 96–100; and inequality, 87–94, 178, 196; in the kibbutzim, 188–89; and rationing programs, 61–64, 123–24; role in agricultural labor, 42–46; role in the kitchen, 86–92, 144–45; and the *totzeret ha-aretz* campaign, 54, 57–58; working outside the home, 129

*The Women's Corner* (radio program), 144–45

Women's Farm (Kinneret), 45–46

Women's International Zionist Organization (WIZO). *See* WIZO (Women's International Zionist Organization)

women's organizations: and army cooking, 177–78; Hadassah, 97–99, 107–8, 139–43, 177–78; work with immigrants, 104–6. *See also* WIZO (Women's International Zionist Organization)

World War II, 220–21

Yakobson, Max, 55

Yaron, A. L., 48

Yemenite immigrants, 18

Yishuv, 12, 39, 50–51, 53–59, 102, 213–15

Yom Kippur War, 228

Yonathan, Nathan, 193

Yosef, Zehava, 71

Yosef, Dov, 64–65, 69

youth movements, 192, 194–95

Zastolie gatherings, 84

Zena rationing program, 19, 64–74, 101, 175, 223, 238n21

Zerubavel, Yael, 11

Zionism: concept of homeland in, 2; establishing historical continuity, 4, 10, 30–34, 37–39; gender inequality in, 87–92; growing criticism of, 228; homogenization attempts, 110, 126, 140–41, 168–69, 203–4, 220; impact of the Second Aliya on, 217–19; and local products, 52–59, 140–43; motivations for, 3; religion in, 11–12; role of agriculture in, 28–29, 37–41. *See also* immigration

"Zionism in the Kitchen" (Schwartz), 52–53

Zionist ideology: ascetic values of, 41–45; creating connections to the land, 6, 10–11, 28–29, 83, 192, 195; importance of agriculture in, 10–11; power of media in transmitting, 120;

productivity ideal, 39, 237n16; in radio shows, 139, 140–43; role in immigration, 231–32; shifts in, 138; use of symbols in, 113; Western culture in, 76

Zionist propaganda: focus on agriculture, 10–11, 39–40, 47–49; focus on local products, 54–58, 140–43; food as tool in, 28, *33*, 47–49, 50, 219; influence of, 106; during the Zena rationing program, 65–73

Ziv-Av, Ytschak, 58

Zukerman, Y., 19